TRANSATLANTIC ENCOUNTERS

Previously published in this series:

23. Multiculturalism and the canon of American culture
Hans Bak, ed. (1993)
24.* Victorianism in the United States
Steve Ickringill and Stephen Mills, eds. (1992)
25. Cultural Transmissions and Receptions
Rob Kroes, Robert W. Rydell, Doeko F.J. Bosscher, eds. (1993)
26. Modern American Landscapes
Mick Gidley and Robert Lawson-Peebles, eds. (1994)
27. Fair Representations
Robert W. Rydell and Nancy E. Gwinn, eds. (1994)
28. Hollywood in Europe
D.W. Ellwood and R. Kroes, eds. (1994)
29. American Photographs in Europe
M. Gidley and D.E. Nye, eds. (1994)
30. American Culture in the Netherlands
D. Bosscher, M. Roholl and M. van Elteren, eds. (1996)
31. Connecting Cultures
Rosemarijn Hoefte and Johanna C. Kardux, eds. (1994)
32. The small town in America
Hans Bertens and Theo D'haen, eds. (1995)
33. 'Writing' nation and 'writing' region in America
Theo D'haen and Hans Bertens, eds. (1996)
34. * The American Columbiad
Mario Materassi and Maria I. Ramalho de Sousa Santos, eds. (1996)
35. * The insular dream
Kristiaan Versluys, ed. (1995)
37. Social and secure?
Hans Bak, Frits van Holthoon and Hans Krabbendam, eds. (1996)
38. * Living with America, 1946-1996
Cristina Giorcelli and Rob Kroes, eds. (1997)
39. Writing Lives: American Biography and Autobiography
Hans Bak, Hans Krabbendam, eds. (1998)
40. Through the Cultural Looking Glass
Hans Krabbendam and Jaap Verheul, eds. (1999)
41. Dynamics of Modernization
Tity de Vries, ed. (1999)
42. Beat Culture
C. A. van Minnen, J. van der Bent and M. van Elteren, eds. (1999)
43 Predecessors
Rob Kroes, ed. (1999)
44. * Ceremonies and Spectacles
Teresa Alves, Teresa Cid, Heinz Ickstadt, eds. (2000)
46. Transatlantic Encounters
David Adams and Maurizio Vaudagna, eds. Vol. I (2000)
Günter H. Lenz and Peter J. Ling, eds. Vol. II (2000)

* These volumes have been produced for the European Association for American Studies (E.A.A.S.)

TRANSATLANTIC ENCOUNTERS
Multiculturalism, National Identity and the Uses of the Past

edited by

Günter H. Lenz
Peter J. Ling

with contributions from

Reinhard Isensee
Richard H. King
Rob Kroes
Günter H. Lenz
Peter J. Ling
Klaus J. Milich
Berndt Ostendorf
Jens Rahbek Rasmussen
Meike Zwingenberger

VU UNIVERSITY PRESS
AMSTERDAM 2000

EUROPEAN CONTRIBUTIONS TO AMERICAN STUDIES

This series is published for the Netherlands American Studies Association - N.A.S.A., and the European Association for American Studies - E.A.A.S.

General editor
Rob Kroes, Amerika Instituut, Plantage Muidergracht 12
1018 TV Amsterdam

This Volume II carries the same main title as its other half:
TransAtlantic Encounters. The Public Use and Misuse of History in Europe and the U.S. (Vol. I)
David Adams and Maurizio Vaudagna, eds.

VU University Press is an imprint of:
VU Boekhandel/Uitgeverij bv
De Boelelaan 1105
1081 HV Amsterdam
The Netherlands
vuuitgeverij@vuboekhandel.nl

isbn 90-5383-711-6
nugi 651

© Amerika Instituut, Amsterdam 2000
All rights reserved. No part of this book may be reproduced, stored in a retrieval system, or transmitted, in any form or by any means, electronic, mechanical, photocopying, recording, or otherwise, without the prior written permission of the holder of the copyright.

CONTENTS

INTRODUCTION   1

PART I. THE POLITICS AND RHETORICS OF DIFFERENCE—MULTICULTURALISM IN THE UNITED STATES AND GERMANY

THE POLITICS OF ETHNIC DIFFERENCE: MULTICULTURAL THEORIES AND PRACTICE IN COMPARATIVE U.S.-GERMAN PERSPECTIVES
Berndt Ostendorf   17

SOCIAL CAPITAL - MISSION IMPOSSIBLE? A COMPARATIVE ANALYSIS OF SOCIAL RELATIONS IN ETHNIC COMMUNITIES IN THE UNITED STATES. AND GERMANY
Meike Zwingenberger   31

TRANSLATIONS OF MULTICULTURALISM: MULTICULTURAL EDUCATION AND PUBLIC DISCOURSE IN THE UNITED STATES AND GERMANY
Reinhard Isensee   46

HISTORIANS, HISTORIES, AND PUBLIC CULTURES: MULTICULTURAL DISCOURSES IN THE UNITED STATES AND GERMANY
Günter H. Lenz   63

PART II. VISIONS OF AMERICA IN/AND EUROPE—AMBIVALENT IMAGES AND THE ROLE OF INTELLECTUALS

AMERICA AND THE EUROPEAN SENSE OF HISTORY
Rob Kroes   107

LOCALIZING THE SUBLIME: CONCEPTS OF CULTURE IN GERMANY AND THE UNITED STATES
Klaus J. Milich   128

BRITAIN AND AMERICA: TWO VIEWS OF MODERNITY IN NINETEENTH-CENTURY DENMARK
Jens Rahbek Rasmussen   152

THE AMBIGUITIES OF ENLIGHTENMENT: GUNNAR MYRDAL AND AFRICAN AMERICAN CULTURE
Richard H. King   167

THE MULTICULTURAL ROUTES OF HISTORICAL MEMORY:
A CRITIQUE OF PIERRE NORA'S CONCEPT OF *LIEUX DE MÉMOIRE*
   Peter Ling   184

LIST OF CONTRIBUTORS   197

INTRODUCTION

In recent decades, the debates about the meaning and the political repercussions of multiculturalism have attracted wide attention in both the United States and Europe. At the time of the America's so-called "culture wars," multiculturalism was condemned by conservative and liberal critics as a threat to the unity and the fundamentals of the nation's political culture, while it was simultaneously celebrated by adherents of an ethnic essentialism, such as some versions of Afrocentrism, who reject orthodox liberal ideas of cultural pluralism as inherently hierarchical. Multiculturalism was also projected and explored by radical critics and minority intellectuals as a new, complex, contested, dialogic and intercultural vision of American society and culture. As such, it was appropriate to an age of globalization and transnationality that had gone beyond liberal pluralism and the conservative ideal of a stable, unitary, common (i.e. national and white) core culture. By comparison, the controversies about multiculturalism in Europe have been less severe and enjoyed less public prominence. They have also often been based on a crude or polemically distorted understanding of both the terms of the debate in the United States and the concepts of society, politics, and culture in the American Republic. Nevertheless, the increasing migration of people from all parts of the world to Europe and the remarkable mobility of citizens across the European nations for many different reasons, notably economic globalization with its wide-ranging, and sometimes contradictory, social and cultural effects, have compelled Europeans to take more seriously the ramifications of the more penetrating contributions to the American debate.

The comparative perspective on the multiculturalism debate has also made us aware again of the crucial differences of the concepts of culture and their social and political implications, as they have developed in European countries and in the United States. The constructions of national identities have always been deeply engaged in often contradictory, ever ambivalent intercultural, transatlantic visions and revisions of the meaning of "Europe" and "America" as the utopian or threatening, negative "Other." Only if we explore these processes of cultural exchange, displacement, and unending transformations in the history of transatlantic intellectual and cultural encounters can we hope to respond in a productive, transnational, and dialogical way to the manifold and highly contested challenges of the current age of globalization and relocalizations.

Part I: The Politics and Rhetorics of Difference—Multiculturalism in the United States and Germany

The contemporary clashes over multiculturalism can be seen as a prime example of the dynamics and dialectics of latest in a long line of transatlantic encounters. They enable us to identify the processes of transculturation that articulate competing concepts of cultures of difference. The first part of this volume offers a comparative case study of transatlantic multiculturalism(s), of the objectives, practical consequences, and discursive strategies of multiculturalism in the United States and in Germany. Due to its traditional citizenship law based on ius sanguinis and its understanding of national culture as basically homogeneous due to this principle of common descent, Germany seems particularly different in outlook to the United States with its inherently heterogeneous culture and society.

The first essay by Berndt Ostendorf compares the complex relationship of the theory and practice of multiculturalism in the U.S. and in Germany, contrasting the ways cultural difference and dealing with the ethnic other are conceptualized and politically implemented in both countries. If the dilemma of dealing with difference, of negotiating universalism and particularism is at the centre of multicultural theory, how can they been held in balance in political practice? Ostendorf points out that the very concepts of "difference" are encoded differently in American and German society. Seemingly similar discourses on the significance and role of difference, he explains, "react to and work over different historical wounds and political cultures" to produce divergent outcomes. The debate over Charles Taylor's proposal for a "politics of recognition," which would complement the traditional procedural form of liberalism (what Taylor calls Liberalism 1) with a "communitarian" version (Liberalism 2), which protects a normative idea of belonging and of group survival, spotlights the difficulty of recognizing group rights based on cultural difference without essentializing them and excluding other groups. But Taylor's proposal also shows the dissonance between the United States and Germany in terms of the organization of cultural identity; that is, in the meaning and relationships assigned to the concepts of "individual" and "community" in the two cultures.

In the United States, Ostendorf argues, individualism is based on the "freedom and integrity or inviolability of the individual," on "voluntarism" and "freedom of choice." As a result, the moral framework of America's civil religion is primarily a matter of the individual, not of the state. In Europe, on the other hand, "equality" and "solidarity" are seen as primary values, particularly in the German case, where they are strongly supported by the normative bond of a Volks- or Abstammungsgemeinschaft. Thus, the "crisis" of multiculturalism in Germany occurred when the children of the Gastarbeiter (guest-workers) came of age during a period of economic recession which brought home to them the precariousness of their situation in a society which denied them political rights. In this case, an American-style model of multiculturalism may be attractive since it offers "the juridical-liberal instruments" and patterns of "ethnic solidarity" that can help groups to "weather the hazards of an economic liberalism." Ethnic solidarity in the United States is conceived to be "voluntary," a matter of personal choice, at least for white ethnics, rather than simply a question of descent. This voluntary, de-essentialized ethnicity constitutes the American understanding of community. It is supported by the majority of Americans who, simultaneously however, reject—as in the case of religious denominations—the establishing or institutionalizing of ethnic difference as political power or what some term a "particularistic multiculturalism." In contrast, since

Germany lacks the liberal constitutional tradition that facilitates such a de-essentialization of difference, cultural difference continues to be highly essentialized in the German debate on multiculturalism. As a result, ironically, cultural difference in Germany, unlike in the United States, finds support in right-wing political circles.

If Berndt Ostendorf's closely-argued essay expounds the ideologizing intricacies of the politics of multicultural theory and practice in the U.S. and Germany, Meike Zwingenberger's contribution uses the same comparative perspective to explore the political implications of the creation and sustaining of voluntary associations as theorized in the popular concept of social capital. How do ethnic communities accumulate social capital in the strikingly different institutional settings of the two countries, and how do "naturalization law and concepts of citizenship shape the character of social relations of ethnic groups"? If social capital relies on personal networks of interacting people in a community, how can it still be accumulated at a time of weakening social relations? Can social capital not only help to solve the economic problems evident in de-industrializing societies but also "build civic solidarity and stabilize a national identity," as some of its proponents claim? Zwingenberger's comparison of the United States and Germany shows the different modes of integration for newly arrived immigrants/foreigners and diverse barriers they face as far as the various aspects of human capital like national origin, political status as a refugee, or ability to speak the language are concerned. These kinds of discrimination encourage a retreat into ethnic enclaves and the accumulation of what Zwingenberger calls "ethnic capital" (that is, the social capital mobilized in a particular ethnic community). In accordance with Ostendorf's account of the dimensions of "ethnicity," Zwingenberger points out that the accumulation of ethnic capital by a group depends both on the suppression of differences within the group and the "invention of traditions" in order to maintain its distinctiveness in relation to other groups and create a program for action.

So, how does the accumulation of social capital in ethnic communities work in practice in the U.S. and Germany? Zwingenberger takes the Korean immigrants in California and the Turkish minority in Germany as her examples, a comparison that highlights the ambivalent position of these ethnic communities in the two nations but in the common context of a fundamental restructuring of the labor market. If the Koreans in California have succeeded in forming ethnic networks which have facilitated the accumulation of material wealth and social capital, the lack of political rights and the absence of bilingual education in Germany have prevented the Turks of the second and third generation from becoming fully integrated into the German economy and society. In both countries, however, immigrants have increasingly been marginalized and forced to find employment in the "informal periphery of the economy." Social capital has undoubtedly been accumulated and invested in dense imagined community structures, but clearly it has failed in R.D. Putnam's terms, to "save the civic virtues of the nation-state."

Zwingenberger's comparative analysis of the social relations in ethnic communities also highlights the crucial role that education plays in the accumulation of social capital in multicultural societies. The history and changing conceptualization of multicultural education in the United States and Germany are the subject of Reinhard Isensee's essay. He shows that the controversies about the meaning, the need, and the objectives of multicultural education reach far beyond the confines of the public school systems and the universities affected. They involve fundamental issues such as the constitution of national identity, the construction of historical memory, the meaning of democracy, and the institutional repercussions of such key categories as race, class, and gender. The "culture wars" that have been waged in the U.S. during the 1980s and 1990s are not uniquely American, but only one spectacular and emotionally highly charged expression of transformations in the global economy and in communications media that have affected all post-industrial societies at the end of the 20th century. As Isensee elaborates, the implications and consequences of these common challenges that have particularly affected the structuring and the social mission of educational institutions have been articulated in very different ways in the United States and Germany. In the U.S., as Todd Gitlin has emphasized, multicultural education has had to confront a "central wound" in American history, the denial of civil rights to African Americans, without falling back on an exclusionary Afrocentrism. Instead, it has to pursue, in Isensee's words, "the dynamics of negotiating diverse and conflicting interests" in the interplay of different groups. Isensee argues that we can avoid being trapped by much of the polemical reductionism of the recent culture wars, if we place the debate about multiculturalism and the canon in a historical perspective and revisit the controversies over the curriculum earlier in this century. He reminds us of the movement for a "Great Books" curriculum and the progressivist educators' struggle for an Integrative Curriculum. Against this background, he analyzes the pedagogical potential of some of the models of multicultural education developed in universities and schools since the late 1960s, their political reform impulse, and the intricate problems of institutional and curricular implementation they have encountered.

As Isensee explains, multicultural discourse has developed in a very different political and social situation in Germany. He traces its course from a largely pedagogical project of integrating or assimilating foreign workers into a German culture (seen as essentially homogeneous and based on common descent) to more recent programs that relate the issue of immigrants to "a more complex analysis of the moral state of society that routinely employed ethnicity as a source of discrimination against particular groups." At least in principle this has resulted in a revision of the traditional concepts of German culture, acknowledging heterogeneity and difference. Isensee perceptively notices the unique situation of Germany in the 1990s. Reunification, in its ambivalent repercussions, has provided a context for reassessing the objectives and institutional consequences of multicultural education among West as well as among East Germans. The effects of this reconstitution of the German nation-state and, at the same time, the challenges faced by the trans- and postnational movement toward a unification of Europe (based on the European Community) have, unfortunately, resulted in a glaring neglect of higher education on the agenda of major political issues in Germany during the last decade, a neglect that more recently has been reflected in public demands for reforms. However, Isensee points out, academic disciplines and programs at German universities like American Studies, Cultural Studies, Anthropology (Ethnology), Political Science, and German Studies have extensively problematized concepts of multiculturalism in their specific implications for German society and culture and explored the cultural and political consequences of ethnicity, race, class, and gender politics in an international perspective.

The final—and longest—essay in the first part of the volume by Günter H. Lenz takes up the issue of the different character, function, and strategies of discourses of multiculturalism in the United States and Germany. It starts from the observation that, unlike their counterparts in Germany, American historians have played a crucial role in the debates about multiculturalism. They have powerfully contributed to reopening the question of the public role of the intellectual, and to reassessing the contours of public culture in the age of post-industrialism, post-modernity, and globalization. They have reconsidered their objectives and reflected upon their modes of conceiving and writing the history of multicultural societies. Lenz characterizes the American approach to multiculturalism, particularly in radical versions and minority discourses, as being based on an open culture concept. This defines the problems of cultural difference and heterogeneity and of interculturality primarily in terms of internal cultural diversity and difference, i.e. as challenges of American history or histories that have to be met in the work of American historians. In Germany, as in other European countries, however, multiculturalism has usually been seen as a challenge coming from outside. It has been understood as an externally generated problem of recent origin that threatens the unity of the national culture (traditionally understood as inherently homogeneous), and that raises new questions of citizenship and the composition of the nation-state. Therefore, multiculturalism has not been a central issue among German historians, nor have demands for revising the historical canon in the various areas of cultural studies in Germany attained the level of urgency they have had in the U.S. over the last decade. Still, the meaning of multiculturalism has been debated in Germany, too, both among the general public and, as Isensee's essay indicates, in academia. Numerous studies have also, to some extent, contributed to a sharper awareness of the inherent heterogeneity of German culture and society throughout its history. By doing so, they have an alternate framework for understanding the impact of the de facto immigration of people from around the world, of the reunification process, and of the ongoing steps towards a united Europe. If multicultural discourse in Germany has been slow to engage in the analysis of intra-cultural differences, American multicultural critique has conversely often lacked a clear recognition of the intercultural, transnational dimensions and interactions that affect all national cultures in our present age of globalization, world-wide migrations, and electronic communication media.

Thus, placed in comparative perspective, multicultural discourses in Germany and the United States pose the question of multiculturalism in ways that mutually correct and strengthen one another. But what is needed most urgently in both cases, Lenz argues, is a much more sophisticated and penetrating conception of the realm and the dynamics of public culture in which the critical concepts of multiculturalism can be articulated effectively. He calls for a radical understanding of the dialectics of multicultural histories and their discursive strategies that engage the various separate group histories achieved in recent decades in a dialogue without falling for a reductive version of a "new" (or old) "synthesis." It is here that the multiculturalism debate among American historians can provide suggestive reflections and provocative models.

In his essay, Lenz closely analyzes Thomas Bender's continuing efforts to define and elaborate the contours and concepts of public culture as a way of reconceiving both the complex interrelationships within American history and the role of the historian as public intellectual in contemporary society. In this respect, the American historical profession's debate over multiculturalism and the fate of cultural differences in the United States (with all its tensions, contradictions, and competing visions) can be seen as a crucial test-case *and* as a practical realization of Bender's project of American public culture as both forum and force-field. In subsequent sections of his essay, Lenz offers detailed readings of influential studies by several American historians that focus on the dimensions, issues, and strategies of multicultural discourses. They range from the politics of multiculturalism (and the implied notion of a common culture as a bulwark of a stable political system), through debates over the meaning of the term "culture" and alternative traditions in American history, to the controversies about the history standards, the canon, and the engagement of historians in the public sphere. Focusing especially on Robert F. Berkhofer's book *Beyond the Great Story*, Lenz addresses the crucial, but usually neglected, question of how a recognition of the crucial importance of cultural difference and a critical multiculturalism (must) affect the representational strategies for narrating and writing multicultural histories of the United States. He concludes positively that the argument among American historians about the meaning of multiculturalism and public culture has been set in a wider context by the various efforts, notably those of David Thelen (editor of the *Journal of American History*), to internationalize American history. Thelen has urged colleagues to see American history in its global setting, and to build up a transnational dialogue among historians of the United States, of "America" in a wider sense, in which comparative, intercultural work can be realized in a more productive way than in the past.

Part II: Visions of America in/and Europe—Ambivalent Images and the Role of Intellectuals

The essays collected in this section consider in diverse ways the complex processes at work in the construction and reconstruction of national identity. In doing so, they enlarge upon the theme of the dynamic and fluid relationships within and between cultures. As Rob Kroes observes in his wide ranging and thoughtful contribution, visions of America in Europe have always simultaneously been visions of America *and* Europe. In seeking to define America and register its differences, Europeans have also, if sometimes unwittingly, defined themselves. Mapping America in this sense has been an exploration of the European self. To use Kroes's terms, "there is always a triangulation going on, in the sense that the reflection on America as a counterpoint to

European conventions functions within a larger reflection on European history and destiny."

The representation of America as "the land of the future" and within that image, the incorporation of anxieties over the destiny of one's own nation is well illustrated by Jens Rasmussen's essay on Britain, America and Danish modernity. Summarizing the writings of Danes at the time of the American Revolution, he comments that they "may be considered a sort of vicarious protest against autocratic system at home," since at that time the democratic liberties, espoused by the American Declaration of Independence and legally embodied in the Bill of Rights attached to the US Constitution of 1783, were not recognized in absolutist Denmark. Rasmussen corroborates another key point of Kroes's discussion: namely, that a comparable pattern of reflection regarding other European nations accompanied the triangulation of American and native images and realities. Rasmussen does this explicitly by highlighting the fact that for most of the nineteenth century, Great Britain, because of its technological and political eminence, rivaled the United States as an exemplar of future trends in Danish eyes.

Rasmussen furthers our understanding of the processes by which envisioning America or any other nation entails an implicit national self-examination. He notes that Danish views of Great Britain were significantly affected by the lasting national resentment against Britain's naval attacks on Copenhagen during the Napoleonic Wars. As late as 1884 the mother of Oscar Wilde reported that Admiral Nelson and the Duke of Wellington were still reviled in Copenhagen. A similar phenomenon is also acknowledged by Kroes when he comments that European reflections on the United States and upon their European neighbours were crucially coloured by the after-effects of the Great War. If traditional antipathies, rooted in memories of past confrontations, restrain and direct the ways in which we conceive of other nations, this process at the same time reinforces the limits upon our capacity to imagine our own nation anew.

The above is just one of many ways in which the world of nations or as Benedict Anderson calls them, "imagined communities" is transfixed. Rasmussen also points out that for Danes, knowledge of both Britain and America was mediated by the preeminence of German as the second language of the bilingual Danish elite during the early nineteenth century. The linguistic barriers that divided continental European nations from each other and from a largely Anglophonic Atlantic sphere (arguably until the Second World War) may seem obvious but their implications are important. Even today, it has tended to mean that the study of language and literature is the major educational route for students from mainland Europe to American Studies whereas in the British Isles, the absence of the language barrier means that historical study equally readily leads a student westward. Moreover, as we shall see, the delicate task of translation—so central to the diffusion of ideas across the West—frequently results in telling, if subtle, changes in meaning that may often reveal the different assumptions and emphases of the national cultures involved. This is particularly the case with cognate abstract terms such as culture and civilization which already have a range of definitions. For poststructuralists, the imprisoning nature of language has become something of cliché, but it is never more binding than when its effects are undetected. Significantly, whereas Rasmussen's examination of Danish reflections on America and Britain from the American Revolution to the Second World War identifies the mediating role of language, Kroes's focus on more general, twentieth-century contacts places the emergence of a new visual culture of global, mass media in the foreground, a development he discusses largely via the observations of the great Dutch historian Johan Huizinga. Ironically, given the limitations of language just noted, Huizinga feared the supersession of the text by the image.

The European visions of America, mediated by distance, language, and the historical legacy of international relations in Europe itself, were also vitally shaped by the phenomenon of emigration to the United States. In Rasmussen's essay, this is demonstrated by the contest between popular representations of America as a golden land of opportunity and abundance, and more skeptical portraits. The latter are well illustrated by the clash between the celebrated Hans Christian Andersen and the less renowned Danish poet Ingemann. Andersen enthused about the technological innovations pioneered in America while Ingemann, although prepared to concede American progressiveness in this respect, doubted whether this trait had elevated American morals and culture. Here, again, Rasmussen's discussion of the Danish case conforms to general principles outlined in Kroes's essay.

Drawing from his own larger work on this topic, Kroes suggests that for all their variety, European views of America may be classified into repertoires with essentially three dimensions that serve to structure a discourse of cultural difference. The first dimension is spatial, whereby European verticality, its hierarchy and emphasis upon the essential interplay between cultural heights and the feeling of depth are contrasted to the purely horizontal flatness of American life and culture, a spatial metaphor for its shallow, inner spiritual life. The second dimension is temporal and contrasts the vital, deep-rooted European sense of the past with the transient immediacy of American life. The third dimension consolidates the main points of criticism evident in the first two by contrasting the organic cohesion of European culture, which nurtures a more holistic outlook, to the American predilection for selective expropriation, for combining cultural components without any reverence for their historic and spatial specificity. Although these dimensions could be readily used to critique American culture, Kroes rightly notes that they have also be used to celebrate America as an example for Europeans to emulate. He adds that the structural features of the discourse he identifies seem more a function of a degree of apprehension about another nation state rather than of Europeanness or Americanness *per se*. As Rasmussen reveals, in Denmark's case this meant that antipathy for Germany for geopolitical reasons was paralleled by a dislike of Britain and America as precisely the kind of large-scale, industrial capitalist societies that the Danes feared might yet be their own fate. However, ultimately, military defeat in 1867 and proximity to a continuing German militarism significantly tempered Danish hostility to Britain and America; with Britain in particular emerging as the preferred model of the future until at least 1945.

While European emigration to the United States provided one spur for reflections upon America's national character, the flow of travellers across the Atlantic and especially of members of the intelligentsia from Alexis de Tocqueville onwards greatly enriched the discourse of national difference to which Kroes refers. In his own essay, Kroes considers Huizinga's ambivalent response to the United States. As a public intellectual, Huizinga tried to interpret America for his countrymen as a commentary upon European trends. Visiting America in the mid-1920s made him more appreciative of Europe, as he set the impersonal scale and scope of American cities and organizations—the epitome of what he termed "the mechanization of life"—against the more personal world from whence he came. Yet the contrast was more accurately between American modernity and the monastic, medieval Europe to which Huizinga was so powerfully drawn; a vision of Europe, which, through its great cathedrals and continuing religious rituals, still offered its own pointed commentary on what Huizinga regarded as the increasingly ugly character of contemporary European life. Thus, visiting America, the quintessential "other" country reinforced Huizinga's sense of the past as another country.

Just as representing another country provided a mechanism for defining one's own land, so the elementary historical process of periodization served to define the present. As Klaus Milich's essay demonstrates, this function has become particularly evident in the contemporary debate over the transition from modernism to postmodernism. Drawing on Niklas Luhmann's article "Why Does A Society Describe Itself as Postmodern?," Milich argues that the new framework of periodization has furthered American global cultural influence by displacing a specific model of modernity "through which particularly German culture has tried to come to terms with *its* [his emphasis] political, historical and philosophical traditions." Examining the intellectual history of postmodern concept, Milich summarizes the position of Jurgen Habermas, who presents "postmodernity as a turn away from the project of modernity, i.e. from Enlightenment ideals, especially a turn against the consensus-building and cathartic effect of reason." The term "modern" itself was sparked by a conscious sense of transition from the old to the new during periods sometimes referred to as renaissances (12th century, and more notably 15th, 16th and 17th centuries). During the Enlightenment, modernity developed two distinct modes of thought. It acquired a faith in human progress, rooted in science and as its antithesis, a romanticism developed which challenged the dominant rationalism and celebrated revelation or intuition. This romanticism sometimes used an idealized image of the Middle Ages to critique the processes of rationalization that had found their own inspiration in an idealized classicism. By the twentieth century, Habermas suggests this romantic spirit had freed itself from specific historical models to express simply "an abstract opposition between tradition and the present." It venerated the new and this future-orientation was exemplified by its celebration of the "avant-garde." As Milich argues, it is this latest mode of understanding modernism that predominated in the post-war United States.

Other German scholars helped to develop a sharper definition of modernity in Germany than in the United States. With America very much in his mind, Max Weber, for example, stressed rationalization as the core process of modernization since the Enlightenment, and one which "differentiated and polarized the sphere of cultural and aesthetic modernism from social and technological modernization under the rubric of the terms culture and civilization." This German distinction between culture and civilization was also central to the work of the Frankfurt School. As recently as 1965, Herbert Marcuse, notes Milich, wrote that civilization was "the realm of necessity" where man was compelled to respond to external conditions and meet involuntary needs. As such, progress in civilization came from operationalist modes of thought that developed the productive rationality of existing social systems. In contrast, culture referred to life's higher dimensions where humanity escaped these external limits to experience a sense of autonomy and fulfilment. Consequently, culture both gave rise to the utopian hopes that civilization derided and offered the critical space from which to indict civilization's compression of human possibilities. At the same time, since this higher culture was divorced from the toil and misery of those most immured by the tasks of civilization, it could also to some degree serve as the ideology of that society, affirming it by disassociating its critique from "real" experience.

If the framework of modernity contained the tensions between culture and civilization that German intellectuals identified, in the United States a similar, containing, ideological function was first served by the concept of the sublime before being superseded by that of postmodernity. In America, civilization, in the German sense of modernization of the social reproductive apparatus, was paramount but was viewed in opposition only partly to culture (since this was displaced as an attribute of Europe). The more pointed opposition to civilization in America was offered by Nature and from this tension came the importance of the concept of the sublime for Americans. Given the extraordinary physical characteristics of the American continent, David Nye has suggested that "had no theory of the sublime existed, Americans would have been forced to invent one." Having grounded the national image in this awe-inspiring encounter with the sublime, Americans successfully transposed it from the pastoral to the technological, enabling the forces of civilization to play a role within the sphere that Germans defined as *Kultur*. European commentators compounded these tendencies by stressing in their own visions of America the wondrous character of its technology and commerce as its principal, distinguishing characteristic. In doing so, they also implicitly underlined their own European, cultured status.

The emigration of European intellectuals, notably including leading members of the Frankfurt School meant that in the post-war era, German concepts of modernism which assumed the distinction between culture and civilization played a larger role than previously in American intellectual debates. In Milich's view, the New York intellectuals associated with *Partisan Review* translated the culture-civilization dichotomy into textual categories to create a new discourse of modernism in the United States. As part of their attack on "mass culture," older figures like Irving Howe and Lionel Trilling celebrated the aesthetics of high culture for the critical distance it displayed from the mundane mechanics of everyday life. Younger figures such as Susan Sontag and Leslie Fiedler, on the other hand, were unhappy with such an exclusionary concept of culture, regarding it as blind to the forms of aesthetic consciousness realizable in performance or via intellectual engagement with forms such as science fiction or pop music that were traditionally dismissed as generic.

By the 1960s, Milich explains, while these new visions of culture in America were at odds with German orthodoxy, they were being significantly bolstered by the work of French poststructuralists. Jacques Derrida's and Roland Barthes's destruction of the notion of the text as a self-enclosed world meshed nicely with Sontag's critique of a high culture in which individual genius operated without the taint of the masses. Significantly, both Barthes and Sontag were intrigued especially by visual culture. This aspect of modern expression was, as Rob Kroes points out, precisely what Huizinga had pinpointed as developing most rapidly in America via advertising and the movies, and doing so in a way that threatened to shift culture permanently from the printed word to the image. The ephemeral, fluid quality of this ideographic culture that Huizinga regarded with such apprehension in the 1920s seemed to have been realized by the 1980s (thanks to a telecommunications revolution) in what Frederic Jameson described as "a new and original historical situation in which we are condemned to seek History by way of our own pop images and simulacra of that history, which itself remains forever out of reach."

Milich identifies a third phase of postmodernity with the incorporation of Michel Foucault's foregrounding of the power relations at work within the production of knowledge. Foucault's work strengthened a growing critique of the Enlightenment project and particularly its assertion of the universality and objectivity of truths attained by rationalist epistemology. When coupled to the assaults upon canon formation by socially marginalized groups in the late 1960s and 1970s, this form of post-modernism became in the United States part of a larger range of multiculturalist critiques. As Richard King points out in his essay on Gunnar Myrdal and African American culture, the Swedish sociologist's curious dismissal of African American culture in 1944 as a potentially valid and vibrant springboard for the struggle for racial equality was itself rooted in "a progressive Enlightenment derived sociology." Although his critique of Myrdal was not published at the time, African American writer Ralph Ellison tellingly rejected Myrdal's denial of black cultural agency. The subsequent rise of black consciousness, with its use of post-colonialism to assert the legitimacy of Afrocentric viewpoints within a multicultural discourse, was accompanied by a growing insistence that modern slavery and racism were key products of the Enlightenment. While acknowledging the truth of such claims, King is keen to offer a more balanced assessment of the Enlightenment's legacy. For Myrdal, a key part of that legacy was the attempt to subject irrational, prejudicial behavior to scientific analysis in order to achieve a more rational future.

Unlike Milich, King is struck by how completely Myrdal shared the intellectual biases of his American collaborators with regard to culture. Chosen by the Carnegie Corporation in 1938 precisely because he was not already known within the citation community of race relations, and because as a Swede he came from a country without a history of imperial domination of non-white peoples, Myrdal brought with him a technocratic inclination derived from the more interventionist, European state experience. Unlike many contemporary American sociologists, he had more faith that stateways could change folkways. Nevertheless, he did not differ from them on the vexed question of race and culture. He was part of a generation of Western social scientists who abandoned the idea of a significant biological differentiation of the races yet largely retained a belief in a hierarchy of cultures that ranked non-white, non-western cultures as backward or underdeveloped. In the case of African Americans, Myrdal concluded that despite some divergences, "American Negro culture is not something independent of general American culture. It is a distorted development, or a pathological condition, of the general American culture."

King goes on to explain this insensitivity to black expressive culture by comparing Myrdal's great work to that of members of the Frankfurt School. For King, it is hard to imagine Hannah Arendt's *Origins of Totalitarianism* without the Kafkaeque motifs that inform it nor to appreciate Theodor Adorno and Max Horkheimer's *The Dialectic of Enlightenment* (published in 1944, the same year as Myrdal's *An American Dilemma*) "apart from the sensibility of the European avant-garde which dominates it." In contrast, reading Myrdal is more reminiscent philosophically of Thomas Jefferson. Reminded by Milich of the importance for German thought of the distinction between culture and civilization, one is tempted to see Myrdal as a disciple of civilization, and therefore of modernization more than modernism.

In another portion of his fascinating exploration of the Swede's encounter with American race relations, King alludes to historian Warren Susman's claim that a central theme of American cultural life during the Great Depression was the rediscovery of local and regional cultural practices, sometimes referred to positively as folkways or folk culture. In the final essay in this collection, King's colleague, Peter Ling looks more closely at this cultural category of the "folk" in the context of another, more recent European thinker, French historian Pierre Nora. Just as the processes of representing other nations or differentiating historical periods tends to entail the rhetorical construction of defining oppositions, so Nora's positing of a crucial historical transition—from the era of the *milieu de memoire* to the modern epoch of the *lieu de memoire*—constitutes a potent rhetorical strategy. Offered in the context of commemorative celebrations of the two hundredth anniversary of the French Revolution, Nora's idea of the *lieu de memoire* as a key feature of modern French culture attracted considerable attention. Superficially, it seemed to follow a Foucaultian emphasis on the centrality of power relations in the process of cultural formation by indicating the artificial and contingent quality of images, places, traditions or events that had operated as stimulants of a supposedly genuine, national memory. However, to bolster the critical claims he wished to make against these *lieux de memoire*, Nora invokes an opposition between his native France and the United States within which he describes the latter as "a country of plural memories and diverse traditions" in which history had a less central "didactic role in forming the national consciousness." As well as endorsing the traditional idea of American exceptionalism, Nora offers an even more sweeping global dichotomy between the modern realm of History and the earlier sphere of Memory by declaring that "independence has swept into history societies recently roused from their ethnological slumbers by the rape of colonization." He adds that at the same time, "a sort of internal decolonisation has had similar effects on ethnic minorities, families, and subcultures that until recently had amassed reserves of memory but little in the way of history." History, as a key aspect of the modernity into which the nations of the world have been swept in this century, is a very different, cultural phenomenon for Nora than its predecessor, unhistoricized Memory.

Like Gunnar Myrdal, Pierre Nora has cultural biases that make it hard for him to comprehend African American culture. The experience of African Americans in the rural South for most of this century seems largely to fit his concept of the *milieu de memoire*. In the absence of widespread literacy, their oral traditions preserved folk memories that were magical and affective, operating in a way that placed "remembrance in a sacred context" that was insensible to the distortions to which it was subject. It is this strong, if implicit, contrast between orality and literacy that prompts Ling to test the validity of Nora's taxonomy by considering the example of the Spirituals. In doing so, he draws on black British scholar Paul Gilroy's emphasis on music and oral culture in the cultures of the black Atlantic. Where Nora speaks of the emergence of *lieux de memoire* as a major rupture in human consciousness, Ling describes a complex pattern of cultural development that reinvigorated the status of African American spirituals through a process in which orality and literacy co-existed and collaborated. The intellectual outlook that prompted leading black scholars such as E. Franklin Frazier to affirm the merits of assimilation in their advice to Gunnar Myrdal had produced an educated African American population that largely rejected Spirituals sung in the traditional style by the 1950s. It was a white folk singer and song collector Guy Carawan who recognized the worth of this music and helped to make it a key part of the emerging Freedom Song repertoire of the Civil Rights Movement in 1960-61. As part of the folk revival of that era, and subsequently as what can quite properly be termed the soundtrack for more recent commemorations of the Southern Freedom Struggle, the songs —most notably *We Shall Overcome*—have become what Pierre Nora would term a *lieu de memoire*.

However, this example of folk music, Ling argues, serves to underline the artificiality of Nora's original distinction between *lieux* and *milieux de memoire*. Drawing on the recent work of ethnomusicologists such as Robert Cantwell, Ling stresses how the folk concept is quintessentially modern, a projected reification of features that successive commentators have perceived, often from a romantic standpoint, as missing in their own modern civilizations. Just as Canadian folklorist Sheldon Posen argues that "items are not intrinsically 'folk'; rather their 'folkness' lies in the functions and processes and ultimately the contexts of which they are a part," so *milieux de memoire* (whose inviolate social memory sets the criteria of authenticity according to which *lieux de memoire* represent for Nora, a decline) are essentially myths that obscure the possibilities within contemporary culture for settings "in which memory was a real part of everyday experience." According to Ling, Carawan's work demonstrates how function, process, and context can fuse—at least for a time—the qualities of *milieu* and *lieu de memoire* that Nora sets irrevocably apart.

Thus, across the several essays of this section, putative binary oppositions—Europe and America, old and modern, modern and postmodern, cultural and economic, folklore and History, culture and civilization—simultaneously proliferate and dissolve. However elaborate the discourse of difference we invoke, they seem to say, we continue in our transatlantic encounters to confront the contradictions in ourselves, and through this engagement, from the expressive confines of our history, we inscribe our identities anew.

The essays in the volume grew out of an international research network in the Human Capital and Mobility Program of the European Community, directed by Professor Maurizio Vaudagna (Centro Piero Bairati, Torino). We would like to thank the Council of the European Community for funding the research network and Professor Vaudagna for his unfailing commitment to turning the often enthusiastic, but also difficult efforts of cooperation among scholars from different countries and different academic disciplines into a successful and challenging common endeavour. We would also express our thanks to Reinhard Isensee, Klaus J. Milich, Karin Sinnema ... for doing the necessary editorial work to transform the various files into a publishable book manuscript.

Günter H. Lenz (Berlin)—Peter Ling (Nottingham)

PART I.
POLITICS AND RHETORICS OF DIFFERENCE—
MULTICULTURALISM IN THE UNITED STATES AND GERMANY

THE POLITICS OF THNIC DIFFERENCE:
THEORIES AND PRACTICE IN A COMPARATIVE U.S.-GERMAN PERSPECTIVE

Berndt Ostendorf

"Lieber französische Sitten als amerikanische Zustände"
(Picket sign of unionized workers in Berlin)

"Daddy, what are we?"
"What do you mean?"
"You know, where are we from? Are we Italian, Irish, Jewish; you know like that?"
"Well, we're from here; we're Americans."
"Daddy!!! What am I going to say in school?"
John Garvey

Frank-Olaf Radtke, a defender of the Enlightenment Project, listed five ways of dealing with the ethnic "other," options which extend from rigid exclusion to complete inclusion.[1]

1) Radical separation and exclusion—which may take several historical forms: repatriation, expulsion, ethnic cleansing and genocide, all based on differences of race, culture, national origin, and religion.

2) Ghettoization or, more precisely, asymmetrical apartheid—the subordinate group in the "host" society is without civil rights and has a special subordinate or "alien" status such as that of guestworkers.

3) Corporate or hard multiculturalism with a political and juridical recognition of group rights effecting the political equality of groups not of individuals.

4) Hyphenate pluralism (or soft multiculturalism) with a (negotiable) division *à la* Hannah Arendt between a private and a public sphere. In terms of political practice the former is particularistic and subordinate, the latter universalistic and dominant. In other words, particularistic group rights are recognized so long as these do not interfere with universal individualistic rights. A graded distinction is made between the private ethnic *l'homme* and the public *citoyen*.

---

[1] John Garvey, "My Problem with Multi-Cultural Education," *Race Traitor*, 1 (Winter 1993): 18-25. Frank-Olaf Radtke, "Multikulturell—Das Gesellschaftsdesign der 90er Jahre," *Informationsdienst zur Ausländerarbeit*. Nr. 4/90: 27-34. See also his contribution "Multikulturalismus: Ein Postmoderner Nachfahre des Nationalismus," in *Multikulturelle Gesellschaft. Modell Amerika?* ed. by B. Ostendorf (München: Fink Verlag, 1994), 229-236.

5) Radical inclusion: the integration of the other regardless of race, culture, national origin and religion.

These options are quite familiar from history, and they are currently operative in political and legal practice all over the world. They range from legal inequality (1) to legal equality (5). In terms of a politics of difference we move from a negative recognition of difference (1) to indifference towards difference (5).[2]

However, both of these radical options discriminate against the men and women who are perceived to be and want to be different, and particularly against those who are given no choice by established patterns of discrimination. The first, exclusion, discriminates in *principle*, the second, inclusion, tends to discriminate in *practice*. This dilemma of difference lurks at the core of the current conflict over multiculturalism. In her book *Making "All" the Difference*, Martha Minow, former assistant to Supreme Court Justice Thurgood Marshall, captures the dilemma well:

> when does treating people differently emphasize their differences and stigmatize or hinder them on that basis? and when does treating people the same become insensitive to their difference and likely to stigmatize or hinder them on *that* basis?... The stigma of difference may be recreated both by ignoring and by focusing on it.[3]

The American moral imagination privileges manichean scenarios and tends to draw the players in this debate into mutually exclusive camps which reinforce and stabilize each other. We might want to divide them into the *ignorers* and the *focusers*, fully armed with a rhetoric of invective: "You nasty focuser, you blind ignorer." Hence the debate is noisy and divided.

Alan Wolfe argues that both the defense and the abolition of difference or of boundaries is an essential part of an unending sociogenesis which unfolds as a negotiation between inevitably particularistic communities within an inevitably universalistic liberal state.[4] This sounds "balanced" in theory. How does this balancing act between a particularistic and universalistic ethos work in practice? How do tacit assumptions in the American and German public cultures control or affect the meaning of difference?

At this juncture a first cognitive dissonance between Germany and America appears in the semantics of difference. Not only does the "ethnic other" have a specific historical ring in Germany, but the two radical options, separatism vs. integration, are grounded in different *pragmatic* political force fields. In short, the two debates, though apparently similar in their rhetoric and utopias, react to and work over different historical wounds and political cultures. In Germany the hidden choreography of the debate is defined by the fall of liberalism after 1848 and by the Holocaust; in the U.S. by the coexistence of

---

[2] The morphology of "gleichgültig" highlights the fact that indifference towards difference presupposes equal rights.

[3] Martha Minow, *Making All the Difference: Inclusion, Exclusion and American Law*, (Ithaca, NY: Cornell University Press, 1991), 20.

[4] Alan Wolfe, "Democracy versus Sociology: Boundaries and Their Political Consequences," in *Cultivating Differences. Symbolic Boundaries and the Making of Inequality*, ed. by Michèle Lamong and Marcel Fournier (Chicago: University of Chicago Press, 1992), 309-325.

the success of liberalism for white males and its failure for Blacks and women, Native Americans and Hispanics. In Germany "to make a difference" stands in the shadow of *Sonderbehandlung* (special treatment), *Endlösung* (final solution) or, more recently, of *Fremdenfeindlichkeit* (nativism) all of which are compounded by unification woes. Hence politically conscious Germans are loath to consider a politics of difference—even as a strategic *countervailing balance* against the excesses or faults of liberalism. With an eye on the failure of liberalism after 1848 and on the Holocaust they argue for the fifth option, complete legal equality and inclusion.[5]

In America the quest of ethnic groups for a politics of difference and cultural autonomy had a positive and a negative motive. After the liberal principle of individual civil rights was achieved in the courts (1954-1965), the economic and social chances of African Americans, Native Americans and Hispanics did not improve as expected. Full political citizenship, Blacks were first to find out, did not protect them against social or economic discrimination under the prevailing neoliberal dispensation with its strong belief in individual achievement. Such victims of social and economic discrimination needed help not as individual American citizens but as members of these groups. The *affirmative* step was to transfer the principle of "equality before the law" from the individual to ethnic groups. At the same time the notion of equality was expanded from an equality of chances (within a liberal economy) to a more substantive equality. This positive push for recognition of group rights and for substantive equality was reinforced by a negative, "republican or communitarian" reaction towards the corrosive effects of a possessive individualism on the one hand and the "stultifying" process of Americanization and mass cultural homogenization on the other. Neo-conservative communitarians worried that core republican values were in decline as an inevitable consequence of "too much" liberalism. Counter-cultural communitarians attacked patterns of hegemony (Gramsci) and power (Foucault) of an all too repressive state and blamed the current crisis of civil society on "not enough" liberalism. Both groups, however, reinforced the positive connotation of difference and defended small communities against the all-powerful state. But are differences inherently good?

The squaring of the circle, as it were, was found in a binary switch. Divisive, negative ascription was changed by an act of consciousness-raising into a positive identity, expressed in the slogan "Black is beautiful," a transformation which worked remarkably well, albeit more effectively in the culture industry than in social or economic relations. A negative recognition of difference, which in Northern Ireland has lead to bloodshed and mayhem, is transvaluated, thanks to the safe liberal frame of the US constitution, into the recognition of "positive" difference. By taking the negative connotations out of difference it became a positive social good and a pillar in the defense of affirmative action. Cultural or ethnic diversity was now a political virtue. Behind this reversal I rec-

---

[5] The former minister of justice and member of the liberal party Leuthäuser-Schnarrenberger was close to tears when the "Lauschangriff" was ratified allowing police to monitor private residences in the fight against organized crime. "This is a black day for liberalism," she said. That this decision could find the approval not only of our liberal party, but also of the Social Democrats is telling.

ognize a specifically American spin, the power of positive thinking that derives from the victorious Armenian heritage in the management of religious difference. When the liberal principle of the equality of individuals was applied to groups, this led inevitably to the problematical assumption that all cultures must be accepted as equally good. America, as opposed to Bosnia or Northern Ireland, has a system of "no-fault cultures." To Europeans this is an instance of American exceptionalism or of exceptionalist optimism.

With one eye on Quebec, Charles Taylor argues in his essay "Multiculturalism: The Politics of Recognition," for such a positive revaluation of cultural difference and for the possibility of a "liberal Quebec nationalism." One of Taylor's approving respondents, Michael Walzer, with one eye on the U.S., formulates the two types of liberal goods which need to be protected in a *post-Civil Rights* state: individual freedom and group or ethnic loyalty.

The first kind of liberalism ("Liberalism 1") is committed in the strongest possible way to individual rights and, almost as a deduction from this, to a rigorously neutral state, that is, a state without cultural or religious projects or, indeed any sort of collective goals beyond the personal freedom and the physical security, welfare, and safety of its citizens. The second kind of liberalism ("Liberalism 2") allows for a state committed to the survival and flourishing of a particular nation, culture, or religion, or of a (limited) set of nations, cultures, and religions ...

In other words, "liberalism one" is, in terms of culture or religion, "contentless" and merely guarantees any pursuit of happiness to a plurality of individual citizen. "Liberalism two" on the other hand protects a normative idea of belonging, of the "good society" and the "right values" which would guarantee group survival. "Liberalism one" represents the classic American position, "liberalism two" the classic German position. This fact is not lost on Walzer. For he feels constrained to add a caveat to liberalism two after a long dash: "—so long as the basic rights of citizens who have different commitments or no such commitments at all are protected."[6] "Liberalism two," which Taylor considers at this time the more urgent policy, keeps its innocence, Walzer warns, only under the stern vigilance of "liberalism one."

Here we run into the communitarian dilemma which not only mirrors a key problem of multiculturalism, but brings out the "American" or "exceptionalist" character of the debate: how to prevent the cultural loyalties of liberalism two from becoming "normative" or "essential" and how to prevent boundaries, designed to protect one minority, from being "exclusive" to other minorities. Though ethnic cultures and boundaries based

---

[6] The title of the second edition adds one word: "Examining" and therewith a note of caution *Multiculturalism: Examining the Politics of Recognition* 1994 with additional essays by Jürgen Habermas and Anthony Appiah. See also Walzer's "Multiculturalism and Individualism," *Dissent* (Spring 1994), 185-191 and Andrew Stark, "Vive le Québec anglophone!" *TLS* (Sept. 22, 1995), 16. Louis Menand unravels some of the contradictions in: "Blind Date. Liberalism and the Allure of Culture," *Transition* (Fall 1995), 70-81. Needless to say the term "liberal" is fraught with transatlantic ambiguity. American and German usage varies considerably: Dietmar Herz, *Republik und Verfassung. Die theoretischen Grundlagen einer liberalen Staatsordnung* Habil. Schrift, Sozialwissenschaftliche Fakultät, München 1995.

on endowment are by any classic anthropological definition normative and are supported by strong essentialist and ethnocentric motives, how can they be made voluntary? Indeed, the "voluntarization" of what in Europe tends to be considered essential, this is the key difference in American and European multiculturalism. Here we have, in Goethe's words, "*des Pudels Kern*," the core of the multicultural and communitarian dilemma: the balance (or imbalance) between the "freedom" and "necessity" of belonging. And here the European and American stories diverge with a vengeance.

Classic American liberalism one abolished the necessity of *primordial* belonging. This did not mean that America rejected the notion of a national "Gemeinschaft." But this national "glue" was not ethnic, but a repository of republican, communitarian values beyond the constitution that Gunnar Myrdal called the "American Creed" and others in the wake of Rousseau a "Civil Religion." This extra-constitutional sense of belonging to a *Wertegemeinschaft* rather than to a descent group, conservative communitarians claim, is now endangered by a rampant liberalism one on the one hand and by a new particularistic congeries of all sorts of quasi-tribalist, pre-national "Gemeinschaften" such as Blacks, Native Americans, Women, Gays. Incidentally, the groups neo-conservatives blame for the fraying of America are the very same groups that were marginalized by the liberal "Creed." Communitarians posit community against the excesses of liberalism one, multicultural groups promote the identity politics of liberalism two as a compensatory strategy against the "blindness" of liberalism one. Both privilege *Gemeinschaft*, but for different reasons.

Apart from this communitarian quandary (whose genesis will be explored below) we run into a profound cognitive dissonance between America and Germany, or indeed between the New World and Europe. There is a marked difference in the organization of cultural identity, particularly as concerns the historically sedimented traditions of "individualism" and "community," that constitute the pillars of liberalism one and liberalism two respectively. In the language of jazz, let me run these key concepts, *individualism* and *community*, through German and American changes.

For Americans individualism rests on a belief in the *freedom* and *integrity or inviolability* of the individual. The rigorous protection of the individual manifests itself best in crises like war. In World War Two it was the U.S. government's policy to minimize the loss of American citizens and consequently the U.S. sacrificed a mere 350000 individuals—much to Stalin's chagrin—whereas Soviet Russia lost forty times as many as cannon fodder. Wherever an American citizen is in danger, as Tom Lehrer has it, America "sends the Marines." The second pillar of the national faith is *voluntarism* (as opposed to coercion) and its corollary, *freedom of choice* rather than unfree fate or deterministic descent. Americans insist that politics be implemented according to the "consent of the governed" rather than the descent of the group. Hence, there is the demand, often observed in the breach, but renewed and reclaimed in the course of American history, of *one man [sic], one vote* and of *no taxation without representation*.⁷ All of this boils down to one important difference. "Amerikaner kann man werden durch freie Wahl. Aber man ist Deutscher." (You may become an American, but you are a German.) Hence the US has had an Ein*bürgerungs*gesetz (naturalization law) since 1800 and Germany has had a Staats*angehörigkeits*gesetz (national membership law) since 1913. When the chips are down Americans favor inclusion on the basis of freedom and voluntaristic choice regardless of culture, religion or national origin, in short, "liberalism one"; when in doubt, Germans favor exclusion on the basis of cultural or religious bonds for the protection of normative *Gemeinschaft* and essential descent groups, in short, "liberalism two." A more moderate, Social Democratic version of a *Solidargemeinschaft* would call for the protection of working class "social capital." A minority of Germans would gladly do without Walzer's caveat as some of the recent attacks on the *Bundesverfassungsgericht* after its crucifix decision, all allegedly based on "gesundes Volksempfinden," amply demonstrate.⁸

Despite frequent jeremiads by communitarian Cassandras who bemoan the effects of a corrosive individualism and the decline of republican virtues, Americans in their role as *political agents* will come up with the following spontaneous free associations when the word individualism pops up. On the plane from Frankfurt to Washington D.C. in March 1995, after watching the in-flight movie *Forrest Gump,* I tried it out on my two neighbors: to my left a Jewish New York liberal, to my right a Polish-American follower of Pat Robertson, who despite their ideological differences got along famously on a first name basis. Germans find this social civility across political divides mildly disturbing, and this very difference in etiquette supports my argument. Although from diametrically opposed ideological camps they agreed that the state should not interfere with or curtail the freedom of choice of individuals. But they also defined the role of the individual in society by stewardship, by duties and obligations. Both stressed the moral framework of a civil religion, both insisted that ethics are a matter of individual responsibility, not of the state. Yet their notion of voluntarism was embedded in a sense of duty towards the public good, the common wealth. How did Jonathan Edwards put it? "Where much is given, much is demanded." Both gave me Gunnar Myrdal's *American Creed.* (I should add that they did disagree on causes and remedies of poverty.)

---

⁷ In other words, America's liberal *Bürgerrechte*, like its Coke, have become so "classic" to the postmodern imagination as to be boring, thus inviting ill-advised attempts to improve them. Moreover, the *virtuous citoyen* living in a *moral* city upon an *exceptional* hill is called upon to be a *model for the world*—much to the chagrin of that world. This missionary habit of the American heart has already affected the international multicultural debate. Benjamin Barber suggests in a recent article that America should export its brand of multiculturalism worldwide. Published fittingly in the *World Policy Journal* 10 (Spring 1993), 47-55, its title, "Global Multiculturalism and the American Experiment," is properly exceptionalist. Barber thinks that the American model of multiculturalism (he means soft pluralism) and a federalism along the lines of the "Articles of Confederation" could be a viable model for multiethnic countries. I detect a note of exceptionalist condescension in wanting to export the constitutional lemon that did not work in America.

⁸ Hans Ulrich Wehler, "Der Kampf gegen Karlsruhe. Wie die Advokaten des gekränkten Volksempfindens die Axt an unsere Verfassungsordnung legen," *Die Zeit* Nr. 49 (Dec. 1, 1995), 73.

For Americans my argumentative line may begin to steer towards neo-conservatism. Not so from a German perspective. I am articulating the envy of a German looking at bipartisan approval of certain principles of enlightened liberalism buttressed by a republican civil religion, principles that according to Helmuth Plessner *"verspätete Nationen"* (latecomer nations) or according to Theodor Adorno democracies without a successful revolution so often lack. And this difference in tacit assumptions is borne out by recent comparative polls on values in western democracies, which *The Economist* reported with understandable envy under the Eurocentric headline "An Odd Place: America."[9] The question "which good do you value higher, 'freedom' or 'equality'" received markedly different responses from Germans and Americans. Indeed the difference would question the allegedly successful Americanization of (West) Germans.

In the U.S., 72% of the respondents opted for freedom, only 20% for equality. In (West) Germany, 37% chose freedom, but 39% would have equality. Raising the ante, the pollsters asked should government equalize income disparities that are due to the free market system. And a whopping 80% of the Americans said no, but 59% of the Germans approved. Of Italians and Austrians a solid 80% called for the state to right the wrongs of the market.[10] Americanization of Germany? Perhaps, but only relatively speaking. American freedom is, in Isaiah Berlin's classic definition, a "freedom from interference of the state" and "freedom to do your own thing." Therefore the state should be weak and inactive, the individual strong and active. In Germany (and Europe), where the state has a history of being strong and active, the individual tends to be weaker and more inactive. This continues to be a habit of the heart across political divides.[11]

What are the spontaneous associations when a concerned student of German history and a reader of the German press considers *Gemeinschaft*, that is Walzer's "liberalism two." *Gemeinschaft* as the majority of Germans including a good part of its intellectuals would define it is constituted by culture, religion, or linguistic or regional ethnicity. You are a German, a Catholic, a Bavarian, a Volga-, or Sudetendeutscher. There is a strong undertow of determinism buttressed by "collective memories" (M. Halbwachs) in the conceptual history (Begriffsgeschichte) and the current popular use of *Gemeinschaft*.[12] The question "Herr Bubis, Sie sind doch Jude," heard in Rostock not so long ago, har-

---

[9] "American values," *The Economist* (Sept. 5, 1992).

[10] *The Economist*, with raised eyebrows, marvels: "in Germany 'solidarity' is an obsession. The constitution itself calls for 'unity of living standards in the federal territory.' In four decades the pursuit of solidarity has not eliminated economic differences among regions, but it has smoothed them out, and it has also given Germany relatively even distribution of income among classes." (Sept. 30, 1995), 21.

[11] Thomas Nipperdey subtitled his *Deutsche Geschichte 1800-1866* "Bürgerwelt und starker Staat." (München 1983). According to a recent poll by the *Süddeutsche Zeitung* East German approval of the German liberal constitutional republic is low and 44% favor a return to a "starker Staat," (Jan. 5, 1996).

[12] Manfred Riedel, "Gesellschaft, Gemeinschaft," *Geschichtliche Grundbegriffe* Band 2, (Stuttgart 1979), 859, comments on the reactionary turn in the understanding of *Gemeinschaft* as an oppositional term to *Gesellschaft*. It needs to be remembered that the Holocaust sensitized post-Germany to questions of racialism or "racial" difference, yet because of the ethnic cleansing post-World War Two Germany is a more homogeneous *Gemeinschaft* than Weimar. On basic differences between German and American notions of community: Hans Vorländer, "Ein vorläufiges Nachwort zur deutschen Kommunitarismusdebatte," *Forschungsjournal NSB* 8 (1995): 39-43.

bours a tacit political agenda quite different from such a query in New York. From the tacit privileging of *Gemeinschaft* in German political culture it follows that the autonomy and self-determination of the collective often takes precedent over the rights of dissenting individuals. Within such *Gemeinschaften*, in crises such as war, the individual serves as cannon fodder for the national, ethnic and religious cause. "Dulce est pro patria mori." You find yourself as a member of a *Schicksalsgemeinschaft* (Carl Schmitt), or as a member of a descent group (*Volks-* or *Abstammungsgemeinschaft*: former Minister of the Interior Kanther) complete with genealogical myths. On the constructivist end you are a member of a *Solidargemeinschaft* or of a *Sozialisationsgemeinschaft* (Habermas), yet all of them are defined by an inevitable membership. What about one man, one vote? Surely, Germans believe in it thanks to a "Westernization" of our basic law after the war, but historical or collective memories and ideological configurations persist. Indeed, in keeping with "liberalism two" the protection of a *deutsches Volk* is part of our basic law, and this legal obligation shows a trickle down effect. When a member of a Bavarian *Trachtenverein* was asked on the radio why he dressed up each week-end and wore a funny hat, he did not answer "Because I like it," but "Der Schutz der Tradition ist Paragraph eins unserer Statuten." (The protection of tradition is required by our by-laws.) How better could one capture the normative bond of *Gemeinschaft* or the legal protection of its cultural content. Hence it follows that Gemeinschafts-oriented people would have a *Staatsangehörigkeitsgesetz* (national membership law) and that candidates for the German civil service have to present a *Staatsangehörigkeitsnachweis* (proof of "membership in the nation") that reaches back several generations into the past.

Let me turn to the spontaneous fantasies of a modal, i.e. statistically average German when s/he hears of individualism within the given ideology of *Gemeinschaft*. Again I use a broad brush for the sake of dragging tacit mind-sets out of their ideological closets. For "gemeinschafty" Germans individualism has often evoked anomie or egotism, narcissism and libertinism. Lack of solidarity and a penchant for hedonism or self-indulgence are traits that Germans over the years have recognized "instantly" as a "fault" in the American system. Not surprisingly the German vote for freedom in the poll of the *Economist* ranked below the vote for "solidarity," and 59% of the Germans wanted the government to equalize income disparity. This has been the tacit objection to America, the land where according to Heinrich Heine, Sigmund Freud and Heiner Müller liberty quickly degenerated into libertinism. Liberty, according to this German view, has by itself no moral or cultural content, is merely "procedure." Robert Bellah and Amitai Etzioni also attack the excesses of liberalism, albeit from a republican American perspective, and call for a new sense of community as a countervailing balance to "liberalism one.

Not that solidarity is in itself an illiberal force or that a consensus on values does not sit well with a liberal polity. Far from it, as Montesquieu, Rousseau and I would argue. Indeed some of the best traditions of German political culture are grounded in communitarian habits which constitute our accumulated social capital. One such virtue, solidarity, is expressed in the higher vote for equality, and it bears directly upon the German multicultural debate. Clearly the "olidaritätsbeitrag" (short Soli) would be quite unthinkable in the US. One reason why the debate on individual and civil rights is underdeveloped in Germany today—even among the ethnic groups themselves—has to do with the consequence of a strong working class solidarity and with a "systemic or structural ethics" of a paternalistic "strong state." Indeed the worry about income disparity and about social capital is a basic element in the concept of "soziale Marktwirtschaft," which all parties including the conservatives embrace and which Germany has been envied for the world over. The fact that those who have a job in Germany, including foreign born workers, enjoy a degree of job security and fringe benefits unheard of in America has in the past reduced their need to claim "civil rights" that would enable them to fight in a competitive, "free" market system over diminishing resources with other citizens under conditions of "equal opportunity." For a Greek or Turkish worker whose safe job at the BMW or Siemens plants is protected by German labor law the question of "civil rights" and "empowerment" within the German political culture are of a decidedly secondary order. You would, in fact, be hard put to find a Turkish BMW worker willing to emigrate to America and exchange a safe job without civil rights in Germany for the sake of civil rights without a job there. Add to this an open and inexpensive educational system and you knock two of the two most powerful motives for the rise of multiculturalism in the U.S. clean out of the German picture. Indeed, it is the lack of job security in the U.S. and the high cost of education that make "individual rights," "equal opportunity" and "access to resources" such important political instruments in American free market competition under conditions of a zero-sum-game. Is it an accident that the multicultural debate gained momentum during a period of a moral and economic slump from the late sixties onward and fully emerged when Ronald Reagan began to deconstruct the Welfare State and the New Deal?

Therefore it is not surprising that the German "crisis of multiculturalism" was first felt when the second generation, the children of *Gastarbeiter*, came of age. This second generation did not enjoy the job safety of their parents and had no rights as citizens although, in marked contrast to their parents, they were born and raised in Germany. Whereas their mothers and fathers rested comfortably in a non-assimilationist attitude nursing their belief in the myth of return, the second generation began to experience an identity crisis, that is, the dual pull of being *de facto* German, but *de iure* Ausländer. They were caught between two "hostile" ethnic environments both blaming them that their ethnic glass was "already" half empty or "only" half full. Their acculturation was (in George Devereux' apt term) clearly "antagonistic" leaving them with a split superego. For, to add insult to injury, their culture of origin tagged them as "the Germans" while their host society called them "Ausländer." Worse yet, they faced the double jeopardy of being unemployed and of having no rights. As the German labor market over the past ten years has become more deregulated and privatized following a global neoliberal realignment, the need for an American-type multiculturalism may indeed increase. The decline of their socio-economic capital (job safety) increases the need to mobilize the ethnic social capital. American-type multiculturalism wants to equip individuals with the *juridical-liberal* instruments on the one hand and with ethnic solidarity on the other to weather the hazards of an *economic* liberalism. In a nutshell, American multiculturalism is a strategic result of economic disparities based on a liberal economic order. Sir Ralf Dahrendorf concedes, "[economic] liberalism can live with a great deal of inequality...as long as the equality of chances is secured."[13] It is because of economic inequality inherent in liberalism one that the entire idea of instrumentalizing the *ethnic* capital becomes so important within the U.S.

Let us return to the notion of community and chart the semantic range of American meanings of *community* by quoting from dissertations defending the American creed. We may begin at the beginning and quote the Mayflower contract, which was "voluntarily agreed upon." Voluntarism was a key concept in the early Republic, when individuals flexed their muscles and exercised their new freedoms guaranteed in the constitution and the amendments. German observers on the Right have always marveled at the strong self help groups and the more encompassing definition of the private sector, and our Left successfully imported civil disobedience and social movements (Bürgerinitiativen) in the late Sixties.[14] Many "voluntary" associations of the "private" sector, let me hasten to add, are too often stabilized by Social Darwinistic advantages such as money, family status, chauvinism and racism. No wonder that Social Darwinism as a social philosophy for the selection of the fittest was so successful in America. Therefore "*gemeinschafty*" Germans will tend to characterize the American principle of freedom as hypocritical, pointing an accusing finger at its Social Darwinist practice.[15] But the point I want to make is that the cultural habit of voluntarism is so deeply embedded in the American unconscious and in political practice that it is simply taken for granted *as being natural*, even by the American Left. It is telling that communitarians, who desire a return to more normative values, still insist that the change in the habits of the heart should be "voluntary."

Even "ethnicity," which is the ultimate determinant of identity by descent (codified in Europe in the *ius sanguinis*), has come under the sway of voluntarism. Mary C. Waters' *Ethnic Options. Choosing Identities in America* (1990) concludes that "ethnicity

---

[13] Die Zeit (Dec. 2, 1994), 13. See also *Die angewandte Aufklärung. Gesellschaft und Soziologie in Amerika* (München 1963).

[14] Robert Bach in his essay "Recrafting the Common Good: Immigration and Community" emphasizes the role of voluntarism as a way of negotiating cultural difference: "Voluntary associations, organized formally or informally, provide the energy, resources, and direction for community building. They mobilized private and group standards, obligations, and responsibilities and are especially important in shaping culture and discourse." *Annals of the American Academy of Political and Social Sciences*, 530 (Nov. 1993), 164. See also Robert Wuthnow, "The Voluntary Sector: Legacy of the Past, Hope for the Future?" in *Between States and Markets: The Voluntary Sector in Comparative Perspective*, ed. by Robert Wuthnow. (Princeton: Princeton University Press, 1991), 3-29.

[15] They are joined by American communitarians: Ann Swidler, "Inequality and American Culture. The Persistence of Voluntarism," *American Behavioral Scientist*, 35 (March/June 1992), 606-629, and of course by Marxists: CB MacPherson. *Die politische Philosophie des Besitzindividualismus* 2. Auflage (Frankfurt 1987). See also Hans Joas. "Gemeinschaft und Demokratie in den USA. Die vergessene Vorgeschichte der Kommunitarismus-Diskussion," in *Gemeinschaft und Gerechtigkeit*, ed. by Micha Brumlik and Hauke Brunkhorst (Frankfurt 1993), 49-62. For a comparative view: Helmut K. Anheier, Lester M. Salamon, and Edith Archambault, "Participating Citizens: U.S.-European Comparisons in Volunteer Action," *Public Perspective,* 5 (Mar.-Apr. 1994), 16-18,34. I owe the coinage "gemeinschafty" to Werner Sollors.

is increasingly a personal choice of whether to be ethnic at all ... it matters only in voluntary ways ... First, I believe it stems from two contradictory desires in the American character: a quest for community on the one hand and a desire for individuality on the other." She quotes the official instructions for the census takers for the 1990 census: "List the ethnic group with which the person *identifies*." How did that get into the instructions for a census which is supposed to form the solid statistical rock for policy making? Through voluntary associations, in this case through the active lobbying on the part of ethnic leaders in Washington.[16] There is an interesting process at work here. The essentialist or primordial quality of descent *(Abstammung)* acquires, in the American political process (that is in the free exercise of white individual rights), an *exceptional* or *voluntaristic* quality, a privilege, I repeat, which extends primarily to white ethnics. You cannot choose *not* to be black though this has been tried close to the color line in the tradition of "passing."[17]

Translated back into the political process, however, voluntary ethnicity becomes essential again (in both meanings) when the division of political spoils along an ethnic or a color line, as in affirmative gerrymandering or quotas, has to be administered and defended as public policy. Voluntary or de-essentialized ethnicity recoups its normative losses in democratic proceduralism under the given patterns of inequality of the market. This curious process of voluntary de-essentialisation and procedural or juridical re-essentialisation is, I believe, the cause of much of the current resentment among white ethnic males and explains the crisis of affirmative action.

Quite clearly African Americans and Native Americans have not enjoyed the privilege of voluntarizing "community." They had no choice or wanted no choice. Continued racism was the dividing line between voluntary white and involuntary non-white ethnicity. Indeed, racism kept African American and Native American communities and community bonding alive (cf. the Black church, secret lodges, Social Aid and Pleasure Clubs etc.). Hence the sense of community among African Americans and Native Americans has an "Un-American," almost Bavarian ring to it, one reason, perhaps, why there seems to be an elective affinity between community-oriented Germans and African Americans or Native Americans.[18] This compensatory role of community as antidote to structural racism within American liberalism explains why the "white ethnic" American Michael Walzer, who enjoys the privilege of an ethnic option, has no choice but to consider the

---

[16] And thereby hangs a tale. Mary Waters writes, "symbolic ethnicity persists because of its ideological 'fit' with racist beliefs." *Ethnic Options. Choosing Identities in America* (Berkeley: University of California Press 1990), 147. On the balance between consent and descent cf. Werner Sollors, *Beyond Ethnicity* (New York: Oxford University Press, 1986).

[17] Shirlee Taylor Haizlip recounts how she restored missing branches of her family tree in "Passing," *American Heritage* (Feb./Mar.1995), 46-54. This problem is heatedly debated in *Lure and Loathing. Essays on Race, Identity, and the Ambivalence of Assimilation,* ed. by Gerald Early (New York: Penguin USA, 1994).

[18] In Bavaria and Baden-Württemberg there are a number of "Indianervereine." These are clubs with a lower middle class membership (often drawn from the crafts) that cultivate and recreate Native American tribal traditions complete with teepees, war paint and corn dances.

protection of minority-community a "liberal" cause.[19] This idea, I submit, is not exportable to Europe without losing its liberal „innocence."

The process of de-essentialization may best be explained by looking at another tacit belief of the American political creed: the role of religion in the public sphere. For I suspect that the voluntarization of ethnicity is modeled on the manner in which "primordial" religious loyalties (as in the absolute dictum "una sancta catholica" or "once a Jew always a Jew") were denominationalized in the young republic. Denominationalism, which has by this time become a deep-seated political faith, is the American way of pulling the political teeth of religious passions (cf. Federalist 10). The two parts of this crucial compromise on religious difference are set down in the First Amendment. First, the two freedoms "from and to": 1) the *free exercise clause*, which gives each individual the *freedom to* exercise his/her religious faith without *interference from* the state and from other individuals and, as a consequence, 2) the *anti-establishment clause*, which aims to prevent the rise of any sort of *unique* ecclesiastic, dogmatic or institutional religious power. Hence America has no *ecclesia*, no state church, no *institutional* religious power. And the power-sharing between church and state—typical of the *Konkordat* (of June 1933) between the German government and the Vatican—is to the average American decidedly "the work of the devil." Not surprisingly, American denominations are notoriously weak on dogma, but high on general morality or on principles of a civil religion. The latter is best characterized by the buzzword of the canon debate, the "Judeo-Christian tradition."[20] In the course of American history, the organization of ethnic difference has fallen in line: the *free exercise* of ethnic difference is widely accepted, but most Americans, including members of ethnic groups, are hesitant, if not wary, of the *establishment* of ethnic difference as political or consociational power. Interestingly, ethnic elites want it more than the rank and file. The quasi-religious nature of the battle over this core value may be explained by its roots in the First-Amendment heritage.

Since our focus is difference, we can now make a difference between "denominational" ethnicity which enjoys general support and "established" or "dogmatic" ethnicity that has so far failed to convince a clear majority of Americans, even of African Americans. A preference for a "denominational" ethnicity is borne out by a poll, entitled

---

[19] Anna Whiting-Sorrell, a member of the Salish-Kootenai tribe, writes that the salient feature of Indianness is "a strong sense of community," "a strong sense of belonging," and a "strong sense of rituals." "Life Is Belonging," *Treatment Today*, 7 (Spring 1995).

[20] B. Ostendorf, "Identitätsstiftende Geschichte: Religion und Öffentlichkeit in den USA," *Merkur* (May 1995) 205-216, and Jürgen Gebhardt, "Amerikanismus—Politische Kultur und Zivilreligion in den USA," *Aus Politik und Zeitgeschichte*, B 49/90 (Nov. 30 1990), 3-18. The old civil religion based on a denominational consensus is in a deep crisis. One consequence has been the rise of the new evangelicalism or televangelism, that is the new fundamentalism, that represents not a regression to the middle ages, but a voluntaristic realignment of denominationalism. The old denominations are breaking apart at the liberal/conservative fault line and realign as pluralist parachurches or megachurches or as electronic communities drawing their members from those established denominations now in decline. This process is driven by voluntarism which continues unabated into a virtual and New Age phase. Cf. Charles S. Clark. "Religion in America," *CQ Researcher* (Nov. 25, 1994), 1035-1041, who says that people, more than ever, "shop around" for a custom-made religion that fits their particular life-style and moral universe. Robert Wuthnow, *The Restructuring of American Religion* (Princeton: Princeton University Press, 1988).

"What Ordinary Americans think about Multiculturalism," conducted among the most postmodern and, in my view, least ordinary Americans, namely Southern Californians. The preliminary results were presented at the annual meeting of the American Political Science Association, Sept 1 1994 by four of our academic colleagues: David Sears, Jack Citrin, Sharmaine Vidanage, and Nicholas Valentino, a research team that represents a properly balanced ethnic ticket like the bomber crews in Hollywood's World War Two movies. This is their—to me quite unsurprising—conclusion:

> We have found that the mass public—*more or less irrespective of ethnicity*—is sympathetic to culturally diverse groups. There is a respectful recognition of diverse heritages. But there is little mass support, at this time, for official recognition of these ethnic differences or for special entitlements attached to them. And this lack of mass support for particularistic multiculturalism holds despite much *more supportive elite-rhetoric* and official policy both in California generally and in the Los Angeles area (my emphasis).

If Southern Californians think so, what about the folks in Peoria? And the authors end somewhat enigmatically: "This gulf between elite and mass creates a dynamic that might have a number of longterm outcomes."[21]

Germany has no First Amendment tradition for the taming of religious difference. But while Germans have accepted the institutional empowerment of religion in the *Konkordat*, they take revenge by freely exercising their right of not going to church and of not confusing personal morality and political talent. Nobody cares whether our political class has affairs or believes in God. And most politicians would not be caught dead quoting the Bible. Yet, without a First Amendment history, no liberal constitutional tradition exists for de-essentializing difference, whence difference in Germany remains inescapably *essential*. Indeed the discourse on the "politics of difference" along the boundary lines of *Gemeinschaft* has an almost exclusive right-wing tradition in Germany. This fact was brought home to me when I presented current American theories of multiculturalism (Charles Taylor, Martha Minow, Iris Marion Young, Michael Walzer) to the Council members of the City of Munich. The person most interested in Walzer's "liberalism two" (including its afterthought) turned out to be the press secretary of the *Republikaner*, who welcomed this unexpected support for his party's platform from the American Left. Therefore Frank-Olaf Radtke is correct when he argues within the given German multicultural debate: "Multikulturalismus bleibt auf halbem Wege stehen." He means "auf halbem Wege" to an enlightened citizenship law and to a political culture honoring consent, not descent, a position that we have yet to fully embrace. Hard multiculturalism is entirely compatible with our right wing's efforts to keep

---

[21] Daniel Yankelovich attributes the birth of the new politics of "Ressentiment" (Nietzsche) to this widening gulf. "Three Destructive Trends: Can They Be Reversed." Lecture presented at the National Civic League's 100th National Conference on Governance, Nov. 11, 1994. Seymour Martin Lipset in turn argues that "clearly, the American political system—though distrusted and ineffective in dealing with major social problems—is in no real danger." "Malaise and Resiliency in America," *Journal of Democracy*, 6 (July 1995), 17. Lipset observes not a decline, but a realignment of voluntaristic energy under post-modern, post-Fordist conditions. See also his *American Exceptionalism. A Double-Edged Sword* (New York: W.W. Norton, 1996).

the difference between Germans and Turks intact. When liberal Germans such as Daniel Cohn-Bendit and Thomas Schmid speak of *multikulturelle Gesellschaft*, they mean hyphenated pluralism (option 4) with a strong tendency toward integration (option 5), in short what the U.S. practiced until 1965.[22] The press secretary of the *Republikaner* would gladly import the more radical politics of difference (option 3) of Taylor, Young and Minow to Germany as a compromise which would allow him to exercise a modicum of nativism without running the risk of being *verfassungsfeindlich*. Indeed the model of a politics of difference or of an "ecological protection of diversity" has by now been adopted by members of the CDU.[23] The current campaign of the CDU/CSU against dual citizenship bears this out.

---

[22] Daniel Cohn-Bendit, Thomas Schmid. *Heimat Babylon. Das Wagnis der multikulturellen Gesellschaft* (Hamburg: Hoffman und Campe, 1992).

[23] Sabine von Dirke presents a cogent analysis of various ideological positions of the Right and Left in "Multikulti: The German Debate on Multiculturalism," *German Studies Review*, 17, (Oct. 1994): 513-536.

SOCIAL CAPITAL - *MISSION IMPOSSIBLE?*
A COMPARATIVE ANALYSIS OF SOCIAL RELATIONS IN ETHNIC COMMUNITIES IN THE UNITED STATES AND GERMANY

Meike Zwingenberger

Intellectuals and policymakers across the political spectrum have recently become enchanted with the concept of social capital in their search for new ideas. Liberals and conservatives alike now celebrate social capital as the key to success in domestic issues from public education to the battle against crime and unemployment. In these discussions, social capital has come to mean the ability to create and sustain voluntary associations, or the idea that a healthy community is essential to prosperity. In the international arena, strong social capital supposedly explains economic success of the Asian countries, while weak social ties are made accountable for the failure of the Soviet republic. The economic future of collective entities like nation-states seemingly depend on the durability and potential of relationships of its' citizens. In regard to citizenship, the United States and Germany represent different models of nation-states, one based on the ideal of cultural pluralism, economically depending on new waves of immigrants, the other based on the assumption that a homogenous "Volk" can only remain pure if immigration is restricted by the bloodline. The political foundations of both nations have consequences for the social reality in which members of ethnic minorities live - not only concerning naturalization and citizenship, but also the perception of oneself as an integrated part of a nation or as a marginalized outsider. In this essay I will provide a rather theoretical approach to what can be defined as social capital, investigate the possibility of its accumulation in two different institutional and political settings and analyze the character of social relations of ethnic groups under the influence of naturalization laws and concepts of citizenship.

Social Capital as a Resource of the Individual

Members of the German Bundestag and affiliated organizations plan a conference on "Soziales Kapital in der Bürgergesellschaft" in 1998. This meeting of social work experts, intellectuals and politicians is meant to find a way of mobilizing and creating social capital, which is supposed to reintegrate a fragmented society and encourage self-help and solidarity of German citizens. The planners of the welfare state and social workers are obviously helpless in view of the high amount of unemployment and the identity crisis of many juveniles in the Eastern part of Germany, of whom many support a right-wing ideology. Can social capital really succeed in the mission to solve not only the economic problems of post-industrial societies but additionally build and stabilize a national identity and civic solidarity? The attempt to utilize social capital for the prosperity of a collective entity which contains all members of a nation-state is plain and simple unrealistic. The following theoretical approaches explain why contact and communication is the basis for the accumulation of social capital. All forms of capital depict a bundle of resources, a stock of accumulated goods or capabilities, but also an aggregate that can be charged and recharged. Material capital comes in different shapes and forms, but is usually something valuable. Physical objects, like jewelry or pieces of art, are material resources. Human capital is a term, mainly used by economists, which describes the individual intellectual resources and dexterities a person has: skills, knowledge but also the ability to speak many different languages and other features. Social capital characterizes the potential of the social relations a person has.

The concept of social capital relies on the personal connection of interacting people in a community—"community" referring to a group of people with common interests usually living in a particular area. The active exchange of material goods and emotions of the members, to realize their interests, results in the development of social relations. The structure of these relations depends on the individuals' resources, how much control they can exert and how strong their social interdependency is. The potential of mobilizing help and support in such a community depends on the creation and strengthening of networks. Efficient information networks supply the members with news about housing, the work situation and important events in the neighborhood. Information networks can also be a source of knowledge: if an individual does not know how to repair a washing machine, a friend who is electrician might be more competent.

Social capital—just like material capital—is something that can be accumulated, but also invested. The accumulation process is marked by an intensification of interaction of the members of a community. As a result, the efficiency of social relations is enlarged; the individual now has a web of resources available which facilitates the accomplishment of a goal. James S. Coleman, one of the first sociologists who defined social capital, described it by its *function* in making the achievement of certain aims easier[1]: For it is very easy to borrow some eggs from a well-known neighbor, if the store around the corner is closed, and the Sunday cake has to be baked.

Trust—in this case social trust—is another basic element of such a social relationship—the more people trust each other, the more will they be willing to help and to give each other credit, financially as well as emotionally. Coleman describes the example of Jewish diamond merchants in New York, who save a great deal in lawyers' fees by conducting their transactions informally. Sacks of jewels worth thousands of dollars are lent for examination overnight without any paper signed. If one of the merchants is found guilty of dishonesty, the gruesome punishment is that he will no longer be able to participate in a lucrative market and is exiled by the community. The aspect of trust also illustrates that tight knit social relations support mutual understanding and intimacy. Alejandro Portes provides the example that many times pupils in Catholic schools fare

---

[1] James S. Coleman, *Grundlagen der Sozialtheorie. Bd. 1 Handlungen und Handlungssysteme* (München: Oldenburg, 1991), 392.

better than those in public schools because a teaching staff imbued with religious ideology sees the school as a closely integrated community rather than a set of bureaucratic structures.[2] The sense of being part of a community can either rely on the achievement of common interests as a group or, as seen in the example of the Catholic school, on a feeling of belonging, created by a common identity, like a religious orientation or ethnic heritage.

The foundation of clubs and organizations strengthens the relationship of members of a residential area. Regular meetings, activities and celebrations bring people together and secure their willingness to be supportive. In the past, churches used to create such a warm feeling of belonging. Today, a neighborhood center with all its affiliated offers of activity might be a solid foundation for the creation of networks. But also a local art club which organizes exhibitions and a political debate circle will have the same function. Robert Putnam is one of the authors who focuses on the weakening of social relations and the loss of social capital in the United States in recent years in his article "Bowling Alone: America's Declining Social Capital" published in the *Journal of Democracy* of January 1993. Putnam describes changing patterns in society and organizational membership which he observes and considers symptomatic for this loss: a decline in turnout in national elections over the last decades, falling numbers of union membership, less volunteering for civic and fraternal organizations. Some critics stress that the actual situation might rather indicate a change in orientation; many international organizations like Greenpeace record increased membership in the last years. Even Putnam has to admit that there is a countertrend, a growth of tertiary and nonprofit organizations, a rapid expansion, for example, of "support" and "self-help" groups like the Alcoholics Anonymous. The scope of social capital might be local or national, formal or informal—the basis for its creation is always the relations of individuals who interact. It can be found in highly formal, national organizations like trade unions or in rather informal associations like the German *Stammtisch*.

Coleman's concept of individual social capital had been stretched by Putnam to a national level: "*America*'s Declining Social Capital." For Putnam a high amount of social capital had become a characteristic of groups and even nations, rather than of individuals. Portes criticizes this vast scope and indicates that collective social capital can not simply be seen as the sum of individual social capital.[3] It links the micro- and macro level of society, but its creation depends on a form of personal contact. The collected data of smaller social units proves the significance of social capital in settings where people have this close direct contact. It is always on the individual level at which social interactions can be measured. Interaction is usually structured by norms and values which provide a framework for what kind of behavior is accepted and what is disapproved. Norms and values are intrinsic aspects of a vivid civil society. Because close and strong social relationships support the maintenance of civic virtues, many

---

[2] Alejandro Portes and Patricia Landolt, "The Downside of Social Capital," *The American Prospect*, 26 (1996), 18-20. http://epn.org/prospect/26/26-cnt2.html (30. August 1998).
[3] Portes, "The Downside," 2.

politicians and social activists ask for the preservation and accumulation of social capital to enforce basic values and norms of society.

Portes stresses that social capital is a resource that some individuals can claim and that comes at the expense of others. He indicates that the preservation of norms and values can therefore only be valid for the interacting members of a community and not for the society on the whole. He discerns a "conspiracy against the public" indicating that the concept of social capital also implicates a strong aspect of social exclusion: The "public," in this sense, are all those excluded from the networks and mutual support of the insiders—those belonging to the group.[4] Additionally to exclusion effects, the concept of social capital does also imply social control of the members. According to Portes, membership in integrated communities restricts individual freedom and business initiative. An ethnic enclave might offer protection against the discrimination from the core society, but it also implies tight control over those employed in enclave businesses—which American Chinatowns around the turn of the century successfully proved.

The Role of the State

It is highly questionable if social capital can really be responsible for the economic success of a nation-state as a collective entity. An ethnic enclave might provide a refuge for those with less human capital but can not evade the social stratification system on which the economy is based. Many Hispanic immigrants working as farm aids in the Southern and Western states of the US—many of whom belong to the growing group of the so-called *working poor*—have often very intense relationships, but can not climb up the social ladder. They are hindered not only by educational barriers but also by social ones. Those on the top usually had all the necessary incentives: not only a very good education, but also efficient information networks and wealthy and influential friends. The less affluent on lower levels of the social hierarchy are usually not as lucky. For newly immigrated members of society in both countries the only way to find work many times is the informal sector of the economy, where knowing the language is not as important and nobody asks for a university diploma. It is obvious that social networks for these migrants exist only on a horizontal level. On a vertical axis these newcomers have hardly any social relation which could provide mobility ladders and if they do, these contacts usually exist through members of their ethnic group.

Although, social capital represents a resource or a commodity, none of the people who profit from it, can consider it his or her personal property. Accordingly the right to social capital can not be sued for. This aspect distinguishes social capital from public commodities like education. The availability is limited and there is no universal right to it. The state protects only the individual rights of its citizens. If, for example, a very active individual or family leaves a residential neighborhood, because of a better offer

---

[4] Portes, "The Downside," 2.

for work somewhere else, it cuts social relations and weakens the community—but none of the community members can do anything. Even if the survival of a whole industry is threatened by the changing patterns of social relations the individual and the state can do nothing about it, as described by Putnam: The bowlers decision to "bowl alone," instead of bowling in organized bowling leagues has not only social, but also economic effects: "The rise of solo bowling threatens the livelihood of bowling-lane proprietors because those who bowl as members of leagues consume three times as much beer and pizza as solo bowlers, and the money in bowling is in beer and pizza, not the balls and shoes."[5]

Public institutions can stimulate the building of social networks: if schools have strong and active parent-teacher-organizations, social bonds develop and the feeling of belonging establishes a more connected community. The parent-teacher association has been an especially important form of civic engagement in twentieth century America because parental involvement in the educational process represents a particularly productive form of social capital, according to Putnam.[6] Stable norms and networks of organized reciprocity and civic solidarity influence the public life and the performance of social institutions.

The state with all its affiliated institutions affects the maintenance of social capital enormously—in two different ways. Nation-states with tax systems and social services distribute and redistribute wealth and secondly immigration and naturalization laws determine who can become an integrated part of the core society—the central majority and not the marginalized edges of society—and can trust the protection of his or her individual rights by state institutions. Many positive measures of welfare organizations are meant to reduce the personal hardship of an individual or family and attempt to succeed in increasing material resources, sometimes at the same time reducing the social capital. The welfare state tries to compensate the negative effects of a social stratification system by moving a person on welfare to an apartment paid by the state. The recipient is relieved of the costs for accommodation, but it cuts his or her social networks and therefore reduces the social capital at the same time. Social isolation might be the consequence. Many social benefits by nation-states are very ambivalent, concerning the accumulation or loss of social capital. On a different level, the constitution and rule of law of nation-states preserves the individual freedom of citizens. The US considers itself a "country of immigrants" and has a tradition of rather fair immigration and naturalization laws, based on quotas, which allow people of different nationalities, religious beliefs and levels of education to immigrate. Nevertheless, *skill* is a category that plays an important role, in who receives the official green card to get in and work. Germany regulates its immigration through the laws of descent—every legal immigrant needs to have a certain amount of German blood. The legal system protects the "citizens," but not necessarily all inhabitants, because not all people do have the same

---

[5] Robert D. Putnam, "Bowling Alone: America's Declining Social Capital," *Journal of Democracy*, 1 (1995), 65-78.
[6] Putnam, "Bowling Alone," 69.

rights and freedoms. Different kinds of discrimination—individual, institutional and structural—persists in most industrial and postindustrial societies.[7] The two structural settings provide various modes of integration for newly arrived immigrants but also diverse barriers on the basis of national origin of immigrants, political status as refugee, ability to speak the language and other human capital aspects.

Mobilization of Ethnic Capital

Structural barriers might support the retreat to the ethnic enclave. Within a given political culture manifold factors influence the chances of accumulation of "ethnic capital." The protection of individual rights by the state and labor law might be a strong impetus to integrate into the core society to profit from these structural incentives. If such a possibility is denied, family resources or ethnic solidarity offer an alternative structure to combat injustice. One basic difference between Europe and the United States is that members of ethnic groups in Europe can depend on a tradition of working class solidarity, and use the equal protection of labor law, but they face higher barriers to citizenship in Germany due to "ius sanguinis." In the US immigrants and ethnic groups have an easier access to citizenship rights, but are left to fend with the social Darwinism of the economic order. The sources for the need of social capital, especially for members of minority groups, are different in the German and American society, but the result of strong ethnic networks are quite similar.

The universal rights of citizens, not their everyday social realities, are addressed by the discussion about politically correct ways of dealing with the ethnic "other." Rights define the parameters of a political culture and its arena for legal action. And yet, the very existence of informal economies and ethnic enclaves is proof for the ethnic "capital" beyond mere rights. "Ethnic capital" is a definition for social capital which is mobilized in an ethnic community. This alternative structure indicates the persistence of social hierarchies, institutional racism, and economic discrimination in the core society. Universal rights are never truly accessible to those who are economically and socially marginalized. The realm of high principles on which America was founded is abstract, universal, and, for a long time under white, male control. The political universalism of white males, so claim the detractors, was mainly observed in its breach and has had a hypocritical history until the Civil Rights legislation of the sixties made blacks full citizens. The domain of popular passions, of warm ethnic feeling, may be of a lower

---

[7] Fred Pincus, *Race and Ethnic Conflict: Contending Views on Prejudice, Discrimination and Ethnoviolence* (Boulder: Westview Press, 1994), 82-162. In his book Pincus describes three distinct forms of discrimination: Individual discrimination refers to the behavior of individual members of one group that is intended to have a differential and/or harmful effect on the members of another group. Institutional discrimination is quite different in that it refers to the policies of majority institutions and the individuals, who implement these policies, that are indented to have a harmful effect on minority groups. Structural discrimination refers to policies that are race-neutral in intent but still have harmful effects on minority groups. For more information see Pincus 82ff.

order in the evolution of the philosophy of government, but it is simpler, more affective, more low-down, and often constitutes the only bond minority communities have. In this sense, we have to discuss ethnic capital as a possible means of mobilization towards a substantive improvement of the social and economic situation of those marginalized, as Martha Minow and Iris Marion Young would argue.[8] Indeed a certain measure of such capital beyond mere rights may be necessary as a stepping stone to reach the level of true and full citizenship. In Irving Howe's words, ethnic enclaves function as "decompression chambers."

The strong persistence of ethnic ties and the amount of solidarity in ethnic communities can be explained by individual interests on one side and by structural incentives on the other. Ethnic enclaves continue to exist because people of a common cultural background share past experiences as "collective memories" and a "myth of origin" as well as present experiences. These people will necessarily define their identity and mobilize solidarity around these shared assumptions. Interest groups within a liberal state may well have to organize around these types of "capital." Kathleen Neils Conzen defines two different levels of ethnicity: while "primordial ethnicity" both generates its own dynamic and is an end in itself, "interest group ethnicity" is instrumental, transitional and situational.[9] Ethnic bonding can be used as a strategy to receive sympathy and solidarity. In stressing the symbolic differences between oneself and the members of the core society, ethnic capital at the same time has a symbolic value. Language, manners, cultural practices might all be used as signs of distinction. For Pierre Bourdieu the existence of a symbolic value of all goods and practices additionally to the economic value is one basic hypothesis of his social theory.[10] In many situations the symbolic capital is responsible for the status of a person in the social hierarchy. One valid example is that of a University professor, who is expected to be a very serious and trustworthy person—his title accounts for symbolic capital. Ethnicity might be used as symbolic capital if the institutional system of a state provides affirmative action for members of minority groups. If the state does not offer that kind of "preferential treatment" ethnicity can at least be used as the common factor for the building of networks and community structures as an alternative to the core society.

But the decision to consider oneself as ethnic is not always a situation of choice. As a category of difference "ethnicity" originates from either a sense of achievement by the actors themselves or from ascription by others. Membership in a group, also brings demands for conformity. The same strong ties that help members of a group enable it

---

[8] Martha Minow, *Making all the Difference: Inclusion, Exclusion, and American Law* (Ithaca: Cornell University Press, 1990) and Iris Marion Young, *Justice and the Politics of Difference* (Princeton: Princeton University Press, 1990).

[9] Just like Werner Sollors, Kathleen Neils Conzen interprets ethnicity as an "invention" because it might be instrumentalized. The primordial base is just a source for solidarity which can be utilized to mobilize a group. Kathleen Neils Conzen, "The Invention of Ethnicity: A Perspective from the U.S.A.," *Journal of American Ethnic History*, 2 (1992), 3-41. See also Werner Sollors, *The Invention of Ethnicity* (Oxford: Oxford University Press, 1989).

[10] Pierre Bourdieu, *Sozialer Sinn: Kritik der theoretische Vernunft* (Frankfurt am Main: Suhrkamp, 1993).

to exclude outsiders. The creation of boundaries and their maintenance between such ethnic groups depends on the suppression of differences within these groups. A constructed in-group homogeneity is the price to be paid for maintaining "different" as a group. In this sense, identity formation may be seen as a program of action acquired by identification, socialization and internalization processes.[11] Such ethnic identity is future-oriented, not retrospective: the construction of ethnic tradition is in line with a "suitable historic past," which is instrumentalized for present goals. Traditions which carry the aura of a venerable age are often quite recent in origin and sometimes invented. These "invented traditions" are sets of practices, normally governed by overtly or tacitly accepted rules and of a ritual or symbolic nature. They seek to inculcate certain values and norms of behavior by repetition, which automatically imply continuity with the past.[12] One good example is the "traditional" ethnic meals that many members of ethnic groups in the United States still cook. Food remains one viable aspect of the folkways of American ethnic groups and a significant way of celebrating ethnicity and group identity: You eat what you wish to be.[13] The Irish-American celebration of Saint Patrick's Day in all major American cities is another symbolic act.[14] Following Pierre Bourdieu these patterns of behavior might also be called "ethnic habitus." The "ethnic habitus" is aligned and in tune with the necessities of every-day life for it is a perfect way to connect the objective—the social structure—and subjective—the ethnic heritage. Reality is a dialectic played out between internalized and objective structures, according to Bourdieu. Objective structures are defined by the exteriority, whereas internalized structures are a system of dispositions. The habitus is a "lex insita" and a possible vehicle for people who want to build a community. As such they develop a social sense or "Le sens pratique."[15]

Social Capital in Ethnic Communities in the United States and Germany

In the US many ethnic communities prove the use of social capital as a means of accumulating material capital. One typical example of acquiring social, material and additionally human capital are the Korean immigrant entrepreneurs in California. The US census lists about one quarter of Koreans in Los Angeles as "self-employed" or

---

[11] Erik Erikson delivers a detailed analysis of the identity formation processes for juveniles in his book *Identity, Youth and Crises* (New York: Norton, 1968).

[12] In their classic book of 1983, *The Invention of Tradition,* Eric Hobsbawm and Terence Ranger are mainly concerned with the constructed characters of nations. But they also indicate that ethnic collectives have the same elements of constructedness. Cambridge: University Press.

[13] Susan Kalcik, "Ethnic Foodways in America: Symbol and the Performance of Identity," in *Ethnic and Regional Foodways in the United States,* ed. by Linda Keller Brown and Kay Mussell (Knoxville: University of Tennessee Press, 1984) 37-61.

[14] Mary C. Waters, *Ethnic Options. Choosing Identities in America* (Berkeley: University of California Press, 1990) 91.

[15] Pierre Bourdieu, *Entwurf einer Theorie der Praxis* (Frankfurt am Main: Suhrkamp, 1976). Also *Sozialer Sinn: Kritik der theoretischen Vernunft* (Frankfurt am Main: Suhrkamp, 1993).

"unpaid family workers." Koreans are nearly three times more frequently in entrepreneurship than are non-Koreans.[16] Residential segregation is still a strong force for controlling the settlement patterns of minorities. Many Korean-Americans suffer of discrimination but utilize the dense living condition to enhance the intensity of their urban ethnic networks. Korean companies tend to service low income, nonwhite neighborhoods generally ignored and underserved by big corporations. Their residential and commercial interests compelled Koreans to combat street crime—one of big cities' most feared problems. In Los Angeles the Korean entrepreneurs are most often seen as a "middleman minority," a buffer between the white residences on Hollywood Hills and the inner city poor.[17] Different sources support the formation of capital and explain their successful social mobility: Koreans were highly educated in their country of origin, often well off upon arrival in the United States, and commonly middle or upper-middle class in social origin. Part of the class resources is human capital, referring to education and skills a person has acquired. On the other hand, Koreans passed business information among themselves, worked long hours, mobilized unpaid family labor, maintained expected patterns of nepotism and employer paternalism and utilized rotating credit associations in financing their businesses. All this is part of the social networks they use to create social capital and to raise money and get their businesses going. Often seen as the new "model minority" the high number of Korean-Americans enterprises are proof for the possibility of accumulating wealth through ethnic networks. Once they made a little money and can afford it, many acculturated Koreans move to the suburbs. This local migration encouraged the relocation of some Korean business firms. This is a perfect example of how acquired human capital in the forms of skills or family workers supports the creation of social capital in form of ethnic networks and finally led to the accumulation of material capital and wealth.

In Germany one can find a variety of ethnic businesses: Greek and Turkish grocery stores and Vietnamese restaurant owners on every corner. They all use their social networks to build their enterprises. At first this economy developed as a supplement which satisfied the needs of the ethnic group. But it also attracted the pastoral wants of local populations for "exoticism." The proprietors of ethnic enterprises soon stabilized their position on the market and developed into an ethnic petite bourgeoisie. The number of self-employed foreigners in Germany is high and their resource of cheap workers are usually helping family members.[18] After years of holding on to the "myth of return" many Turks decided they might as well try to fulfill their dreams in Germany and accept their legal status as "Gastarbeiter" while they were de facto permanent residents with a limited chance of naturalization. The loss of jobs in the industrial sector accelerated the enormous growth of ethnic enterprises in Germany. Self-employment mushroomed to secure an existence and to escape unemployment. The resources for ethnic enterprises

---

[16] Ivan Light and Edna Bonacich, *Immigrant Entrepreneurs: Koreans in Los Angeles 1965-1982* (Berkeley: University of California Press, 1988) 3.

[17] Edna Bonacich, "Class Approaches to Ethnicity and Race," in *Majority and Minority*, ed. Norman R. Yetman (Needham Heights: Allyn and Bacon, 1991) 59-76.

[18] Friedrich Heckmann, *Ethnische Minderheiten, Volk und Nation* (Stuttgart: Enke, 1992) 89.

include cheap labor through family members and high work motivation. The capital base of these enterprises depends on relatives or friends, or other members of the ethnic network.

The density of social networks in a community can be shown by measuring the frequency of interaction between its members. Many interactions usually mean tighter networks and more social capital, which is represented by a higher standard of mutual trust. With such a solid base people are more willing to help each other. Where interaction is limited, social networks are weak and people mistrust each other. The situation of the urban poor in American inner cities provides an example of such incipient nihilism[19]: The disappearance of work and the lack of opportunity are characteristic of these inner city communities—the so-called "urban underclass." But inner city youth gangs, for all their negative connotations also have social networks that provide access to resources and affection. For a ghetto teenager, membership in a gang may be the only way to obtain self-respect and material goods, but in the long run the conformity and pressures from the group may hold him down rather than raise him up.[20] Such problem areas persist due to the larger social structure, not because of the socialization of individuals or their lack of character. The inner city poor live in a social and spatial concentration of poverty-inducing factors. A stable working class has followed the jobs out of the inner city and the remaining residents find themselves confronted with a closed opportunity structure because "[...] the social networks of parents, friends, and associates, as well as the nexus of social institutions, have seen their resources for economic stability progressively depleted."[21] Residents of these extreme-poverty areas have fewer social ties. They also tend to have ties of lesser social worth, as measured by the social position of their partners, parents, siblings and best friends. Social clubs and organizations which usually support the emergence of social networks also fail in these areas—social networks serve as information networks only if there is valuable information to be transmitted.

Most immigrants in both settings expect to find better working conditions and higher wages outside their ghetto-communities. But to get these jobs they need human capital such as education, on-the-job-training and work experience. The amount of human capital a person has accumulated defines the level at which he or she enters the labor market. Starting positions of white workers in the United States tend to be better, due to structural advantages, which make it possible for them to accumulate more human capital. They have greater access to quality education and job training programs; they are more literate and proficient in English—a critical labor market skill for high-

---

[19] Cornel West, "Nihilism in Black America," *Dissent* (1991), 221-226. See also the influential book by William Julius Wilson, *The Truly Disadvantaged: The Inner City, the Underclass, and Public Policy* (Chicago: The University of Chicago Press, 1987).

[20] Portes, "The Downside," 3.

[21] Loic J. D. Wacquant and William Julius Wilson, "The Cost of Racial and Class Exclusion in the Inner City", in *Majority and Minority*, ed. by Norman R. Yetman (Needham Heights: Allyn and Bacon, 1991) 498-509. See also William Julius Wilson, *When Work Disappears: The World of the New Urban Poor* (New York: Knopf, 1996).

paying jobs; and they exercise greater political leverage to protect their advantaged economic and social status. Because of their lack in human capital and the structural racism in the labor market, many ethnics have a hard time finding a job in the mainstream economy; the only alternative for them are the jobs which they can acquire through their community.

The same effects of globalization are perceptible in both countries but Republican Presidents Ronald Reagan and George Bush in the United States were quicker to give up many labor law regulations and union contracts in the 1980s. As a consequence the economic situation in the 1990s in the United States is described as a "segmented labor market," a "mixed economy" or a "split labor market."[22] All these concepts indicate that there are certain boundaries between different sections of the economy. Co-ethnics often work in the enclave economy and accept low wages because they can improve their skills and increase their human capital as compensation. Today sweat shops in San Francisco, where Asian immigrants sew for piece wages, recall the older immigrant labor markets of a hundred years ago. This does not mean that all ethnics are dependent workers. In fact, the self-employment rate is much higher for immigrant US workers than for all US-born workers.[23] Nor is dependency on welfare higher for immigrants than for all American-born persons in general. The important point is that there is much variety between ethnic groups: Puerto Ricans are a lot more dependent on welfare than, for example, Asian immigrants.

For certain groups the ethnic labor market really offers the only perspective. Sometimes immigrants possess material resources as well as social capital—as the Korean entrepreneurs. Sometimes their status as legally accepted political refugees in the US provides symbolic capital: Cuban immigrants received substantial help from the American government through the Cuban Loan program for years. Today the Cuban ethnic enclave in Miami reflects the economy of the core society. A Cuban entrepreneur can get judicial advice from a Cuban lawyer and can visit a Cuban doctor for medical advice. Moreover, workers in the Cuban economy received returns on their human capital—education, knowledge, experience—equivalent to those paid in the mainstream center economy and far superior to those paid in the secondary labor market, a junkpile of dead-end jobs. Enclave employment did not disadvantage immigrant workers and

---

[22] For Victor Nee the segmented labor market theory posits closed boundaries between primary and secondary labor market sectors, which results in a fundamental dichotomy between the jobs of migrants and the jobs of natives. He questions the distinction of the primary and secondary sectors of the labor market as real or nominal and therefore prefers the term "mixed economy" in his article "Job Transitions in an Immigrant Metropolis: Ethnic Boundaries and the Mixed Economy", *American Sociological Review*, 1 (1994), 849-872. Edna Bonacich delivers an analysis of class relations and dynamics in the American labor market and discusses the labor competition as the center of the split labor market in her essay "Class Approaches to Ethnicity and Race", in *Majority and Minority*, ed. by Norman R. Yetman (Needham Heights: Allyn and Bacon, 1991) 59-76.

[23] Vernon M. Briggs and Stephen Moore, *Still an Open Door? U.S. Immigration Policy and the American Economy* (Washington: American University Press, 1994), 108.

probably made better opportunities available than they would have found on the general labor market.²⁴

The meaning of ethnic communities is ambivalent. On one hand the community is a refuge with stable norms, on the other it is a barrier to mobility in the core society. The second generation, the children of immigrants, develop a reactive or antagonistic subculture. Gang members in a Californian high school differentiate between doing well in school and being Chicano: to study hard is to "act white."²⁵ Seeing their parents and grandparents confined to menial jobs, and becoming increasingly aware of discrimination by the white mainstream, many US-born children of earlier Mexican immigrants have readily joined a reactive subculture as a means of protecting their sense of self-worth. Three features of the social context are responsible for the "segmented assimilation," especially of the second generation: the first is racism, the second is inner city-location and the third is the absence of mobility ladders. For Putnam, dilemmas of collective action can be resolved when "incentives for opportunism are reduced" and "networks of civic engagement foster sturdy norms of generalized reciprocity and encourage the emergence of social trust."²⁶ This generalized version of social trust and civic engagement does not necessarily accompany social capital. For the groups which are excluded from the core society only trust people in their own community. Those who are marginalized can not participate as a fully accepted member of society—without the necessary papers—and will not "trust" the core society.

For the second and third generation of young Turks in Germany, the ambivalent situation leads to a problematic identity crises: merely tolerated, these young people are not sure if their "investments" in their parents' enterprises or the accumulation of human capital will ever pay off. While most Islamic centers loose members in Germany, the fundamentalist organization *Milli Görüs*, which supports the *Refah*-party, the party of Islamist Necmettin Erbakan, is doing well: attracted by study groups, computer or Karate classes, camping trips, sport centers or soccer clubs and intensive help for people who have been in prison, these groups have many young members.²⁷ Left alone with their problems, those children and grandchildren of the Gastarbeiter—as "ausländische Mitbürger" not at home in Germany and as "Alemanci" excluded in Turkey—search for a cultural identity. Crucial to acquiring a cultural identity are social networks, as the ones these religious groups offer. The young Turks find their community in the Islamic centers and mosques.

Assimilation to and integration in the German society is not attractive for these juveniles. In an extreme formulation one of them says: "Assimilierung an deutsche

---

[24] Alejandro Portes, "The Rise of Ethnicity: Determinants of Ethnic Perception Among Cuban Exiles in Miami," *American Sociological Review*, 1 (1984), 383-397.

[25] Alejandro Portes and Min Zhou, "Should immigrants assimilate?," *Public Interest*, 116 (1994), 18-33.

[26] Putnam, "Bowling Alone", 67.

[27] In his book *Verlockender Fundamentalismus*, Wilhelm Heitmeyer makes very clear that the attraction of "religious fundamentalism" has a lot more to do with the social realities in which the studied juveniles in Germany live, than with religious orientation per se, (Frankfurt am Main: Suhrkamp, 1997).

Trinker und Schweinefleischfresser, die im Sommer nackt an türkischen Stränden liegen?"[28] ("Assimilation to German alcoholics and voracious pork eaters, who sunbathe naked on Turkish beaches during the summer?") Turkish juveniles developed a reactive subculture just like their Hispanic counterparts did in the US. Their legal status in the Germany is so weak that after a vicious fight between young immigrants from Turkey and a group of mostly Albanians in Munich in January 1998, no official institution has tried to clarify the motives of the young offenders. The media reflected the popular view that the "solution" of the problem is, deportation of all people who are residing in Germany without the necessary papers. The office in charge ordered procedures to take seventeen people out of the country, nine others were taken to prison. The fact that only two of the thirty-five offenders had a German passport and many came to Germany after their tenth birthday received most coverage. Instantly there was a loud cry asking to stop the possibility for family members to come to Germany. Hardly anyone asked about the social situation in which those immigrants lived or about the conflict between these ethnic groups.

The Islamic centers are located in the poorer parts of the cities where not only Turks, but also many borderline Germans live. Growing up in these problem areas, security and safety are very relevant for the young people: German style public health insurance and "fundamentalist" organizations are considered equally important, because they are good and valuable for the people. A growing number of "fundamentalists" are academics and professionals. They focus on better education possibilities for young Turks. There is nothing like a federal bilingual education act in Germany: only some cities have measures for children with a different mother tongue than German, but these programs are not standardized. Being "different" can hardly be instrumentalized as symbolic capital, if there are no governmental agencies which enforce "equal" education.

The leaders of organizations like *Graue Wölfe* or *Türkisch-Islamische Union in Europa* (ATIB), which usually represent their ethnic group in city councils like the *Ausländerbeirat*, have an especially tight social network. Both groups support not only a mosque, but also a tea room, a grocery store and a cultural center. They offer assistance for getting financial help from the state, concerning pension, child support and residence permits.[29] A very attractive aspect for juveniles: both of the organizations have soccer teams in Dortmund sponsored by Turkish companies. The growing influence of "fundamentalist" Islamic groups in Germany might at least partly be explained by the tight social networks they offer, connected with precise values and rules of behavior. But the religious orientation and ethnic identification of this community represent a nightmare for the liberal German state.

In Germany as well as in the US the changing labor market and the loss of industrial jobs has led to a stronger dependence of immigrants on their ethnic communities. If these enclaves can provide their members with employment and some kind of "social

---

[28] Wilhelm Heitmeyer, *Verlockender Fundamentalismus*, 16.
[29] Wilhelm Heitmeyer, *Verlockender Fundamentalismus*, 16f.

security" their ethnic identity will be stabilized. However, dealing with the "difference" of such group members by governmental authorities relies on very different philosophies in the two countries. In the US "difference" may account for affirmative action, which might mean "preferential" treatment and therefore the liquidation of symbolic capital. Even if there are certain similarities in one sphere—the one which Jürgen Habermas calls "Lebenswelt"—for ethnic groups in both countries, the second sphere which he defines as the "System" accounts for the differences.[30]

The quest for integration of minority members and their reliance on the social capital of their ethnic community are interrelated aspects. Integration is not a one-way street, as many German politicians like to stress, but a mutual process of interacting, understanding and accepting. The responsibility for creating and sustaining a pluralist society lies on the individual members—those belonging to the core society but also the members of ethnic communities—their political representatives, and the governmental decision makers. A recent report of the German government states that the German "Ausländerpolitik" is based on two goals. The first is to integrate the fellow-citizens who live in Germany as fast as possible, and the second aspect is to limit the additional moving in of foreigners. The terminology of the report can be traced back to the official message of the parties in office in November 1981 in which they state that Germany is not an "immigration country" and neither will be one in the future.[31] Part of this policy has been the unlimited stop of recruitment of Gastarbeiter since 1973. Those already in the country are now officially induced to integrate: "Das bedeutet, daß sie sich nicht absondern oder in eigene Zirkel zurückziehen."[32] (This means, that they should not separate and withdraw into their own circles.) Governmental institutions offer little help to integrate and learn the German language, which would function as an inducement. Of course, compared to all other European countries Germany admits more persons seeking political asylum, but for many, their status in Germany leaves them in a state of confusion and insecurity. Which is especially true for the civil war refugees from Bosnia, of whom many have to return, because their native towns and villages are now considered "save" territory. For the German state and the parties in power migration around the globe is more of an economic problem than a human tragedy: "Für weitere Zuwanderungen besteht auch aus arbeitsmarktlicher Sicht kein Bedarf."[33] (There is no economic need for more immigration.) Those who come anyway will have to find employment in the alternative structure of the informal economy. Whole segments of the informal economy are taken over by a certain ethnic groups—for example the apparel industry in Miami is a Cuban enclave. The United States and Germany provide manifold examples for intense social relations based on ethnic origin. Social capital is

---

[30] Jürgen Habermas, *Theorie des kommunikativen Handelns* (Frankfurt am Main: Suhrkamp, 1981).

[31] "Die Bundesrepublik setzt ihre Ausländerpolitik konsequent fort," http://www.bundesregierung.de/05/0507/98073001/ (31. August 1998).

[32] Die Bundesrepublik setzt ihre Ausländerpolitik konsequent fort," http://www.bundesregierung.de/05/0507/98073001/ (31. August 1998).

[33] "Die Bundesrepublik setzt ihre Ausländerpolitik konsequent fort," http://www.bundesregierung.de/05/0507/98073001/ (31. August 1998).

accumulated and invested in these dense community structures. Social capital clearly is on "Mission Impossible" and has to fail in the attempt to save the civic virtues of a nation-state, as portrayed by Putnam, but in providing an alternative social and economic structure for many immigrants and members of ethnic communities in the second and third generation it is a real success.

TRANSLATIONS OF MULTICULTURALISM: MULTICULTURAL EDUCATION AND PUBLIC DISCOURSE IN THE UNITED STATES AND GERMANY

Reinhard Isensee

I. Controversies about Multiculturalism and Multicultural Education in the U.S.A.

In the United States, the continuing debate over concepts of multicultural education is part of a much larger critical discourse on the philosophy, direction, function and structure of education. This debate rages in the context of a redefining of American culture(s) at the end of the 20th century. Multiculturalism is one of the most controversial constituents in this debate. It emerged historically as a project in the field of education, and has been informed by several key contemporary, cultural categories such as race, ethnicity, and gender. The controversies were originally confined to education in the public schools and were prompted by the political and social emancipatory movements of the 1960s and the accompanying judicial rulings and legislative acts requiring equal access and opportunities for minorities. The present discourse, however, goes far beyond public school system. Although education remains a crucial site of debate for the theoretical and practical implications of multiculturalism, a polarization over issues regarding American national identity, the construction of historical memory, and the meaning of democracy now fuels the central struggles of the so-called "culture wars."[1]

Publications such as Allan Bloom's *The Closing of the American Mind* (1987), E.D. Hirsch's *Cultural Literacy: What Every American Needs to Know* (1987) and Arthur M. Schlesinger's, Jr. *The Disuniting of America: Reflections on a Multicultural Society* (1992) provided a powerful inspiration for these struggles in general and for the curriculum debate in higher education in particular. The concepts of education defended in these volumes were essentially based on a (homogeneous) definition of culture that confined it to national boundaries and thus adhered to traditional notions of a "national culture." The argument for this conservative defense of an educational philosophy that centered itself around Western or white American values was spurred by the claim that US educational institutions supposedly no longer provided this common foundation of knowledge that was needed to give students an adequate understanding of the nation's past and a vision of its future. In addition, the conservative critique raised fundamental

---

[1] Henry A. Giroux, "Insurgent Multiculturalism and the Promise of Pedagogy," in *Multiculturalism: A Critical Reader*, ed. by David Theo Goldberg (Oxford/Cambridge: Blackwell, 1994), 325.

questions about the very basis of modern education and thus has started "a war of ideas" within the academy as well as the public.

Bloom's and Hirsch's basic concern was to urge a change in direction for American education. They articulated a defense of "classic standards" and values, thus starting a new round in the long-running dispute over the function of a democratic education in the academy. But their critique gained added weight in the public discourse through powerful endorsements from politicians, notably William Bennett, Secretary of Education in the Bush Administration. Equally important to public interest was the response from advocates of multicultural curricula that attempt to take the constant transformations in (American) society more properly into account. The most recent responses include historian Lawrence W. Levine's *The Opening of the American Mind* (1996) in which he forcefully confronts the conservatives' charge of an academic disintegration in American higher education by providing a historical perspective on the present controversies about universities, history, and American identity. According to Henry A. Giroux the current debate is increasingly taking place on two fronts:

> First, multiculturalism has become a 'tug of war over who gets to create public culture.' Second, the contested terrain of multiculturalism is heating up between educational institutions that do not meet the need of a massively shifting student population and students and their parents for whom schools increasingly are perceived as merely one more instrument of repression.[2]

While this view acknowledges the special role that education plays as the primary space, both academic and public, for today's cultural struggles over the direction of American society, it seems to suggest that this debate is specifically American grounded in the historical and cultural idiosyncracies of the United States. From an international perspective I will argue, however, that the "culture wars" we observe in America —although notable for their vehemence and visibility—are the result of vast economic transformations that all postindustrial societies are experiencing at the end of the millennium. Hence, the United States represents but one model of how these transformations are translated into (national) political and cultural discourses.

If the present economic challenges facing Western societies are seen as the underlying *common condition*, with differences a matter of degree rather than of essence, both the differences *and* the similarities—as well as the theoretical implications and practical consequences of the "culture wars" on both sides of the Atlantic can be more adequately grasped. As Todd Gitlin convincingly argues in his discussion of identity politics, there are several currents at work that constitute the *condition* for the "culture wars":

> The stability of communities is undermined by the expatriation of capital, the migration of peoples, and the bombardment of images. Never before have hope, greed, and fear had so many channels through which to rush so fast. Jet planes transport immigrants overnight from Seoul to Los Angeles, while back in Seoul, engineers clone computers from Silicon Valley, taking the jobs of workers in San Jose, and the computers they build in Kuala Lumpur move capital instantly from Los Angeles to Tokyo

---

[2] Giroux, "Insurgent Multiculturalism," 325.

> ... The collisions and suspicions feel all the more intense within a dynamic of economic decline. Under pressure from globalization, the nation-state loses its will and capacity to remedy what the conservative economist Joseph Schumpeter called the 'creative destruction' that the un- bridled market brings. Such controls as Western societies succeeded in imposing on capital's license during a century of reform have weakened. Growth is wildly uneven, inequality is immense, anxiety is endemic. The state, as a result, is continually urged to do more but deprived of the means to do so ... Observing the state's incapacity, resentful of those worse off than themselves, people blame the government, refuse to vote, hate taxes, doubt democratic institutions. Political Parties are hollow shells for the convenience of contributors. People withdraw from public life altogether.[3]

Whereas Gitlin's analysis particularly points to parallel aspects of the problematic conditions confronting Western societies the question still remains why have certain issues moved into the center of academic and public debates while others have not.

An attempt to explain these incongruities first has to explore respectively the concepts of multiculturalism and education in the context of their *national meanings*. The current struggles over the concept of multiculturalism in the United States demonstrate the remarkable inconsistencies of the cultural meanings and political intentions assigned to the term itself. But they also seem to strike a vital chord in terms of the perception and construction of America as a societal model. In many ways, multiculturalist discussions thus serve as an umbrella for reconsidering social and cultural essentials of the not-so-common American past and present. When Gitlin, for example, maintains that contemporary multiculturalism "evades a central wound in American history," he highlights the most prominent argument in favor of an (earlier) project of multiculturalism, namely "that for centuries, in a culture that affirmed the rights of the individual, American blacks were subject to slavery ... and that slavery was followed by more than 125 years of frequently violent discrimination."[4]

In relation to race, the perspective of Afrocentrism has been widely discussed and used as a key model for conceptionalizing the notion of multiculturalism. Advocates of this perspective assert that: "The key concept of any discussion of Afrocentricity is *place*—where you are standing culturally and psychologically when you act or make a statement about anything."[5] By moving beyond categories of race, they suggest that: "While Afrocentrism reflects a particular cultural reaction to the egregious application of Eurocentrism, multiculturalism brings into focus the democratic stirrings of other determinisms, in an ongoing renegotiation of civil, social, economic and cultural rights."[6]

---

[3] Todd Gitlin, *The Twilight of Common Dreams. Why America Is Wracked by Cultural Wars* (New York: Henry Holt, 1995), 224.

[4] *The Twilight of Common Dreams*, 228-229.

[5] Molefi Kete Asante, in Phil Petrie, "Afrocentrism", *American Studies Newsletter*, 36 (1995), 7.

[6] James Early, quoted in Phil Petrie, "Afrocentrism," *American Studies Newsletter* 36 (1995), 7. For a more extensive discussion of the concept of multiculturalism in the context of the "culture war" see Guenter H. Lenz, "American Culture Studies: Multikulturalismus und Postmoderne," in *Multikulturelle Gesellschaft: Modell Amerika*, ed. by Berndt Ostendorf (Muenchen: Fink Verlag 1994), 176-187; Guenter H. Lenz, "Transnational American Studies: Negotiating Cultures of Difference. Multicultural Identities, Communities, and Border Discourses," in *Multiculturalism in Transit: A German—American Exchange*, ed. by Klaus Milich and Jeffrey Peck (Providence, RI, 1998, in print).

It is this move beyond issues of race and ethnicity that elevated the multicultural project to the forefront of academic and public debates in the late 1980s and 1990s since it was now open to address other salient issues of power and identity related to gender, sexual orientation, and age. Multiculturalism as an emancipatory project thus became involved in the dynamics of negotiating diverse and conflicting interests by raising "the question of whether people are speaking within or outside a privileged space, and whether such spaces provide the conditions for different groups to listen to each other differently to address how the racial economies of privilege and power work in American society."[7]

It is not surprising that in the United States the academy has emerged as a prominent place for the ideological debates on multiculturalism. As members of groups, whose culture had been largely excluded for a long time from school, college and university curricula, entered institutions of higher education as students and faculty in increasing numbers, intense struggles over educational opportunities, racial equality, gender, curriculum content as well as the organizational structure of departments and institutions began to shake the academic turf. At the same time, critical theoretical concepts like postmodernism and poststructuralism enhanced the debate not only over what is taught and by whom but over the very nature of knowledge and the possibility of objectivity.[8] As a result, tremendous changes occurred on most American colleges campuses, which—according to John Arthur and Amy Shapiro—responded to these two developments in at least four directions:

> First, faculty and students on many campuses have demanded more women and minority professors, ethnic and gender studies departments ... Second, many universities have promulgated codes of banning sexual harassment and date rape. Third, some institutions have abandoned the insistence on free speech ... and enacted codes punishing racist, sexist, and harassing speech. Fourth, ... many schools have adopted affirmative action policies that give preference in hiring and admissions to women and persons of color.[9]

The emotional intensity and the fierce polarization of positions that has accompanied these struggles from the beginning reflected the fact that both multiculturalists and their critics realized the larger repercussions of the debate. The whole issue of how to define contemporary America and the future implications of that definition as to who or what is properly American or somehow un-American were at stake.

One of the central disputes over values involved the canon or the content of curricula in higher education. While this discussion appeared to be new in its thrust towards an integrative curriculum at the time, it can, however, be traced back in the United States at least to the beginnings of our century. For the purposes of this essay, two sources will be discussed in particular as they seem to be of special importance for

---

[7] Giroux, "Insurgent Multiculturalism," 327.

[8] John Arthur and Amy Shapiro (eds), *Campus Wars. Multiculturalism and the Politics of Difference* (Boulder/San Francisco/Oxford: Westview Press, 1995), 1.

[9] *Campus Wars*, 1-2.

the historical grounding of the curriculum debate in particular and multicultural education in general.[10]

The movement for a "Great Books" curriculum instigated by Robert Hutchins and Mortimer Adler more that 60 years ago can be perceived as the first of several counterattacks against modernizing tendencies in education. In many respects, the questions that were raised in this movement anticipated the current debate. As the old-time classical curriculum of colleges and universities gave way to the more utilitarianly-minded, elective system of the new universities in the 1920s, the so-called "Great Books" began to lose their place in teaching. Many colleges and universities throughout the United States had adopted a more fragmented curriculum. The modern Great Books curriculum originated at Columbia University in New York in 1919 when John Erskin, professor of English, offered his General Honors course for the first time. In Erskin's view the deficiencies he detected in the knowledge of students were a reflection of the new style of higher education in the 1910s and of the more heterogeneous social composition of the student body at Columbia. His course was designed to acquaint students with the so-called great texts of Western culture in order to give them with a common intellectual grounding. Thus, the project sought to create a course which would provide a means of safely sharing the mantle of culture with the brightest of these immigrant sons.[11]

Erskin's project was later continued—with some alterations—by Robert Hutchins and Mortimer Adler. When Robert Maynard Hutchins became president of the University of Chicago in 1929, he immediately initiated discussions about the university's curriculum. Hutchins' conviction was that higher education in America suffered from acute confusion over means and ends. He was determined that the cure for this illness should be administered first to the University of Chicago.[12] He secured the introduction of a new curriculum for the first two years of undergraduate education. Intended to organize teaching and learning along the lines of the medieval universities, this New Plan abolished both attendance requirements and the course credit system. In their place, students intending to proceed to Honors were asked to prepare themselves for comprehensive examinations which they could take whenever they felt ready. The philosophy underlying these changes in the "New Plan" curriculum was strongly opposed by the faculty and academic critics, who eventually prevented the university from fully implementing it. What remained though was the successful introduction of a reading course by Mortimer Adler that was the forerunner of a much expanded Great Books program based on volumes entitled the "Great Books of the Western World" (GBWW). This new curriculum—despite faculty misgivings—was taken up, for instance, by St. John's College in Annapolis, where a completely prescribed four-year curriculum based on the teaching of the Western classics was instituted.

---

[10] A further discussion of other sources is provided by Lawrence W. Levine's *The Opening of the American Mind. Canons, Culture, and History*. Boston: Beacon Press, 1996, a cogent and powerful in-depth study of the history of the curriculum in American higher education.

[11] Benjamin McArthur, "The Education of America. A Continuing Debate", *American heritage*, Feb. 1989, cited in *American Studies Newsletter* 24 (1991), 25.

[12] McArthur, "The Education of America," 27.

The post-World War II decade witnessed a great expansion of Great Books discussion groups supported by the emergence of the Great Books Foundation in 1947. Another important development that kept the academic debate over the role of Western classics in the curriculum alive was the effort to produce another high-quality set of so-called Great Books to be marketed along the same lines as the *Encyclopedia Britannica*. Conceived in 1943, this project came to fruition when the thirty-two-thousand-page collection *Great Books of the Western World* was published in 1952. Since then there have been continuous attacks by academic critics and educators against the philosophy of the Great Books curriculum for its endorsement of a high-culture approach. But the appeal of a single curriculum for a diverse student body, with its implicit orientation towards the education of an elite, and the assumption that there are universal truths accessible from exclusively Western culture perspectives, continues to resonate with proponents of the New Right agenda.

The educational reforms in the 20th century and the struggle for an *Integrative Curriculum* can also serve throw light on the current debate about multicultural education. In contrast to supporters of the Great Books concept, progressive-experimentalist educators in the early decades of the 20th century endorsed a view that educational opportunity should be extended to all children through universal secondary education and the restructuring of the curriculum "so that it would be attuned to the nature of the learner and the ideals of a free society."[13] Thus, they followed John Dewey's argument that the tradition of twin-track education with *basic education* or *literacy education* for the masses and *liberal education* for the privileged was not acceptable in a democracy. Via their concept of general education progressivist educators suggested a new integrative curriculum that would replace the fragmented subject curriculum. Although the aim of replacing the fragmented curriculum was similar to the advocates of the Great Book courses the means proposed were starkly different.

Daniel Tanner, an educational specialist in the history of the curriculum, concludes that the aims of the envisaged integrative curriculum consisted of systematic efforts "not only to correlate subjects that heretofore had been treated in isolation, but to provide integrative learning experiences that cut across the traditional subject cocoons and were more life related."[14] After World War II these efforts met strong opposition from tax saving politicians who favored a so-called cheap curriculum of basic education in school and higher education. Moreover, McCarthyism with its rigid censorship of school materials had a negative impact on the integrative curriculum insofar as it demanded that controversial issues or subjects were avoided.

With the introduction of the National Defense Education Act in 1958 projects aiming at an integrative curriculum were further undermined by a return to fragmentation. The "New National Curriculum" projects emphasized a "disciplinary doctrine

---

[13] Daniel Tanner, "A Brief Historical Perspective of the Struggle for an Integrative Curriculum," in *Education 91/92*, ed. by Fred Schultz (Guilford, Conn.: Dushkin, 1991), 61.

[14] Tanner, " A Brief Historical Perspective," 61.

of knowledge purity and abstraction at the expense of knowledge application and synthesis... Scholars in the social sciences and arts sought to imitate the discipline-centered model, with the result that social studies and history gave way to the social sciences, while feeble efforts were made to refashion the arts as 'academic disciplines'."[15]

While the aim of this national, discipline-centered curriculum was to produce more scientists, there was in fact a sharp decline in the numbers of students in higher education majoring in the sciences. Because of the failure of the science-oriented, national curriculum, the 1960s saw a renewed interest in developing an integrative curriculum that would link the concept of subject interdependence to the theme of relevance to the life of the student. The key words in this debate led by educators and representatives of the student protest movement were "curriculum relevance" and "humanizing the curriculum" both in schools and colleges or universities. In practice, however, this debate did not lead to an integrative curriculum but rather a shift in the classroom didactics rather than in the constituent subjects of the curriculum itself. What emerged in the 1960s and early 1970s then was the so-called "open classroom" approach characterized by less authoritarian teaching methods. This tended to produce a less rigid curriculum or no curriculum at all. Not surprisingly, by the mid-1970s this approach was countered by a concept that called for a "back-to-basics" education.

Based on numerous studies comparing the educational achievements of American students to those in Western Europe and Japan, the newly designed school curricula particularly advocated the teaching of basic skills. Competency was to be assured by standardized tests that were regarded as a major aid to national educational improvement. The projects introduced under this philosophy throughout the 1980s centered around various concepts of literacy that encouraged further fragmentation of the traditional curriculum into isolated subject components, as for instance, cultural literacy, computer literacy, scientific literacy, aesthetic literacy, political literacy, technological literacy etc.

While these numerous efforts for educational reform were basically intended to improve academic standards at the level of the universities the project of multicultural education that entered the public and academic discourse in the late 1960s forcefully argued for a more fundamental reconsideration of the functions and structures of both school and higher education in the United States. With regard to schools, multicultural education has particularly emphasized ethnic diversity since its emergence as a concept approximately 25 years ago. The first official statement of introducing multicultural education into mainstream American educational programs was adopted by the American Association of Colleges for Teacher Education (AACTE) in 1972. It attempted both to define multicultural education and to indicate major directions for its practical implementation:

---

[15] "A Brief Historical Perspective," 61.

> Multicultural education is education which values cultural pluralism. Multicultural education rejects the view that schools should seek to melt away cultural differences or the view that schools should merely tolerate cultural pluralism... It affirms that major education institutions should strive to preserve and enhance cultural pluralism. To endorse cultural pluralism is to endorse the principle that there is no one model American... Education for cultural pluralism includes four major thrusts: (1) the teaching of values which support cultural diversity and individual uniqueness; (2) the encouragement of the qualitative expansion of existing ethnic cultures and their incorporation into the mainstream of American socioeconomic and political life; (3) the support of explorations in alternative and emerging life styles; and (4) the encouragement of multiculturalism, multilingualism, and multidialectism ...[16]

Despite variations in approach and focus, all conceptions of multicultural education share a common concern over the incompatibilities and discontinuities between the culture of the school and those of the different ethnic groups from which its students are drawn. This is based upon the assumption that teaching and learning are culturally specific processes that are embedded in a particular social context. If the early discussions of multicultural education more or less equated the concept with the liberatory aspirations of ethnic groups, the present debate has broadened its scope to encompass the still larger political and cultural identity issues that face contemporary American society.

Geneva Gay, in an attempt to develop a systematic understanding of the numerous approaches, goals and politics within the multiculturalism movement in school education, suggests that because of the present social realities in the United States: "Diversity in education, based on ethnicity, social class, language, non-Western national origins, economic status, cultures, and interests, is no longer a luxury or a matter of choice—it is a necessity for the survival of society." [17]

Furthermore, Gay maintains, that the need for a multicultural approach to education arises from the new situation of global interdependence in which "successful interactions and relationships require the use of knowledge, attitudes, and skills about cultural diversity within a global context."[18] Against a backdrop of slowly changing and rigid school administration, educators subscribing to this view of multiculturalism have called for a radical revision of the traditional functions of schools so that education is no longer equated with formal schooling and standardization. Instead, as Danielle R. Moss articulates in a review of Diaz Carlos' study *Multicultural Education for the 21st Century*, they argue that "Educators need to identify certain universal purposes for education that are in keeping with the democratic ideals that keep people in this country despite its complexities and inequities."[19]

---

[16] American Association of Colleges for Teacher Education Commission on Multicultural Education, "No one model American", in *Journal of Teacher Education*, 24 (19973), 264.

[17] Geneva Gay, "A Synthesis of Scholarship in Multicultural Education," 1994. http://www.ncrel.org/sdrs/areas/issues/envrnmnt/go/leogay.htm (21 Oct. 1997), 6.

[18] "A Synthesis of Scholarship," 6.

[19] Danielle R. Moss. " Review of Diaz Carlos. *Multicultural Education for the 21st Century*." (Washington, D.C.: NEA Professional Library, 1992). htpp://newlinks.tc.columbia.edu/pluribus/danielle.htm (24 Sept. 1997), 1-2.

Acknowledging the need to educate a citizenry that can promote democratic ideals, Ricardo L. Garcia—among others—argues in the same direction, emphasizing the role value systems play in a globalized world:

> While schools will reflect the prevailing values and cultures of their local communities, and while transmission of the basic skills and knowledge of academic disciplines may prepare students to live within their local communities, the schools and their teachers are challenged to prepare their students to live in a pluralistic, globally interdependent human community. Schools should not be mirrors that reflect the values and beliefs of their local communities; rather they should be windows to the world that exists beyond their own community.[20]

The agenda that follows from such a shift in teaching values in school strongly focuses on the institutions and learning environments themselves rather than upon changes in curricula and didactics. Advocates of such an agenda go so far as to suggest a "total reevaluation and dissolution of the institutions which were created within the Eurocentric, male dominated context which no longer serve society's need."[21] What is suggested here is the dismantling of the traditional institution of the school as the primary space for transmitting standardized social norms and values. In its place, a pedagogical praxis is proposed that substitutes the knowledge students gain by experiencing the contributions of various groups to politics and government, science and art etc for the more rigid pattern of textbooks and teacher-brokered learning.

In contrast to this agenda, others have proposed more modest steps for the practical implementation of multicultural education in American schools Gay, for example, maintains that an endorsement of multiculturalism does not imply "that the entire education system should be destroyed or that the Anglocentric cultural dominance existing in schooling should merely be replaced with the dominance of other ethnic cultures ... Rather, it simply says that the education system needs to be improved by becoming less culturally monolithic, rigid, biased, hegemonic, and ethnocentric. The prevailing norm in educational decision-making and operating procedures should be cultural pluralism and heterogeneity, instead of cultural hegemony and homogeneity."[22]

Since the late 1960s, practical attempts of teaching multiculturalism have generated several models that not only reflect diverse theoretical positions but at the same time demonstrate the subsequent development of the American debate on multicultural education. According to Sleeter and Grant, the models that have been implemented in American schools in the past years are essentially based upon five approaches.[23]

---

[20] Ricardo L. Garcia in Moss, "Review," 169.
[21] "Review," 2.
[22] Gay, "A Synthesis of Scholarship," 16.
[23] Christine E. Sleeter and C. A. Grant, *Making Choices for Multicultural Education: Five Approaches to Race, Class and Gender*. 2nd ed., (Columbus: MacMillan, 1993). C. McCarthy suggests a similar paradigm in her discussion of three distinct models of multicultural education: the cultural understanding, the cultural competence, and the cultural emancipation or social reconstruction models. P. Rudi Mattai, "Rethinking the Nature of Multicultural Education: Has it Lost ist Form or is it Being Misused?" in *Journal of Negro Education*, 1 (1992), 68.

Probably the most widely applied model derives from the once pervasive assumption that culturally different students should be taught to fit into mainstream society. In this model it is the educational process rather than the content that is privileged in teaching. A second, similar model favors a human relations approach that stresses the goal of teaching strategies that permit diverse people to live together harmoniously. While these two models mainly focus on the "other" in individuals, more recent schemes advocate either a single group studies approach that emphasizes the teaching of awareness, respect, and acceptance of one group, or use teaching strategies to reduce prejudice, provide equal opportunities and social justice for all groups, but at the same time to make visible the effects of power distribution on ethnic or cultural groups. Finally, Sleeter and Grant describe a teaching model that acknowledges the potential of multicultural education for political and social reform. It strives to teach students "to become analytical and critical thinkers and social reformers who are committed to redistribution of power and other resources among diverse groups."[24]

In his essay "Insurgent Multiculturalism and the Promise of Pedagogy," Henry A. Giroux develops a theory of multiculturalism that similarly links the current controversy to the field of pedagogy. Based upon a critical discussion of the notions of democracy and education that reviews the major liberal and conservative positions, Giroux argues that today public schooling and higher education function as crucial sites for acknowledging and incorporating the relationship between multiculturalism and democracy.[25] His argument is built on Bhikhu Parekh's definition of a critical multiculturalism. In his powerful discussion of what he calls demagogic or fundamentalist multiculturalism, Parekh concludes that:

> Multiculturalism doesn't simply mean numerical plurality of different cultures, but rather a community which is creating, guaranteeing, encouraging spaces within which different communities are able to grow at their own pace. At the same time it means creating a public space in which these communities are able to interact, enrich the existing culture and create a new sensual culture in which they recognize reflections of their own identity.[26]

Based upon these theoretical premises of a critical multiculturalism Giroux argues for a more radical concept of education that he calls *insurgent multiculturalism*. This concept takes as its starting point the question of what it means for educators to treat schools and other public sites as border institutions in which teachers, students, and others engage in repeated acts of cultural translation and negotiation. Perceived in this way, education or schooling becomes "an introduction to how culture is organized, a demonstration of who is considered worthy of valorization, and what forms of culture are considered invalid and unworthy of public esteem."[27] The move here is to force pedagogy away from its exclusive emphasis on classroom management and to define

---

[24] Sleeter and Grant in Gay, "A Synthesis of Scholarship," 14-15.
[25] Giroux, "Insurgent Multiculturalism," 329.
[26] Homi K. Bhabha and Bhikhu Parekh, "Identities on Parade: A Conversation," *Marxism Today* (June 1989), 3-4.
[27] Giroux, "Insurgent Multiculturalism," 329.

it as a form of political leadership and ethical address: "A democratic or insurgent multiculturalism is one that offers a new language for students and others to move between disciplinary borders and to travel within zones of cultural difference."[28]

Moreover, Giroux maintains that the continuing debate on multiculturalism, if taken out of the polemical clashes between liberals and conservatives, become particularly relevant to the pedagogical context. Educators can use the underlying concepts of multiculturalism as tools for a critical understanding and pluralizing of differences. They can apply multiculturalism as an ethical and political referent to understand how power is constructed in the interest of the dominant pattern of social relations, and how such relations can be challenged and transformed.[29]

II. Public Discourse and Multicultural Education in Germany

Despite an increased public interest in the state of contemporary education spurred primarily by the recent nationwide student-protests, the debate on multiculturalism and education in Germany, is still characterized by a disjuncture between the academic multicultural discourse and the cultural practices it describes. Initially, the (West) German discourse on multiculturalism was largely framed as a debate over the "foreigner" or the "other" with the aim being to integrate or assimilate this "other" into a more or less clearly defined national culture. Although the terms used were the "integration of foreigners" or "guest-workers," the first German institutions to show an interest in questions of multiculturalism in the 1970s were the state social welfare agencies. By the beginning of the 1980s, a somewhat broader interest became visible when the churches, political parties and academia began to problematize the status of foreigners in the political, social and cultural life in Germany. At the same time concepts of multiculturalism increasingly entered the leading academic debates due to the considerable influence of reports on multiculturalism controversies abroad, especially in the United States. These debates on multiculturalism—although small in scope—not only instigated a growing awareness of the idiosyncracies of the German situation in comparison to the United States, the United Kingdom or Australia, for example, but also prompted a critical reconsideration of traditional notions of the nation state, national culture and national identity. The focus of multicultural discourse began to shift from the earlier concept of a pedagogic project of integration or assimilation towards issues of negotiating difference in terms of ethnicity, gender, class and age. Crucially, pedagogic projects, began to emphasize ethnicity as an essential category for describing the social situation of immigrants in Germany. By giving ethnic differences a prominent role in determining the social status of groups, such programs strongly related the issue of immigrants to a more complex analysis of the moral state of a society that routinely employed ethnicity as a source of discrimination against particular groups. Thus, the

---

[28] "Insurgent Multiculturalism," 329.
[29] "Insurgent Multiculturalism," 336-337.

ideal of a culturally homogeneous society was undermined by a moral argument that endorsed diversity as a desirable alternative. In this view, cultural differences based on ethnic characteristics were to be considered enriching because of their strong impact on identity formation in cultural communities.

While these discussions emerged due to practical political and social circumstances, they have been eagerly adopted and theoretically elaborated by the social sciences since the 1980s, especially in such disciplines as ethnology and education. One of the central research projects within the theoretical framework of phenomenology has been the exploration of the role of the "other" or "foreigner" in everyday life as experienced by Germans themselves. These efforts to theorize "otherness" eventually resulted in a shift in the perception of contemporary society and its culture. It was now explained in terms of a (re-defined) community ("Gemeinschaft") consisting of diverse groups with different ethnic and cultural as well as social characteristics and values. This model of describing society by highlighting its heterogeneity—a model that also reflected critical discussions in the fields of sociology and social pedagogy ("Sozialpaedagogik")—soon surpassed the political and social praxis that still adhered to a concept of assimilating immigrants into a common German national culture. Instead, the multicultural discourse in academia—despite internal controversies based upon differences in political and theoretical approaches—suggested a new and attractive approach to countering societal deformations such as isolation and alienation. Therefore, the debate on ethnicity, difference, and identity not only articulated a cultural critique but also a political program that revised traditional concepts of German culture.

In contrast to other countries, the debate in Germany has also occurred against the background of its fascist past and neo-Nazi activities and anti-foreigner violence at the beginning of the 1990s. The physical attacks on foreigners and non-German citizens can be interpreted as an indicator of the gap between academic efforts to introduce multiculturalist concepts into a wider public discourse and the social and political reality that is still apparently informed by a need to cling to the idea of a culturally monolithic nation state. Since theories of multiculturalism particularly emphasize the interrelationship of ethnicity, race, class, gender, and age claims to the question of democracy and therefore include moral dimensions (for example, principles of human dignity), the German discussions have occasionally equated the uses of multiculturalism with a "social technique" ("Sozialtechnik") that helps to create spaces for negotiating diverging cultural interests.[30] In the final analysis, however, such a view seems to imply the notion that multiculturalism is only acceptable as long as it works in harmony with the older model of a dominant homogeneous culture.

The critique of multicultural theories in the current debate in Germany has repeatedly centered around the question of what are the "effects" of such a position on society as a whole? The most interesting issues that have been raised in this context include the problematics of ethnic particularization and the revival of ethnic and cultural

---

[30] Frank-Olaf Radtke, "Zur Konstruktion des Fremden im Diskurs des Multikulturalismus," 1991. http://trieb.phys.chemie.uni-frankfurt.de/~stefan/multikulti.html (12 Feb. 1998), 4.

as well as social differences. Also important have been debates over the different forms of fundamental multiculturalism and their impact in terms of privileging single cultural groups or identities, and over the possible loss of national solidarity as a basic mechanism for consensus-building in society.[31]

The special relevance of these issues as well the debate on multiculturalism in general derives from the unique situation of Germany in the 1990s. The process of unification with its goal of establishing one economic and social German entity was initially relied on orthodox national approaches to history and culture. But the ambivalent repercussions of unification, both inside and outside Germany, gradually helped to create an awareness of the need to reconsider such concepts. Formerly regarded as of interest only to the academy and limited to questions related to foreigners and citizenship in political science and sociology, to intercultural learning and teaching in education, or to ethnographic and anthropological issues, the multicultural debate now aroused a broader public interest. This interest increased particularly as the political and economic contradictions and psychological disparities accompanying the process of unification became more evident. Germans on an everyday basis acknowledged that there were social and cultural differences between West and East Germans. This challenged the validity of previously accepted ideas of cultural homogeneity and called for a new understanding of (multi)culture. A second factor influencing the German debate on multiculturalism was the concurrent debate over the political and monetary foundations for a United Europe, a discussion that fostered a greater awareness of the problematic nature of national cultural boundaries.

Relatively speaking, education has been largely absent from the agenda of major public issues in Germany for the past decade. In the 1960s and 1970s, it was a hot topic and radical reforms were introduced to both school and higher education. This resulted in a democratization of access to university education. Subsequent years saw continuing academic debates over the deficiencies of the educational process in terms of course contents, structure and funding, but with little visible impact on the wider public. This public apathy disappeared after 1989 when enormous efforts were made to restructure the former East German educational system according to the West German model. However, educators and academics across various disciplines enthusiastically welcomed this phase of restructuring as an opportunity to reconsider and reform the German educational system as a whole, both East and West. Thus, in many of the former East German universities at the beginning of the 1990s, there was an ironic process of introducing an "old" model of higher education just when that model was being called into question or even declared obsolete by the educators themselves. The contradictory nature of this process was made even more problematic by the severe cuts in university funding in the mid-1990s. This more or less halted the (material) restructuring of the universities in former East Germany and resulted in unprecedented financial shortfalls in the West.

---

[31] "Zur Konstruktion des Fremden," 5.

These enormous shocks, which were felt to a lesser extent in the schools as well, triggered the large student protests against the deteriorating educational conditions at universities in 1997. In combination, the crisis and the protests renewed public concern in educational issues. Even if the debate seemed at first to be dominated by controversial proposals regarding educational funding, it nevertheless gave an important impetus to public and academic discussion of the proper aims and functions of the German educational system. In an address to the Berlin Educational Forum in November 1997, the President of the Federal Republic of Germany, Roman Herzog, similarly wondered why education in Germany was almost exclusively debated by specialists in the field and why it had not entered the public discourse.[32] He concluded that the limited character of the debate on education explained why it had not led to substantial changes or a visible renewal of the German educational system. In his view, a national discourse that included parents, teachers, and students was needed to cope with the challenge of the current economic, political and cultural developments in a global context. What Herzog outlined in his speech was a profound reform of the concepts (content and curricula) and functions (relationship of theory and practice) of both school and higher education as a crucial prerequisite for securing a democratic society in Germany in the 21st century. Acknowledging widely articulated demand for a substantial increase in state funding of education, he focused on problems related to the German educational concept itself and called for the dismantling of longstanding taboos and myths. His discussion of these taboos very clearly revealed the present crisis in the German educational system but at the same time demonstrated the differences and parallels that have triggered the comparable debates in the United States.

Starting from the assumption that education is directed towards human beings as individuals with different talents and gifts, Herzog advocated an educational system that reflected these differences by offering a wide choice of training paths. He also emphasized the importance of a grading system that rejected the idea of pleasing every student but was instead based upon both goal-orientated academic standards on the one hand and a character-building value system on the other. In the latter respect, he assigned a key role to the teaching of religion in school. The model that Herzog envisaged for German education both in school and higher learning would have the following essential attributes: it would be value-oriented, praxis-relevant, international, versatile, competitive, and time-effective.[33]

His discussion of core educational values is particularly illuminating because it sheds some further light on the similarities and divergences of German and American approaches to education at the end of the 20th century. While five attributes mentioned above are in line with the positions articulated in the American discussion in many ways, the question of how to inculcate certain values via public education highlights key differences in the debates in the two countries. On the one hand, Herzog strongly

---

[32] Speech by the Bundespraesident Roman Herzog at the Berliner Bildungsforum on November 5, 1997. Bulletin Nr. 87, Presse- und Informationsamt der Bundesregierung, Bonn 5. Nov. 1997.
[33] Herzog, Speech, 1002.

endorsed traditional values such as reliability, punctuality, discipline, and respect for other people, values that illustrate his "Back-to-Basics" approach. On the other hand, however, he advocated a value system that, in his view, helps to create a culture of self-reliance and responsibility. This is grounded first in an awareness of one's own cultural traditions and heritage as the prerequisite for understanding the value of other cultures. Even though he did not explicitly elaborate a notion of multiculturalism, Herzog emphasized that the new challenges of a "multicultural cosmos" of global markets required the recognition of social competencies as a primary educational goal.

The present structure of the German educational system is built on the concept of uniform guidelines for education regulated by the federal government respectively and the *Laender*. In his critique, Herzog advocated a less bureaucratic and more flexible organization of education with a higher degree of autonomy and responsibility for the educational institutions themselves. He also stressed the role that private educational institutions can play in the quest for the best models of education. Roman Herzog's line of argument throughout his address reflected the agenda of the current educational debate in Germany. It included issues such as institutional structures, curriculum contents, teaching situations, student support systems and evaluation of educational results.

Since the 1980s theories of multiculturalism have been more extensively debated in the German academy. Among the first disciplines to problematize concepts of multiculturalism were American Studies, Cultural Studies, Ethnology, and German Studies. While initially these projects focused on ethnic, class and gender politics outside of Germany, especially in the United States, there were soon attempts to relate concepts of multiculturalism to the German context, notably by exploring the differential impact of particular cultural concepts on identity formation in West and East Germany.[34] It is exactly at this point that the debate in Germany genuinely contributes to the theory of multiculturalism deriving from its unique situation in the midst of a process of (national) unification that is paradoxically predicated upon the still larger project of dissolving the nation state in a transformed European Union.

Partly because of the controversies surrounding the definition of multiculturalism and partly due to its political relevance and applicability to German culture, this more recent debate has resulted not only in the implementation of new courses on multi-cultural issues in university curricula but also in the introduction of new interdisciplinary subjects, notably gender studies. With regard to schools, concepts of multiculturalism have also played a more prominent role. Like their American counterparts, the multi-culturalist, pedagogical projects in Germany have attempted to develop teaching tools that acknowledge cultural differences and didactic strategies for coping with these differences in the classroom. The theoretical premises of these projects mainly relied on concepts of interculturality, transculturality and empathy as well as communicative strategies. In contrast to the various models of multicultural education in the United

---

[34] *American Studies in Germany: European Contexts and Intercultural Relations*, ed. by Guenter H. Lenz and Klaus Milich (Frankfurt/M.: Campus, New York: St. Martin's Press, 1996).

States, the projects discussed in Germany argue less radically for a reformation of curricula content and didactic strategies in school education without questioning the institution of the school itself.

In terms of a multicultural agenda the didactic concepts of "understanding the foreign" or the other ("Fremdverstehen") are mostly directed towards a critical revision of the notions of cultural difference and its impact on educational processes.[35] This revision is based on a complex approach to cultural difference that includes within it issues of ethnicity, gender, and identity. The models proposed for implementing such approaches of encountering and understanding typically involve strategies of negotiating cultural conflicts from a basis of intercultural competence.

Since the end of 1980s the debate on multiculturalism and education has resulted in an increased interest in research projects exploring a wide array of intercultural issues such as identity formation and cultural contact, intercultural knowledge and cultural conflicts, acculturation of teachers in multicultural classes, intercultural curricula, intercultural competence and communication as well as images of the other.[36]

Employing various approaches, these projects address either specific issues in case-studies or deal with more comprehensive, theoretical questions. Over the past ten years, the German Institute for International Educational Research has published a wide range of studies that explore three major areas of multicultural education. The first area includes projects that focus on problems of learning through cultural contact, the significance of collective experiences through intercultural contacts and the competence needed to solve intercultural conflict as well as cultural encounters and their impact on school education.[37] Essentially, these are comparative studies that are based on empirical cases and that make use of psychological approaches in an effort to explain how intercultural competence works. " By analyzing the cultural cognition and conflict resolution strategies of people living in settings of permanent culture contact "these projects aim

---

[35] The concept of *Fremdverstehen* is extensively discussed by Lothar Bredella in Lothar Bredella/Herbert Christ/Michael K. Legutke.eds., *Thema Fremdverstehen*. Tuebingen: Gunter Narr, 1997, as well as in Lothar Bredella/Herbert Christ.eds., *Begegnungen mit dem Fremden*. Giessen: Ferber, 1996, and in Lothar Bredella and Herbert Christ.eds., *Didaktik des Fremdver-stehens*. Tuebingen:Gunter Narr, 1995.

[36] These issues are explored in publications and research projects of the German Institute for International Educational Research. http://www.dipf.de/sp2/s2_pub.htm (12 Feb. 1998), 1-2. These are some of the problems dealt with in a larger research project by graduate students at the University of Giessen, Germany. The title of this project (Graduiertenkolleg) directed by Lothar Bredella is "Didaktik des Fremdverstehens." htpp://www.uni-giessen.de/~ga52/kolleg/prod01.htm (12 Feb. 1998), 1.

[37] Kerstin Goebel. "The Handling of Conflict by Adolescent Female Youth: The Difference Made by Experiences in Acculturation," in Hermann-Guenter Hesse and Kerstin Goebel.eds., *Forschungsbericht Nr. 5 aus dem Projekt "Lernen durch Kulturkontakt."* Frankfurt a.M.: Deutsches Institut fuer Internationale Paedagogische Forschung, 1997; Hermann-Guenter Hesse. "Experiences in Acculturation: What Is Being Learned?," in H.-G. Hesse, ed., *Forschungsbericht Nr. 3 aus dem Projekt "Lernen durch Kulturkontakt."* Frankfurt a.M.: Deutsches Institut fuer Internationale Paedagogische Forschung, 1995, 1-14; Kerstin Goebel and Hermann-Guenter Hesse. "Interkulturelles Wissen und die Behandlung von Kulturkoflikten: Zur Akkulturation von Lehrern in multikulturellen Schulklassen," in H.-G. Hesse and Kerstin Goebel.eds., *Forschungsbericht Nr. 5 aus dem Projekt "Lernen durch Kulturkontakt."* Frankfurt a.M.: Deutsches Institut fuer Internationale Paedagogische Forschung, 1997.

at contributing to the improvement of intercultural training methods."[38] A second area of concentration for these research projects deals with questions of cultural contact among Germans, exploring the experiences and expectations of German immigrants ("Aussiedler") from such countries as Poland and the former Soviet Union in the social and political context of contemporary Germany.[39] Finally, a third major area of research consists of projects that evaluate the perceptions of school from the perspective of nationally diverse students.[40]

At German universities, theories of multiculturalism and multicultural education have been equally recognized as an important part of educating future teachers. At the university of Giessen, for instance, a research project on the didactics of "understanding the other" ("Didaktik des Fremdverstehens") has been running for several years. Based on a critical examination of various concepts of multiculturalism relevant to school education, this project aims at describing the prerequisites of intercultural learning from different perspectives (linguistic, cognitive, communicative, institutional, social, cultural etc.) in an effort to develop didactic strategies of intercultural learning.[41] Although these projects, mostly located at universities and research institutes, very clearly demonstrate the productivity of multicultural theories, they also indicate the discrepancy that still exists between the academic and public discourse on multiculturalism in Germany.

---

[38] Deutsches Institut fuer Internationale Paedagogische Forschung, Intercultural Research. http://www.dipf.de/sp2/e-s2_12.htm (12 Feb. 1998), 1.

[39] Ines Graudenz and Regina Roemhild, "Kulturkontakt unter Deutschen: Zur interaktiven Identitaetsarbeit von Spaetaussiedlern. Eine Projektskizze," *Bildung und Erziehung*, 43 (3, 1990), 313-324.; and Graudenz and Roemhild, "Fremde Deutsche. Aussiedler und Fremden-feindlichkeit—eine Herausforderung an das bundesrepublikanische Selbstverstaendnis." in *Fremdenhass und politischer Extremismus —Was kann die Schule tun?*, ed. by Peter Doebrich and Georg Rutz (Frankfurt a.M.: Deutsches Institut fuer Internationale Paedagogische Forschung, 1993), 17-29.

[40] D. Randoll and Ines Graudenz, *"The Perception of School from the Perspective of Pupils—A European Comparison."* 1996. http://www.edfac.usyd.edu.au/projects/wcces96/wcces96.html. Ines Graudenz and D. Randoll, "'So daenisch wie moeglich, so deutsch wie noetig.' Eine vergleichende Untersuchung zur Wahrnehmung von Schule durch Abiturienten." *Studien und Dokumentationen zur vergleichenden Bildungsforschung*, (Boehlau, Koeln, Wien 1997).

[41] The project explores, for example, the following issues: Warum "Fremdverstehen"? Anmerkungen zu einem leitenden Konzept innerhalb des interkulturellen Sprachunterrichts (Adelheid Hu) Zum Potential von Lehrwerken fuer das Verstehen anderer Kulturen (Dagmar Abendroth-Timmer) Negotiating Common Ground: Ein wesentliches Element (interkultureller) kommunikativer Kompetenz (Annegret Gick) Das Aushandeln einer bikulturellen Identitaet: Aimee Lius *Face* (Sharon Wotschke).
http://www.uni-giessen.de/~ga52/kolleg/Thema%20Fremdverstehen.htm (12 Feb. 1998), 1-3.

HISTORIANS, HISTORIES, AND PUBLIC CULTURES MULTICULTURAL DISCOURSES IN THE UNITED STATES AND GERMANY

Günter H. Lenz

Since the 1980s, debates on multiculturalism and minority discourses have played a crucial role both in the general public and in academia in the United States. In recent years, the issues have also been taken up, though in a more subdued manner, in Germany. However, the same terms that travelled from the United States to Germany have taken on different meanings, reacting to a different social and cultural situation and performing different functions in the discourse of cultural heterogeneity.[1] The recent controversies over the meanings of "multiculturalism" have revealed the strikingly different and conflicting understanding of the foundations and the boundaries of Western nation-states and cultures, of their ways of recognizing, accepting, or incorporating other cultures, and of their ways of dealing with cultural heterogeneity within their societies.

In my essay, I will first give a critical account of the discussions on multiculturalism in Germany and of the meaning of history and of the limited role of historians in this debate, in striking contrast to the situation in the United States. I will then introduce the notion of public culture as it has been proposed by historian Thomas Bender as providing a vision and arena for dealing with the question of a new "synthesis" in the writing of a multicultural history of the United States and for reassessing the public role of the historian in a heterogeneous culture and society. The remaining parts of the essay will deal with the discourse among American historians on the meaning and the repercussions of multiculturalism for the profession of American history, particularly for reconceiving the story or narrative of U.S.American history and for writing versions of a critical multicultural history. I will analyze the various dimensions and perspectives of history and historians in the multiculturalist United States as they have been elaborated and accounted for by American historians in their contributions to a theory of history and multiculturalism and its discursive repercussions. The conclusion will open up the debate and move beyond the confines of national history of the United States to a trans- and international perspective.

---

[1] A concise analysis of the German discourse on multiculturalism as a case of "traveling theory," written from the perspective of cultural anthropology, is given by Gisela Welz in her essay "Multikulturelle Diskurse: Topoi der Differenzerfahrung in Deutschland und den Vereinigten Staaten," *Amerikastudien/American Studies*, 38 (1993), 265-72.

The Debate on Multiculturalism in Germany and the United States

In public debates on multiculturalism in the United States, historians and questions of history have played an important role. Arthur M. Schlesinger's *The Disuniting of America: Reflections on a Multicultural Society* (1991, 1992) focused on the debates of the late 1980s in terms of striking a balance between "fragmentation, resegregation, and tribalization of American life" on the one hand and unity, synthesis, and a common culture on the other hand. David A. Hollinger's more recent book *Postethnic America: Beyond Multiculturalism* (1995), on the contrary, explores the vision of a cosmopolitan democratic society that acknowledges ethno-racial differences and multiple identities without reifying or institutionalizing them and sets out to understand "these various and shifting affiliations as publics nested within a larger public that is the polity of the United States." Representatives of various minority groups continue to contest these "synthesizing" notions and have proposed alternative versions of a multicultural society (beyond ethnocentrism in reverse or ethnic essentialism). But they share with their opponents an emphasis on the reconstitution and the crucial role of public culture(s) as well as on the need of rewriting American history and revising the (idea of the) canon in American cultural studies in universities and public schools.

As multiculturalism is seen in the United States primarily as a challenge to the historical constitution and the traditional understanding of the national culture (*e pluribus unum*), questions of cultural difference, interculturality, and of transgressing national boundaries have been defined as problems of *intra*cultural diversity or heterogeneity—in terms of race, ethnicity, gender, class, religion, region, language, or age, even though these dimensions of multiculturality have often been reduced to ethnicity and race. The demands of multiculturalism are seen as problems of American *history or histories* and of revisioning and revising *historical discourses*. In European countries multiculturalism has also been a response to a fundamental crisis of legitimation of the traditional concept of national cultural identity and the nation-state. It has been a response to the globalization of economic processes, an unprecedented influx of foreign workers and of refugees seeking asylum and the mass migration from former colonies, as well as of the open labor market of the European Community. Yet this challenge of multiculturalism has been conceived, particularly in Germany, as a challenge to the national culture coming *from outside*, as an *external, inter*cultural problem of recent origin that raises *new* questions of citizenship and of the assimilation and cultural and social integration of foreigners into the national culture and the nation-state. Germany has traditionally defined its national culture as more or less homogeneous and—in contrast, however, to other European countries such as France—based its notion of the nation-state (*Volksnation*) and the right to citizenship primarily on *ius sanguinis*, on ethnic descent. During the 19th century a notion of *ethnos* (*Volk*) as homogeneous cultural identity was conceived and used to legitimize a form of *ethnic nationalism* that was seen as transcending social differences and political conflicts. With the founding of the political nation-state in 1871 it functioned as a powerful unifying political ideology that turned heterogeneous or ethnically different groups of people living within the borders of the German nation-state or entering its national territory into (unwanted) "ethnic minorities" that were forced to assimilate or, later, most radically during the Third Reich, expelled or persecuted.[2]

Therefore, multiculturalism has not been a central issue among German historians, nor have demands for revising the historical canon in the various areas of German cultural studies attained a similar kind of urgency they have had in the U.S. over the last decades. Still, the implications of multiculturalism have been hotly debated in Germany, too, both in the general (political) public—though almost exclusively by Germans, less by the "Ausländer/innen" or "Gastarbeiter/innen" themselves—and in academia, but in disciplines other than history, such as political science, sociology, or educational sciences.

The impact of global migrations, of successive waves of millions of foreign workers, of people seeking asylum, and of so-called "repatriated nationals" during the last decades have finally forced Germans—in spite of strong opposition not exclusively from conservative quarters—to challenge and hopefully to reject this closed concept of culture and fully acknowledge the reality of having become an "immigrant country" and of having to revise the restrictive notion of citizenship and face the problems of a "multicultural" society.[3] However, the strong emphasis on questions of citizenship and

---

[2] For a historical account and critical analysis of the highly problematical implications of the German notion of the "ethnic nation-state" (*Volksnation*) or "ethnic nationalism" and a discussion of alternative foundations of a "politically constituted nation-state" (*Staatsbürgernation*) or "civic nationalism" see, e.g., Friedrich Heckmann, "Ethnos, Demos und Nation, oder: Woher stammt die Intoleranz des Nationalstaats gegenüber ethnischen Minderheiten?," in *Das Eigene und das Fremde*, ed. by Uli Bielefeld (Hamburg: Junius Verlag, 1991), 51-78; Wolfgang Kaschuba, "Nationalismus und Ethnozentrismus: Zur kulturellen Ausgrenzung ethnischer Gruppen in (deutscher) Geschichte und Gegenwart," in *Grenzfälle: Über neuen und alten Nationalismus*, ed. by Michael Jeismann, Henning Ritter (Leipzig: Reclam Verlag, 1993), 239-73, 378-80; Claus Leggewie, "Ethnizität, Nationalismus und multikulturelle Gesellschaft," in *Nationales Bewußtsein und kollektive Identität: Studien zur Entwicklung des kollektiven Bewußtseins in der Neuzeit*, Bd. 2, ed. by Helmut Berding (Frankfurt/Main: Suhrkamp, 1994), 46-65; and, with different distinctions, Dan Diner, "Nationalstaat und Migration: Zu Begriff und Geschichte," in *Politik der Multikultur: Vergleichende Perspektiven zu Einwanderung und Integration*, ed. by Mechthild M. Jansen, Sigrid Baringhorst (Baden-Baden: Nomos Verlagsanstalt, 1994), 17-30.

[3] The public debate on multiculturalism in Germany has often been conducted in the political realm in terms of the question *if* we *want* a multicultural society or not. A critical analysis of these debates and a proposal for realizing a "multicultural society in an emancipatory perspective" is offered by Axel Schulte in his essay "Multikulturelle Gesellschaft: Chance, Ideologie oder Bedrohung?," *Aus Politik und Zeitgeschehen*, B 23-24, 1. Juni 1990, 3-15. A more skeptical assessment of the foundations and the political potential (or dangers) of (the German versions of) multiculturalism (and the program of "multicultural or intercultural education") is Frank-Olaf Radtke's "Lob der Gleich-Gültigkeit: Zur Konstruktion des Fremden im Diskurs des Multikulturalismus," in *Das Eigene und das Fremde*, 79-96. The most wide-ranging accounts of a politics of multiculturalism, or multicultural politics, are Claus Leggewie, *Multi Kulti: Spielregeln für die Vielvölkerrepublik* (Berlin: Rotbuch Verlag, 1990), his essay "Vom Deutschen Reich zur Bundesrepublik—und nicht zurück: Zur politischen Gestalt einer multikulturellen Gesellschaft," in *Schwierige Fremdheit: Über Integration und Ausgrenzung in Einwanderungsländern*, ed. by Friedrich Balke, et al. (Frankfurt/Main: Fischer Verlag, 1993), 3-20; Daniel Cohn-Bendit, Thomas Schmid, *Heimat Babylon: Das Wagnis der multikulturellen Demokratie* (Hamburg: Hoffmann & Campe Verlag, 1992); and the comparative studies in Jansen, Baringhorst, eds., *Politik der Multikultur*. A rich and provocative critical discussion of the political implications of the multiculturalism debate in the United States is Berndt

social policies concerning foreigners living in Germany (*Ausländerproblematik*) that has dominated German debates on multiculturalism has often led to a reductive understanding of the fundamental challenges to traditional concepts of society that multicultural theory has tried to articulate in American cultural studies, anthropology, historiography, political studies, and minority discourses. All too often, the discourse on multiculturalism in Germany has been limited to the problem of the "integration" of foreign workers (*Gastarbeiter/innen*) and their descendants born in Germany[4] or of other, foreign "ethnic groups" into an ethnically "homogeneous" German society. Or it has been reduced to the polemical rejection of multiculturalism as a fashionable exoticism in culinary or musical taste. In contrast to the United States representatives of the "immigrant groups" or women rarely have taken part in the multiculturalism debate as yet. Nor should the emphasis on intercultural differences too quickly be read as the "designer model" (Frank-Olaf Radtke) of the corporatist strategy for the global capitalism of the 1990s or simply as a questionable "culturalist" displacement of social and political inequalities.

The charge of "culturalism" is a valid critique of versions of multicultural theory that offer "cultural diversity" instead of structural change and that are based on closed concepts of culture characterized by stable, quasi-inherent traits in values and behavior of more or less homogeneous traditional "ethnic groups."[5] But the critique of multiculturalism as a "culturalist" displacement of the "real" structural inequalities in society often tends to rely on a more or less clean-cut distinction among the various "spheres" of modern societies such as the economy, politics, and culture that is no longer adequate for conceptualizing the complex and heteronomous social processes, interactions, and representations in post-Fordist, postmodern Western societies that force us to redefine the concepts of culture, the boundaries of the political, and the meaning of multicultural identities and communities in crucial ways. Therefore, a self-reflective critique of the dynamics of contemporary culture must articulate in its discursive strategies a crucial *doubleness* or *ambiguity* in the use of the term "culture." On the one hand, cultural critics today are asked to see the various "realms" of a society in a common focus or, better, address their interrelations and their differences as a network of complex and often conflicting interactions and not limit their analysis to the traditional sphere of "culture" in the narrower sense. On the other hand, it is exactly the seeming "omnipresence" of these processes of cultural mediation and the increasing economic, social, political, and public role "cultural processes" have acquired in American and other

---

Ostendorf's essay *The Costs of Multiculturalism*, Working Paper No. 50, John F. Kennedy-Institut für Nordamerikastudien, Freie Universität Berlin (1992), 1-30; for a comparative analysis cf. his essay in this volume.

[4] See, e.g., the critical essays in Hermann Bausinger, ed., *Ausländer—Inländer: Arbeitsimmigration und kulturelle Identität* (Tübingen: Tübinger Vereinigung für Volkskunde, 1986).

[5] For a critique of "culturalism" as a displacement of social conflicts in current discourses of the humanities and social sciences see Wolfgang Kaschuba, "Kulturalismus: Vom Verschwinden des Sozialen im gesellschaftlichen Diskurs," in *Kulturen—Identitäten—Diskurse: Perspektiven Europäischer Ethnologie*, ed. by Wolfgang Kaschuba (Berlin: Akademie Verlag, 1995), 11-30.

Western and non-Western societies over the last decades in the context of the post-Fordist economy of postindustrialism and of postmodernity that challenge cultural critics to reassert distinctions and differences and carefully analyze the *specific* historical modes of representation at work in the public sphere.

Multicultural discourse in Germany must deal with the questions of the social and political organization of cultural heterogeneity, of the constitution and the political repercussions (and also the potential) of multiple intra- and intercultural differences, and of the new manifestations of public culture that are the inescapable consequences of recent globalizing, transnational, as well as localizing processes of economic, social, and cultural mediations. But these challenges have taken on a specific urgency and a unique historical configuration in the difficult processes of "reunification" of West and East Germany after the demise of the German Democratic Republic.[6]

Obviously, the political, social, and cultural questions addressed in public and scholarly debates on the theory and the practical consequences of a multicultural society cannot be answered in the context of a nation-state or a national culture, but ask for a comparative, intercultural approach. The political as well as the theoretical issues of multiculturalism in the United States have often polemically been rephrased in terms of "synthesis" or "core culture" vs. "fragmentation" of American culture, society, and the political system, or as an instance of fashionable "postmodern" commodification. In its "affirmative," often "essentialist" versions as cultural group interest politics, multi-culturalism has frequently been fixed in a simple reversal of valorization of the old oppositions and dichotomies of dualistic thinking. However, in its more radical and multi-faceted versions and strategies American multicultural discourse has offered, and continues to offer, important ways of reconceptualizing the historical workings of heterogeneous nation-states and of the social construction of the culture concept and its political implications in Germany. A *critical multiculturalism*, in this sense does not claim that it can take the place of social and political movements or solve the problems of glaring economic inequality. It must accept its limited power, and it will continue to be a *dialectical* and *open* discourse that responds to and represents political, social, and cultural processes that *are*, and will always be, ambivalent and multidimensional. But it can provide, it seems to me, crucial insights into the radically changing dynamics of societies and public cultures, investigate the political role of dimensions of social and cultural difference and heterogeneity such as race, class, ethnicity, or gender, and their often conflicting interrelations, and reassert and project alternative models of social and cultural construction.[7]

---

[6] A reading of the problems of "reunification" of Germany after 1989 in terms of the problems of a "German-German multiculturalism" is offered by Dieter Thomä in his essay "Multikulturalismus, Demokratie, Nation: Zur Philosophie der deutschen Einheit," *Deutsche Zeitschrift für Philosophie*, 43 (1995), 349-63.

[7] Cf. Avery F. Gordon and Christopher Newfield's program of a "strong version of multiculturalism" developed in their own contribution to the volume they edited as *Mapping Multiculturalism* (Minneapolis: University of Minnesota Press, 1996), 76-115; David Theo Goldberg's notion of "multicultural heterogeneity" in his introduction to the collection of essays he edited *Multiculturalism: A Critical Reader*

American multicultural critique, in its most productive and provocative forms, that is forms of critical multiculturalism beyond liberal pluralism as well as beyond ethnic or racial absolutism and essentializing interest politics, is motivated by an *open* concept of culture and by a notion of a "civic nation-state" (*Staatsbürgernation*—M. Rainer Lepsius) that bases the right to citizenship, with some important qualifications, on *ius soli,* on the country of birth and/or extended residence. As argued and elaborated in minority discourses or in studies by American historians such as Joan W. Scott, David Hollinger or Lawrence W. Levine, it attempts to account for the *inherent* diversity and complexity of what is called "American culture" (or American cultures in the plural) and for their social and political repercussions on the political culture(s) of the United States. However, it is crucial to realize that this exceptional complexity and diversity of American culture cannot be adequately grasped in a "nationalist" discourse limited to the boundaries of the United States, an attempt all too often found in contributions to the American multiculturalism debate. This "nationalist" framing of the problems and implications of multiculturalism in the United States is not exclusively an expression of a typically self-centered and parochial American perspective, but also frequently the consequence of the definition of the issues of multiculturalism as an "*intra*cultural" challenge, a challenge of confronting the multiple global differences *within* the borders of the American nation-state. Yet, in the contemporary world, the problems and the potential of multicultural societies are in their very dynamic also inherently *inter*cultural and have to be analyzed in an explicitly *transnational* perspective. That is, instead of "comparing" cultures seen as more or less independent and stable units, an intercultural approach is distinguished by the insight that cultures reproduce, represent, and reshape within themselves multiple axes or fault-lines of difference that are energized by, and manifested and transformed in, "transcultural" interactions. It is at these points of intersection, of confrontation and difference that "impure," multicultural identities and communities are envisioned, constructed, and re-constructed. Defined in this way, an intercultural approach attempts to account for the inherent hybridity and self-difference of both cultures and transcultural interactions, opening up multicultural discourse to critical dialogues articulated from different, often conflicting perspectives.[8]

Multicultural critique in this sense can also help Germans—and especially German historians—to recognize more fully that "German culture" is not only becoming increasingly "multicultural" and "intercultural," but that it has always been much less stable and homogeneous and much more heterogeneous and internally differentiated by various dimensions of multiculturality than adherents of the German closed culture concept have been willing to concede.

(Oxford: Blackwell, 1994), 1-41; and Peter McLaren's "critical and resistance multiculturalism" in his essay "White Terror and Oppositional Agency: Towards a Critical Multiculturalism," in Goldberg, ed., *Multiculturalism*, 45-74.

[8] See my essay "Transnational American Studies: Negotiating Cultures of Difference—Multicultural Identities, Communities, and Border Discourses," in *Multiculturalism in Transit: A German—American Exchange*, ed. by Klaus J. Milich, Jeffrey Peck (Providence, RI: Berghahn, 1998), 129-66.

The opponents of a "multicultural society" in Germany have based their position on the "allegedly insurmountable differences between ethnic cultures and peoples" or on a less overtly racist notion of an ethnopluralism of incompatible closed cultures that have to be kept apart, a notion that demands the affirmation of German nationalism and the exclusion of other, foreign cultures. All these positions are versions of a reductionist distortion of the complex historical development of peoples to their supposedly unchangeable genetic or ethnic origins. On the other hand, the advocates of a multicultural society have tried to legitimize their multicultural vision of Germany through a different historical narrative which "emphasizes and idealizes historical examples of immigration to Germany," as Sabine von Dirke writes.[9] Important as these—contested—historical examples are for revising the concept of an ethnically homogeneous German people and culture in terms of origin and for rejecting the apocalyptic scenarios of the imminent dissolution of the German nation-state as a result of the influx of foreigners, as they have been painted by the opponents of a multiculturalist society, they tend to argue in terms of the *integration* of *Ausländer/innen into* a German national society conceived of as a fundamentally stable, unified culture. What is more consequential is the question in how far the ideas and political strategies proposed by Daniel Cohn-Bendit, Thomas Schmid, and Claus Leggewie of the historical dialectic of the "continuing emancipation of the individual which results in higher geographic and social mobility, and at the same time as traumatic experience for the individual due to this increased mobility,"[10] can be turned into "postnational" and "postethnic" forms of a multicultural society that acknowledges, negotiates, and productively organizes in an institutional frame the inescapable conflicts of social heterogeneity and cultural differences. Cohn-Bendit, Schmid, Leggewie, and others have elaborated the concepts of "civil society" and of *Verfassungspatriotismus* in order to project the vision of a new definition of citizenship, of the social contract, and of the political process in Germany (in the wider context of Europe).

Crucial as these efforts are, there still remain many problems that have to be pursued more persistently. One vital issue, it seems to me, is a much more cogent reassessment of the meaning and the functioning of the contested public sphere, of the reorganization of *public culture*, or *public cultures in the plural*, in a multicultural society that has to come to terms with intracultural diversity, a multiplicity of group histories, intercultural boundary-crossings, and the move beyond the traditional nation-state. Clearly, the historical, political, and cultural context in Europe, particularly in Germany, is very different from the American one. They cannot directly be compared or explained through each other, but demand a careful attention to the intercultural conditions and the processes of transculturation. But I think the debate among American historians on the political constitution and potential of public culture(s) and their engagement with the meaning, the public drama, and the directions of multiculturalism

---

[9] Sabine von Dirke, "Multikulti: The German Debate on Multiculturalism," *German Studies Review*, 17 (Oct. 1994), 513-36; 518, 525.

[10] Von Dirke, "Multikulti," 525.

in American society, past, present, and future, are in many ways exemplary and a provocative challenge to the languishing, increasingly purely polemical multiculturalism debate on this side of the Atlantic. Seen from the critical perspective of cultural distance or difference, American Studies in Germany can help to mediate and "transfer" the dynamics of American multicultural critique to the different German situation and hopefully to redefine and refocus the public discourse on the notion of culture, the historical contours of the nation-state, and the specific political and cultural implications of a *multikulturelle Gesellschaft*.

The multiculturalism debate among American historians has to be placed in the wider contexts of the more recent quest for a new synthesis in American historiography after the strong emergence of histories of various groups and subcultures in American society since the 1970s and of the demands for reclaiming an important place for history and historians in the public realm of a deeply changing postmodern and post-Fordist world. In the next part of my essay, I will discuss Thomas Bender's continuing efforts to redefine and elaborate the contours and the potential of a notion of *public culture* as a way of reconceiving American history in its complex interrelationships and of the role of the historian in contemporary society. The critical analysis of the potential meaning and the political dynamics of public culture in historical discourse will provide the context for posing, then, a sequence of critical questions concerning American historians' readings of American (multicultural) history at large and for reconstructing the argument of some of their most challenging and influential contributions to the debate on multiculturalism and the writing of a multicultural history of the United States.

The Quest for "Synthesis": American Historians and the Notion of Public Culture

In 1986, Thomas Bender published in the *Journal of American History* his essay "Wholes and Parts: The Need for Synthesis in American History." It was a revised and much longer version of an earlier essay of his that had appeared in the *New York Times Book Review* in the preceding year, which was a response to a question posed by the radical social historian Herbert G. Gutman in *The Nation* in late 1981 in his provocative essay "The Missing Synthesis: Whatever Happened to History?" In his earlier piece, Gutman praised the achievements of the new social history of the 1970s, but pointed out that the focus on "segments (such as blacks, workers, or women)" had also "reinforced the disintegration of a coherent synthesis in the writing of American history." He concluded: "A new synthesis is needed, one that incorporates and then transcends the new history"—a *new* synthesis that could also succeed in creating a different, critical understanding of American history in the public at large. Thomas Bender's response in "Making History Whole Again" to Gutman's challenge acknowledges the multicultural constitution of American society and emphasizes that "the *interrelations* of races, classes and sexes in the formation of American society and culture—or in the making of individual lives" have not been studied in sufficient detail. He proposes that the "new synthesis" can be achieved by studying the "public realm," by "reconceptualiz[ing] public culture," that "essentially civic arena where groups interact, even compete, to establish the configuration of political power in a society and its cultural forms and their meanings." But in this early essay he still tends to oppose the histories of segments, of minorities, of ethnic groups to "American history" as something synthetic or whole, as if the histories of groups and segments (and their interrelations) *are* not "American history" or do not constitute manifestations of what is called the American experience. Therefore, his demand to "restore the center" and "to make history whole again" seemed to stand for an ambiguous undertaking.[11]

However, in his later essay, Bender is much more precise and challenging and quite rightly received a lot of attention in the profession. He registers the deep uneasiness among American historians in the mid-1980s about two, interconnected problems: first, the lack of a new synthesis of the remarkable insights achieved in the various new subfields of the discipline of American history in terms of race, class, gender, region, etc. that were the result of professional specialization, of crises in society, and of the political pressure of minority and oppositional movements, and, second, worries about the declining significance of history and historians in the general intellectual culture, in the general public of our time. Therefore, his objectives are, first, to project a new understanding of American history as a whole that would acknowledge and fully incorporate the approaches and achievements of the new labor, political, social, urban, and cultural histories and their focus on variously defined group histories. But at the same time, it would transcend the fragmentation of the field *in the sense of* isolated, quasi-autonomous areas and reified, essentializing histories that ignore the manifold interrelationships among them and the complex workings of difference in the context of multicultural American history at large. His second aim is to regain a central place for history and historians in the U.S. American national culture, a public role and voice in the interpretation and the shaping of American history.[12]

Bender's notion of *public culture*, which he has revised and elaborated in numerous essays over the following years, provides the frame of reference, the forum and the institutional and public space for combining and interrelating his two objectives. In Bender's reading, "public culture" as a "principle of synthesis" "crystallizes in narrative form" an "image of society" and brings together politics, power, and their forms of "symbolic meaning." "At the center of such a synthetic narrative, as a focus and as an analytical device," he writes in "Wholes and Parts," "we must develop a historical notion of public culture, at once an arena for the play of cultures and interests in society and the product of that play—the constituted definition of power and meaning."[13] "Public culture" is *not* a fixed realm of the public sphere and its institutions as defined by the dominant white establishment, by those in power. *Neither* does it refer to a traditional,

---

[11] Thomas Bender, "Making History Whole Again," *New York Times Book Review*, Oct. 6, 1985, 1, 42-43.

[12] Thomas Bender, "Wholes and Parts: The Need for Synthesis in American History," *Journal of American History*, 73 (June 1986), 120-36; 120.

[13] Thomas Bender, "Wholes and Parts," 131.

stable "common core culture" as something possessed by members of society, *nor* is the quest for synthesis conceived as a return to, or re-enactment of, a stable unity, one single story told by a voice situated at the "center" of society. For Bender, "public culture" is always public culture *in the making and remaking*, a contested, multiplicitous, emergent, and *relational* process of the construction, deconstruction, and reconstruction of the boundaries and the divisions between public and private, society and the individual, the core or center and the periphery, "the field where contingent and multiple identities ... are formed into distinctly American identities."[14] It "illuminate[s] the relations of groups to each other and to the prevailing definitions of public culture" and explores "how power in all its various forms, including tradition itself, is contested, elaborated, and rendered authoritative."[15]

These processes of the making and remaking of public culture have to be situated, however, not in an ideal realm of free democratic discourse, but in a world permeated by inequalities in power and the resistances and the fight for articulation in the public sphere that historians have to realize and analyze in their repercussions on American society at large. "It is this always-changing public culture, and not a series of distinctive group experiences, that reveals and establishes our common life as a people and a nation."[16] Bender carefully tries to distinguish his project of exploring a "historicizing" notion of American public culture in the making and remaking from a conservative quest for reclaiming an authoritative single, substantive synthesis, but he still holds on to the vision of some frame, some forum, a "heterogeneous center" that engages the various groups and voices in a public dialogue: "The point is not to homogenize the experience of various groups, but rather to bring them, with their defining differences, into a pattern of relationships. Once they are in such a relational frame, it is possible to get beyond the parts to a sense of the whole, and of the larger issues of the American society."[17] Bender does not look for one new overarching synthesis which somehow incorporates all the heterogeneity in American history, but he also insists on public culture as one forum and frame that forces historians to see the various groups and their discourses in their interrelations: "I am not proposing a single synthesis that will win universal assent from *the* public, though I believe ... that there is *a* public. Within the public there may be varied readings, but that does not imply a multiplicity of publics."[18]

The tension that Bender dramatizes in his various essays between "a relational sense of differences that mark and make our society" and the vision of a "single compelling narrative" necessarily entails a revisionary view of the concept of the "nation" which

---

[14] Thomas Bender, "'enturesome and Cautious': American History in the 1990s," *Journal of American History*, 81 (Dec. 1994), 992-1003; 995.

[15] Thomas Bender, "Public Culture: Inclusion and Synthesis in American History," in *Historical Literacy: The Case for History in American Education*, ed. by Paul Gagnon (New York: Macmillan, 1989), 188-202; 200.

[16] Bender, "Public Culture," 201.

[17] Bender, "Public Culture," 200.

[18] Thomas Bender, "Wholes and Parts: Continuing the Conversation," *Journal of American History*, 74 (June 1987), 123-30; 126.

is understood not as a "fixed container into which everything and everyone must be fitted," but as "the ever changing, always contingent outcome of a continuing contest among social groups and ideas for the power to define public culture, thus the nation itself."[19] It is a *tension* that reasserts itself in his efforts to describe ways in which studies addressing the vision of a historical synthesis could be written: "I am not anxious to encourage *the* synthesis, but rather works of a synthetic character."[20] What this leads to is the notion that historians should work and write from different competing perspectives and positionings, yet all of them should address American history in its complex relational dynamics, be guided by a "cosmopolitan recognition of particularism,"[21] and engage in a dialogue with one another and with other outside voices in the public realm.

American Historians and the Discourse on Multiculturalism

It is in this context of the quest for a new "synthesis" in the writing of American history by way of exploring and redefining the making and the remaking of political culture in the United States and for reclaiming a formative role for history and for historians in the public realm that the heated debate about multiculturalism in the United States is a crucial test-case and practical realization of Bender's project and vision of American public culture. At the same time, the multiculturalism debate is an historical elaboration of the cultural and political dynamics that energize Bender's urgent call for reconceiving the writing and the teaching of American history. It is, of course, not accidental that in the United States historians and scholars from neighboring disciplines such as political science and sociology writing from the historian's, or a historical, point of view have been most prominent in the controversies about multiculturalism and the revisions of the canon in understanding American society and the teaching objectives and strategies in the humanities and the social sciences in the universities and in the public schools. The public debate on the meaning and the repercussions of multiculturalism, the revisions of the canon, and the contours of a new vision of American society as constituted by cultural differences and social heterogeneity is the most recent collective effort to come to terms with "the centrality of history to the nation's debates about itself" (David A. Hollinger),[22] that is, the specific dynamics and the specific achievements and problems of U.S. culture and society. It sets out to "(re-)invent" a national identity and define a vision of democratic American society, moving beyond earlier models such as the melting-pot or the version of cultural pluralism as an ensemble of stable ethnic cultures. Multiculturalism is seen as a challenge growing out of the *intra*cultural differences and the heterogeneity of American society in a period of radical change and

---

[19] Bender, "Wholes and Parts," 126; "Public Culture," 198, 201; "Negotiating Public Culture: Inclusion and Synthesis in American History," *Liberal Education*, 78 (March/April 1992), 10-15; 15.

[20] Bender, "Wholes and Parts: Continuing," 128.

[21] Bender, "Negotiating," 10.

[22] David A. Hollinger, "National Solidarity at the End of the Twentieth Century: Reflections on the United States and Liberal Nationalism," *Journal of American History*, 84 (Sept. 1997), 559-69; 568.

the emergence of many new, differently constituted groups, movements, or minority cultures demanding a fuller participation in the political process and in public culture, even though there clearly have been tendencies among conservatives to redefine the intracultural differences as being produced by a threat to an otherwise stable, common culture coming from outside the national borders.

Thus, the term *multiculturalism* has been used in many different and contradictory, often polemical ways in the United States, depending on the political and ideological positioning and the goals its representatives stand for. If the highly controversial discussion on the consequences and the potential of multiculturalism among American historians is the most powerful and far-reaching practical case-study of the constructive and reconstructive workings of public culture in the U.S., Thomas Bender's thoughtful reflections on the dynamics of public culture and the potential role of history and historians can help us clarify the objectives and the methodological strategies of the often confusing versions of "multiculturalism" in public debates. In one of his more recent essays, "Negotiating Public Culture: Inclusion and Synthesis in American Culture" (1992), Bender explicitly asks historians to confront the questions of multiculturalism "at home" and places them in the wider context of a cosmopolitan vision (drawing on Randolph Bourne) that acknowledges the "syncretic" and "impure" character of "Western and *all* other traditions." If "multicultural" is used not as describing a diversity of "tightly bounded, self-contained, pure, and fixed" ethnocentric group cultures, but in a "genuinely multicultural" way, it is "cosmopolitan in impulse. It respects the complexity of lived experience and embraces the rich possibilities of multiple and shifting identities. Particularlisms are recognized, but so is their relation to larger, more heterogeneous wholes—what I call public culture."[23]

Bender's remarks not only show the crucial limitations of versions of "multiculturalism" like the radical form of Afrocentrism that insist on the separate and purist identity and tradition of racially or ethnically defined groups and their essentialist interest group politics. They also indicate the shortcomings of the liberal versions of a multiculturalism of "cultural diversity" that still are based on a notion of the predominance of a white, Western, mostly male common core culture and its "values" to which all kinds of newly emergent cultural groups, as defined by race, ethnicity, gender, or class, etc., are allowed to make selected "contributions" as long as they are not seen as threatening" the unity of American society and the consensus of the political system. Bender's more recent reflections on the making and remaking of public culture as the arena for, and the outcome of, the always contingent processes in which different groups and individuals articulate themselves in contexts of an unequal distribution of power question and replace the traditional notion that U.S. society, because of its social and cultural heterogeneity, has to be based on a broad normative, "substantative" consensus that constitutes the *unum* in the *unum e pluribus*. Bender, instead, reclaims and proposes an alternative critical tradition in social and cultural theory that he finds characteristic of New York City, an urban theory in opposition to the predominant anti-urban,

---

[23] Bender, "Negotiating," 12.

consensus-ridden political and cultural notions that have been propagated since the days of the early Republic. It is an urban, metropolitan, and cosmopolitan theory that does not reject differences, but embraces and elaborates "difference, diversity, and conflict" and organizes "a symbolic representation of diversity and difference" in the public culture.[24]

These reflections on public culture and a cultural theory of difference open up a sequence of issues and questions on the dimensions and the implications of the debates on multiculturalism among American historians and their contributions to reconstituting American public discourse. They can complement, correct, as well as substantiate empirically the powerful theoretical reflections offered in recent years in poststructuralist and postmodernist literary and cultural theory and in the various minority discourses. Let me define some of these issues and pose some of the crucial questions as they have grown out of a critical engagement with more recent multicultural discourses among American historians. My intention is not to give a full overview of publications on multiculturalism written from a historical perspective or to reconstruct the fascinating debate or controversial conversation among American historians on these issues in a chronological sequence, but to focus in a more systematic way on contributions that have engaged in critical reflections on the fundamental challenges posed by radical social and cultural changes today. My particular emphasis will be on questions concerning, on the one hand, redefinitions of history standards and of a multicultural canon and the role of the historian in the public sphere, and, on the other hand, the writing of multicultural histories "beyond the Great Story" in a radically changing, postmodern, and globalizing world.

The Politics of Multiculturalism: Common Culture, Dissensus, and the Political System

A set of questions to be addressed in this section: What do American historians mean by "multiculturalism"? Which political and historical questions have the various versions been supposed to answer? Do the United States need a "common core culture" as the condition of achieving and safeguarding the unity of society and the working of the political system? Does "culture" work through common, shared values and a basic substantive consensus or through contested values, debates, and dialogues? Is there a necessary interdependence between something like a common culture and a consensus on fundamental procedural rules of the political process of common culture, of society, of the nation (Anthony Appiah)? What is the (changing) relation of the "cultural sphere" to "politics"? Does the center-and-periphery model still work?

Among leading American historians Arthur M. Schlesinger, Jr. in his book *The Disuniting of America: Reflections on a Multicultural Society* (1991, 1992) and David

---

[24] Thomas Bender, "New York as a Center of 'Difference': How America's Metropolis Counters American Myth," *Dissent*, 34, no. 4 (Fall 1987), 429-35; 433, 435.

A. Hollinger in *Postethnic America: Beyond Multiculturalism* (1995) offer somewhat alternative answers to these questions. Arthur Schlesinger, Jr. analyzes the debates of the 1980s about multiculturalism in terms of striking a balance between "fragmentation, resegregation, and tribalization of American life" propagated by minority groups of different kinds on the one hand and the (re-)assertion of unity, synthesis, and a common culture on the other hand. He acknowledges the deep gap between the democratic, egalitarian ideals of the American republic and economic, political, and social reality, particularly the continuing devastating effects of racism. Yet his approach in steering a middle course is based on more or less reified notions of the stability of ethnic group cultures (and their separate interest politics) and a kind of universalist core of a common American culture based on consensus—without revising the notion of "culture(s)," of what "American culture" and what "the American political system" could mean in a fundamentally changing world today.[25]

David A. Hollinger, on the contrary, tries to move "beyond" the limitations of multiculturalism of ethnic group interest politics toward a "postethnic society" ("ethnic" in the sense of stable, "ethnocentric," semi-autonomous groups defined by national origin or descent), toward a multiplicity of overlapping and conflicting identities *qua* voluntary and often temporary group affiliations and a plurality of competing public cultures. He envisions a *cosmopolitan* democratic society that *acknowledges* ethnoracial differences, internal diversity, and multiple identities *without* reifying or institutionalizing them. He replaces stable communities constituted by descent by voluntary affiliations and, recognizing that group affiliations are not always simply "voluntary," but ascribed and enforced from outside, especially in the case of "race," sets out to analyze and organize "these various and shifting affiliations as publics nested within a larger public that is the polity of the United States."[26] He also knows that the nation-state is under attack and in a historic crisis, and he addresses the issue of post- or transnationality as raised by anthropologist Arjun Appadurai in his essays on the disjuncture of the public sphere and public economy in a world of globalization. Hollinger recognizes the increasing replacement of national by transnational or global processes and interconnections (as well as their "relocalizing" repercussions), produced by multi-/transnational corporations as well as by diasporic consciousness resulting from global migration patterns. But he argues that the idea of the nation-state in the form of a "civic" nationalism continues to be a necessary and inescapable frame of reference for working out and institutionalizing a "civic" "transethnic national consciousness" in the sense of a genuine cosmopolitan vision of American society beyond the narrow confines of multicultural interest group politics or a "multiplicity of ethnocentrisms."[27] For Hollinger, cosmopolitanism is, in contrast to pluralism, "willing to put the future of every culture at risk through the sympathetic but critical scrutiny of other cultures," and

---

[25] Arthur M. Schlesinger, Jr., *The Disuniting of America: Reflections on a Multicultural Society* (New York: W. W. Norton, 1992).

[26] David S. Hollinger, *Postethnic America: Beyond Multiculturalism* (New York: Basic Books, 1995), 155.

[27] Hollinger, *Postethnic America*, 106, 134, 149, 151-56.

he draws a clearer distinction between culture and politics and between ethnic and civic principles of nationality. His vision of a "postethnic America" manifests itself in a multiplicity of differently constituted "we's," of "overlapping" and conflicted communities and voluntary (or non-voluntary) affiliations informed by the various dimensions of multiculturality. This approach also entails a fundamental revision of the definitions of what he calls "ethno-racial blocks" as used in the American census, accounting for an increasing number of marriages across the dividing lines of the five "ethnic" groups. Still, in his strong effort to save—in a new form—the (postethnic) Euro-American nation-state, Hollinger may still give too little attention in his arguments to non-Euro-American and dialogical perspectives.[28]

It is in this context that philosopher Kwame Anthony Appiah's effort, in his lecture *Identity Against Culture: Understandings of Multiculturalism* (1994), to clarify the terms often mixed up in multiculturalism debates and to distinguish more cleary terms like "state," "nation," "common culture," "common institutions," "social identities," and "cultural identities" can be helpful. "My point is that the notion what held the United States together historically over its great geographical range, is a common culture, like the common culture of a traditional society, is *not* sociologically plausible."[29] For Appiah, multicultural education is "to equip all of us to share the public space with people of multiple identities and distinctive subcultures." Multicultural American society does not work through enforcing a commitment to the *substance* of a common "core culture," but through a "shared commitment to certain *forms* of social behavior: "To live together in a nation what is required is that we all share a commitment to the organization of the state—the institutions that provide the over-arching order of our common life."[30] Certainly, Appiah's proposal raises a number of questions that have been discussed in recent years, most prominently in Charles Taylor's *Multiculturalism and the Politics of Recognition* and by his respondents, including Jürgen Habermas, but he provides incisive distinctions for the analysis of the workings of "political culture" and the repercussions of "multiculturalism."

Critical Multiculturalism:
the Meaning of Culture and Alternative Traditions in American History

Questions: How can a *critical multiculturalism* be defined? In which respects does it differ from earlier models of American society such as "cultural pluralism"? In how far is the charge by radical critics justified that the emphasis on questions of "culture" are "culturalist" displacements of the "real" economic and social (class) conflicts in a post-Fordist society or of questions of "race"? Or do we have to redefine the very notion of

---

[28] Hollinger, *Postethnic America*, 85, 106, 108, 128, 132.
[29] Kwame Anthony Appiah, *Identity Against Culture: Understandings of Multiculturalism*, Avenali Lecture (Berkeley, CA: Doreen B. Townsend Center for the Humanities, 1994), 8.
[30] Appiah, *Identity Against Culture*, 30.

a (limited) "cultural sphere" in contradistinction to the "spheres" of the economy or politics? Which concept of "ulture" is used? How are "ultural identities" and "communities" to be reconceived today? Is there some kind of critical multiculturalism in American history, what Gary Nash calls a "mestizo counter-ideology" in historical discourse? How does it relate to the universalist ideal of the early American republic and its inherent fundamental contradictions like the toleration of slavery?

John Higham, in his thoughtful essay on "Multiculturalism and Universalism: A History and Critique" (1993), reconstructs the heritage of the "egalitarian ideology" forged by the Enlightenment and in the American Revolution and tries to recover and renew this "American universalism" as a philosophy that could give direction to American society and culture in a time of highly charged controversies about the meaning of cultural differences and the demands of multiculturalism. Higham acknowledges the "crux" of the idea of "American universalism," as the supposedly universal human rights had systematically been denied to parts of the population in historical reality. This contradiction has been turned, however, he argues, into an "invigorating narrative," an "enduring tension ... between closure and openness, between separateness and inclusion" that Americans have managed in a productive manner by again and again "extend[ing] the circle of those who are acknowledged as makers of an American nationality and project[ing] each incremental addition as a promise of still wider inclusiveness."[31] He points out the inherent tensions and setbacks of this process, but considers the years of the Civil Rights Movement and the early 1960s as a time when "the renewal of American democracy made impressive headway." Yet the 1960s were also the years of the resurgence of "ethnicity" and the demands for recognition and respect for "ethnic diversity" and of specific ethnic groups rights. Higham concludes that this "multicultural movement" that became a strong power in national politics and educational debates during the 1970s and 1980s has failed to offer any viable "multicultural theory of society."

Higham's charge is that the multicultural movement has given up the fight against class inequalities in favor of "cultures of endowment" and dissolved the "enabling paradox" of the American universalist creed by exclusively focusing on cultural differences in terms of race, ethnicity, and gender, or by replacing the idea of cultural pluralism with that of the "separateness of ethnic cultures." He finds a tremendous confusion of terms in the multiculturalism debate and quite rightly criticizes some reductionist, or absolutist, versions. As the multiculturalism idea, in his reading, was "shaped by its explosive emergence from clashing ethnocentric demands and antagonisms: Afrocentric, Eurocentric, phallocentric, and so on," it has failed to engage in a critical explication of the "limitations" and the "incompleteness" that "the pluralist perspective has never lost." It has not worked out a vision of society yet that defines multiculturality not so much as something that "has to do with marginal groups and oppositional attitudes," but as energizing the "common arena," as "a center of gravity

---

[31] John Higham, "Multiculturalism and Universalism: A History and a Critique," *American Quarterly*, 45 (1993), 195-219; 197-98, 214.

in a centerless space where outsiders resist and simultaneously enrich an overall national culture." He insists that "[a]n adequate theory of American culture will have to address the reality of assimilation as well as the persistence of differences.'"[32]

Higham cannot discover these critical efforts of clarifying the unexamined dilemma in cultural practices among the proponents of multiculturalism, and he finds them "lack[ing] a vision of what [multiculturalism] wants the country to become." Yet his conclusion is optimistic, based on his observation that, though truncated and fragmented, "an indispensible heritage of equality lives on amid the contradictions of the multicultural movement." However, his own version of "rebuilding American universalism" has its own problems: "If multiculturalism can shake off a fixation on diversity, autonomy, and otherness, the vision that American universalism sustained and enlarged through two centuries can be renewed. It can teach us that we are all multicultural and increasingly transnational—that minority and majority cultures alike are becoming more and more interconnected, interpenetrative, and even indistinguishable."[33] He tries to do justice to the experience and the discourse of inequality and difference as well as of postnationality and include them in his notion of the "invigorating paradox" of American universalism. But I think he is too much guided by his own ideal of an all-inclusive, general systematic theory of the unity of American culture and society that does not permit him to face the real philosophical (and practical) challenges that the versions of a *critical* multiculturalist theory beyond pluralist diversity and separatist group interest politics have posed to the ideas of cultural identities and of the unity of culture and the nation-state.

Social and cultural historian Elizabeth Fox-Genovese, in her essay "Between Individualism and Fragmentation: American Culture and the New Literary Studies of Race and Gender" (1990), responds to the same situation of a severe crisis of "American identity," of "an American national culture," and the "modern Tower of Babel" characterizing American Studies and the "larger struggle that encompasses all of the Humanities." To her, the crucial question today is "whether any new synthesis is possible, or even desirable. How, in other words, are we to weave the various cultures that we are learning to recognize and appreciate into a general view of American culture?"[34] If this sounds pretty close to Higham's project, she approaches the question of "synthesis" more cautiously and fully engages in a critical discussion of the powerful new work in the historical and, particularly, literary studies of race and gender that force her to confront somewhat more fully the radical challenges of poststructuralism and postmodernism to the traditions of "univeralist" ideas of social and cultural synthesis. Therefore, she carefully discusses a wealth of recent scholarship on race and gender and addresses the revisionary notions of "identity," "culture," and "community" as having notoriously permeable boundaries and as being interactive concepts that pose the

---

[32] Higham, "Multiculturalism," 200, 201, 204, 208, 209.

[33] Higham, "Multiculturalism," 214.

[34] Elizabeth Fox-Genovese, "Between Individualism and Fragmentation: American Culture and the New Literary Studies of Race and Gender," *American Quarterly*, 42 (1990), 7- 34; 7-9.

question "whether we can appropriately speak of a unified culture at all." In her readings of new feminist and African American studies she pursues in detail how they have rediscovered and pursued the power of the sense of twoness, of their "unequal and bilingual experiences," of the "tragedy of twoness" which cannot be divorced from its potential richness, their historical need to "speak in a double tongue." She also notes their attacks on "our inherited notions of a unified American culture" as largely white and male and their continuous "negotiations" with the ideals and forms of representation of the dominant culture and their own group experiences and cultural traditions. Nevertheless, she finds too strong an emphasis on "alternate" senses of self and community and "alternate cultures" in the sense of separation, isolation from the contexts of the larger society, and the illusions of the integrity of essentialist identity.[35] By almost exclusively focusing on cultural distinctiveness, on difference, marginalization, and fragmentation, on recuperating their distinctive voices that the dominant culture had silenced, they weaken, in her view, their political thrust, neglecting the (changing role of) class and the actualities of power in the United States. Like Higham, in the end she complains that most of these new studies of race and gender—she indicates some recent exceptions—have reconfirmed the "commitment to individualism advanced by the dominant culture," in spite of their strong insistence on strengthening "community." They fail to offer, having hastily dismissed Marxism, "a systematic view of the central dynamics of American society and culture" and to engage "the battle of American culture as a whole." She concludes: "The challenge remains to understand the pattern of marginalized cultures in relation to each other as well as in relation to the canonical culture and the ideal of a national culture."[36]

Still, in her essay, Fox-Genovese moves beyond the hope of somehow simply "rebuilding" the unity of an "American universalism" by turning the challenges of the new literary studies of race and gender into new visions and definitions of community and culture: "Whatever we may view as the boundaries of their immediate, affective communities, both African-Americans and women have lived in and belonged to more than one communitiy—frequently to several interlocked social and cultural communities ... Culture must be understood as a manifestation of interlocking and hierarchically related communities. Relations of power inescapably color the ways in which we perceive ourselves in relation to others, ourselves in relation to the past, ourselves in relation to humanity."[37] Yet, again, her conclusions remain somewhat ambivalent when she reiterates the need of "a new synthesis in literary studies" that even the most recent suggestive work she discusses fails to reach due to what she calls in a polemical, undifferentiated mannner "the expanding influence of postmodernism and poststructuralism." She quite rightly insists on the "inescapable relations between culture and power" and reminds us that "American identities, like American culture, have always been shaped by the (conflicted) relations of class as well as gender and race" and that

---

[35] Fox-Genovese, "Between Individualism," 11-13, 16, 22.
[36] Fox-Genovese, "Between Individualism," 10, 23.
[37] Fox-Genovese, "Between Individualism," 24, 25.

American culture is *not* "a multiplicity of unrelated cultures and selves."[38] But her final affirmationm of "our culture" and "national identity" seems to cling to the old ideal of the unity of a nation-state: "To be an American is forthrightly to acknowledge a collective identity that simultaneously transcends and encompasses our disparate identities and communities. Unless we acknowledge our diversity, we allow the silences of the received tradition to become our own. Unless we sustain some ideal of a common culture, we reduce culture to personal experience and sacrifice the very concept of American."[39]

Another contribution by a feminist historian to the debate on the future of American Studies in the age of multiculturalism, Alice Kessler-Harris' Presidential Address, "Cultural Locations: Positioning American Studies in the Great Debate" (1992), responds to the same question posed by Arthur Schlesinger, Jr. and others of how we "preserve unity and still do justice to the multiplicity of American culture" by explicitly attempting to redefine "what we mean by identity" and "how we construct ourselves as a nation." She situates these debate in the context of a critical engagement in the "struggle over multiculturalism as a tug of war over who gets to create the public culture."[40] Kessler-Harris also points to the shortcomings of the recent "shift to a new pluralism" and to its concomitant disavowal of "notions of common identity," but she emphasizes much more strongly the powerful potential of the (re-)construction of "our multiple identities" in the "continuing and unending process" of creating a "democratic culture" in the United States. At the end of her essay she writes: "Far from undermining the search for unity, identity, and purpose, the multicultural enterprise has the potential to strengthen it. It provides a way of seeing relationally that is consistent with the early founders of American Studies as well as with its more recent protagonists. If it redefines identity from a fixed category to a search for a democratic culture, if it refuses to acknowledge a stable meaning or precise unchanging definition of America, multi-culturalism nevertheless opens the possibility of conceiving democratic culture as a process in whose transformation we are all invited to participate."[41]

Like Alice Kessler-Harris, Joan W. Scott discusses multiculturalism in the context of the heated debate on the politics of identity, the revisions of the canon, and the charges of "political correctness." She not only rejects the "hypostatization" of a plurality, or "diversity," of (individual and collective) "identities" conceived of as referential signs of "a fixed set of customs, practices, and meanings, an enduring heritage, a readily identifiable sociological category, a set of shared traits and/or experiences," as they characterize the "pluralist" framework of stable identities as well

---

[38] Fox-Genovese, "Between Individualism," 25-28.

[39] Fox-Genovese, "Between Individualism," 28-29. For a further elaboration of her argument in a wider, and different, context see her book *Feminism Without Illusions: A Critique of Individualism* (Chapel Hill, NC: University of North Carolina Press, 1991).

[40] Alice Kessler-Harris, "Cultural Locations: Positioning American Studies in the Great Debate," *American Quarterly*, 44 (1992), 299-312; 303, 310.

[41] Kessler-Harris, "Cultural Locations," 306, 307, 311.

as the fetishization of personal "experience" in essentialist group cultures.[42] Instead of seeing ethnic and cultural difference as existing attributes or traits of (groups of) human beings, as a "matter of biology or history or culture," she draws on her incisive and crucial work on gender as a category of historical analysis and defines cultural identities as the "effect of an enunciation of difference." Cultural identities are historically produced through "multiple identifications" in continually changing processes of discrimination, in the sense of both being discriminated against and of asserting your own acts of discriminating cultural differences. Paradoxically, it is this move of radically "historicizing" the process of the "construction" of interrelational cultural identities that seems to offer a more viable perspective for pursuing the quest for a more inclusive and more "unified" view of the complex and contested interplay of the various, ever changing group cultures, the multiple cultural identities every person has to negotiate, and the wider horizon of national, transnational, or postnational multicultural social processes. What historians should teach their students, she concludes, is that "identities are historically conferred, that this conferral is ambiguous (though it works precisely and necessarily by imposing a false clarity), that subjects are produced through multiple identifications, some of which become politically salient for a time in certain contexts, and that the project of history is not to reify identity but to understand its production as an ongoing process of differentiation, relentless in its repetition, but also—and this seems to me the important political point—subject to redefinition, resistance, and change."[43]

It is this project of "historicizing" the production and enunciation of cultural identities and differences as it has worked in American history itself that Gary B. Nash pursues in his Presidential Address to the Organization of American Historians in 1995, "The Hidden History of Mestizo America." He responds to the charges brought against the multiculturalist movement that it threatens the unity of a pluralist American culture, and the common core culture at the heart of the American republic by arguing that there have not only been some important examples of "deep intercultural contacts" and "cultural merging" in the course of American history or cases of "mestizaje" and "hybridity" at its boundaries, but that American culture and society have from the beginning been permeated by multiple processes of cultural mixing and transculturation. He replaces the notions of one-sided acculturation and assimilation by the idea of the encounter of cultures, of two-way or multiple-way processes of intercultural exchange and recovers what he calls the "mestizo counter-ideology" in American history. This mestizo counter-ideology has tried in many different and conflictual forms from Emerson and Melville to Randolph Bourne to promote the idea of a "federated, transnational, transracial democratic culture" in order to counter the doctrine of racial purity and a homogeneous American core culture or the prevalent notion of cultural

---

[42] Joan W. Scott, "Multiculturalism and the Politics of Identity," *October*, 61 (1992), 12-19; 14.

[43] Scott, "Multiculturalism," 19. These issues of redefining the notion(s) of "identity" have most cogently been discussed by Stuart Hall; see, e.g., his Introduction, with references, to the volume *Questions of Cultural Identity*, ed. by Stuart Hall, Paul du Gay (London: Sage Publications, 1996), 1-17.

pluralism that "envisioned a United States full of durable ethnic blocs."[44] Nash's version of a "post-ethnic America" in this sense engages more emphatically than David Hollinger's proposal in the contemporary *reality* of a "Mestizo America" that has been "a happening thing" through an unprecedented number of marriages across racial lines of division and the effects of global migrations, a "mestizo America" that has also moved beyond the neat opposition of "black" *versus* "white" in racial politics. Nash does not draw a clear distinction between the uses of *mestizaje* and *la raza cósmica* (José Vasconcelos) in Latin America and its theoretical use as "a social and intellectual construction" in the U.S.American culture(s) of difference, but he rejects the ideology of "racial absolutism" or the reduction of multiculturalism to "multiracialism." Instead, he conceives of "hybridity" as a "shared pride in and identity with hybridity"[45] and draws on Salman Rushdie's powerful vision of a migratory intellectual who celebrates "hybridity, impurity, intermingling, and transformation that comes of new and unexpected combinations of human beings, cultures, ideas, movies, songs. It rejoices in mongrelization and ... is for change-by-fusion, change-by-conjoining."[46]

Nash understands his address as a contribution to "a social and intellectual construction of modern America" badly needed in a time of "multicultural wars," of "sometimes violent arguments about American culture and identity, about courses, canons, and holidays, about entitlements and contemporary programs."[47] It was this hot and higly polemical debate on new standards in the teaching of American history and on the role of the historian in the public culture of the United States at the end of the 20th century that Gary B. Nash became prominently involved during the mid-1990s as co-chair of the National Center for History in the Schools at UCLA.

History Standards, the Canon, and the Historian in the Public Sphere

Questions: How is an explicitly critical "public culture" to be organized? How does it reconstitute political and cultural institutions? What are its repercussions on the restructuring of curricula in universities and the public schools? How is the canon to be revised, what are the principles justifying the idea of a canon? What kind of teaching strategies have to be developed? How is the public debate about these issues to be evaluated? How is the public role of the historian to be redefined?

In his wide-ranging essay, "Multiculturalism and the Politics of General Education" (1993), historian Michael Geyer points out that at the core of the debate on multiculturalism are the highly contested issues of a contemporary politics of representation: "Multiculturalism is not a body of academic thought but a contested politics of social

---

[44] Gary B. Nash, "The Hidden History of Mestizo America," *Journal of American History*, 82 (Dec. 1995), 941-64; 954, 956, 958.
[45] Nash, "Hidden History," 959, 960, 962.
[46] Quoted in Nash, "Hidden History," 958-59.
[47] Nash, "Hidden History," 960-61.

and cultural transformation in which academics participate."[48] It is this insight that permeates Gary B. Nash's essay, "The Great Multicultural Debate" (1992), in which he reminds his readers of a statement by Leon Litwack in his Presidential Address to the Organization of American Historians of 1992 that clearly posed the challenge—and the responsibility—historians have to take up in the public culture of the United States: "[N]o group of scholars was more deeply implicated in the miseducation of American youth and did more to shape the thinking of Americans about race and blacks than historians."[49] Since the early 1970s, in the new social history, labor history, and cultural history as well as in the new fields of Women's Studies, African American Studies, Hispanic American Studies, Native American Studies, and others a whole generation of American historians, coming from all parts of American society, had made powerful contributions to revising the history of the United States. But as Herbert G. Gutman, Thomas Bender, and others had argued, it remained the task of the late 1980s and the 1990s to bring these new insights together in a reconceptualization of the general history of a multicultural United States, to extend their influence beyond the realm of the profession of history and academia to the teaching of American history in the public schools, and to re-establish historians in their "guiding" role in the public culture at large. Gary B. Nash defines multiculturalism as "the integration of the histories of both genders and people of all classes and racial or ethnic groups" and shows how pronouncedly multicultural history and social science curricula have been introduced in many parts of the country over the last years.[50] He takes up the hostile and demagogic distortions of the curricula debates on American campuses put forward by many of the conservative critics in their denunciations of what they construct as "multiculturalism." He also rejects the radical and "retrogressive" forms of Afrocentrism, but situates them in the context of the deteriorating situation of black Americans during the Reagan-Bush years. To Nash, what multicultural education in the universities and the schools has to teach is nurturing mutual respect and an appreciation of cultural differences. But this can only be achieved, he argues, if "parents, teachers, and children reach some basic agreement on some core sets of values, ways of airing disputes, conducting dialogue—in short, some agreement on how to operate as members of a civic community, a democratic polity."[51] His emphasis on "central, defining values of the democratic polity" or a "common commitment to core political and moral values" is not theorized in an adequate manner. His defense of the "ideal of a common core culture" clearly is based on the universalist principles put forward by the "Founding Fathers" in the Enlightenment tradition, even though his remarks on the *common project* of all the different individuals and cultural groups in the United States who have to "reach" some basic agreement and who must want to "participate" in a common civic culture could

---

[48] Michael Geyer, "Multiculturalism and the Politics of General Education," *Critical Inquiry*, 19 (Spring 1993), 499-533; 513.
[49] Quoted in Gary B. Nash, "The Great Multicultural Debate," *Contention*, 1 (Spring 1992), 1-28; 2.
[50] Nash, "Great Multicultural Debate," 11.
[51] Nash, "Great Multicultural Debate," 24.

be developed in the direction of a notion of public culture that transcends the frame already set by the dominant culture of the past.[52]

The attack on "multicultural" curricula and the various committees of scholars and educators to work out new standards for the teaching of history and the social sciences on the national and the state levels (esp. in California and New York) are too well known to need rehearsing. Gary B. Nash, Charlotte Crabtree, and Ross E. Dunn have given a very detailed account of the controversy over the setting of voluntary standards for the teaching of history in American elementary and high schools and defined their involvement and their own position in their book *History on Trial: Culture Wars and the Teaching of the Past* (1997). The book shows graphically how a wide-ranging, collective effort that included "virtually all stakeholders in history education," a project funded by federal agencies, was turned into the most bitter example of the "culture wars" that put historians on the public stage of the media in the United States again. But it also helps to historicize the debate and sets out to show that "contention over the past is as old as written history itself, that the democratizing of the history profession has led to more inclusive and balanced presentations of American and world history, and that continuously reexamining the past, rather than piously repeating traditional narratives, is the greatest service historians can render in a democracy."[53] American "history wars" are as old as the Republic, and they have always been about the interpretation of the meaning of "America" and the difficult processes and fights over the more inclusive democratization of American culture and society. What has been crucial in recent years is the new awareness among historians that their longterm disengagement from the public debate should come to an end and that they should take up the difficult task of transferring their critical insights to the teaching in the public schools and to the forum of the public culture at large. "Broadly construed," Nash, Crabtree, and Dunn write, "'multiculturalism' refers to the many cultural affiliations that Americans hold and to the complex fusion of cultural identities and attitudes that each of us carries in our mind ... Multicultural perspectives in history involve intersecting pathways of historical scholarship in which no one's social and cultural experience is off limits to investigation, not that of women, nor slaves, nor dirt farmers, nor CEOs."[54] The multicultural perspective is not something that came up in recent decades in the context of political fights over affirmative action or "cultures of endowment," or, put differently, as a consequence of the tremendous output of new historical scholarship in women's history or the history of all kinds of minorities, but has to be seen as having been *inherent* in American history from its beginnings. What the authors of *History On Trial* set out to do in their scholarly and educational work is to make teachers and the general public aware of an understanding of history as an ongoing conversation without final truths,

---

[52] Nash, "Great Multicultural Debate," 25.
[53] Gary B. Nash, Charlotte Crabtree, Ross E. Dunn, *History On Trial: Culture Wars and the Teaching of the Past* (New York: Alfred A. Knopf, 1997), x, 8.
[54] Nash, Crabtree, Dunn, *History On Trial*, 77.

an endless sequence of competing revisions of exploring the meaning of history that places American history in the wider, transnational context of the world.[55]

It is significant that two recent books on the multiculturalism debate written by influential sociologists and public intellectuals, Todd Gitlin's *The Twilight of Common Dreams: Why America Is Wracked By Culture Wars* (1995) and Nathan Glazer's *We Are All Multiculturalists Now* (1997), take the controversies about the History Standards and Gary B. Nash's position as the starting-point and context for reassessing the meaning of American history or the historical idea and dynamics of the American Republic in order to account for the problems and the culture wars the United States face today and will have to face in the future.[56] Todd Gitlin reads American history as an ever new fight between the forces for "individual freedom" and the forces for "equality," a fight about unity and difference, about the "perennial dilemma of American identity." It is a fight, however, that was, in spite of glaring shortcomings and injustices in society, embedded in some kind of consensus, in a "culture of commonality," in the vision that "there was in principle, at least, the possibility that we would become a unity, one rising from the many."[57] However, for Gitlin, this conviction that "America *would* be, was *coming* to be, was on its way" has severely been weakened during the last decades as a result of fundamental social changes, but also, ironically, of the crisis of the Left. He criticizes the Left for a tendency to renounce the common Enlightenment project of a universalist rhetoric and a "sense of common citizenship" in favor of a focus on, and a celebration of, cultural difference, fragmentation, a multiplicity of identities, and identity politics, or, put differently, for having given up the realm of politics and power ("the White House") in favor of cultural identity "politics" in academia.[58]

Gitlin's sketch of American history to the present and his account of the changing models of American culture and society or of the competing positions in the contemporary multiculturalism debate are sometimes rather sketchy or reductive, but his book is driven by his commitment to the vision of a "culture of commonality" that *can* be realized in the United States. He has tried to show the contestants in the culture wars, esp. the American Left, that there is "no necessary contradiction between a recognition of difference and the affirmation of common rights": "Mutuality needs tending. If multiculturalism is not tempered by a stake in the commons, then centrifugal energy overwhelms any commitment to a larger good."[59]

Gitlin does not promise a utopian American society, and he knows that "there is no golden past to recover." What he defines as the most crucial and far-reaching failure in American history, "the wound in all American dreams, the question of race," the

---

[55] Cf. Nash, Crabtree, Dunn, *History On Trial*, 275-77.

[56] Glazer also refers to his own involvement in the writing of the controversial Report of the New York State Social Studies Review and Development Committee *One Nation, Many People: A Declaration of Cultural Independence* (1991).

[57] Todd Gitlin, *The Twilight of Common Dreams: Why America Is Wracked by Culture Wars* (New York: Henry Holt, 1995), 3, 46, 217.

[58] Gitlin, *Twilight*, 65, 87, 101, 127-28, 147-48, 151-52, 159, 215ff.

[59] Gitlin, *Twilight*, 228, 236.

"central wound in American history," the "crime of slavery," racism as the "core of our current predicament,"[60] is also the driving force in Nathan Glazer's perceptive and engaging book *We Are All Multiculturalists Now*. In a self-critical vein concerning some of his earlier work, he writes: "I have come reluctantly to the conclusion that the position of blacks (and perhaps Hispanics, though there I would still resist the conclusion) is different from that of immigrants in some radical way. While one can dispute the need for either the old immigrants or the new immigrants who now flood our schools to 'see themselves in the curriculum,' for blacks it is different."[61] He considers the history of racial discrimination in the United States as the fatal shortcoming of the American democratic project, a failure that was bound to produce among frustrated blacks the provocative challenge of "multiculturalism" to the notion of assimilation as the traditional ideal for all Americans: "But the difference that separates blacks from whites, and even from other groups 'of color' that have undergone a history of discrimination and prejudice in this country, is not to be denied. It is this separation which is the most powerful force arguing for multiculturalism and for resistance to the assimilatory trends of American education and American society."[62] Even though Glazer tends to reduce "multiculturalism" to some kind of anti-assimilationist, separatist ideology, he clearly realizes and refers to the much wider social, political, and cultural changes that have been happening in the United States and in the world at large and that have necessarily made the teaching of history even more of a battlefield than it was in the past. But it is this acknowledgement of *difference* that separates blacks from whites and other immigrants and that feeling of (white) guilt that has brought Nathan Glazer to accepting the demands of "multiculturalism" by African Americans, in contrast to those of other groups, as justified in principle and as a "price America is paying for its inability or unwillingness to incorporate into its society African Americans in the same way and to the same degree it has incorporated so many groups."[63] The deteriorating situation of their economic and social situation thirty years after the Civil Rights Movement asks Americans, particularly in the field of education Glazer's book focuses on, to confront this "national wound" and finally take measures to end this history of un-American discrimination, before the United States can really move "beyond ethnicity" to a "postethnic perspective" (Hollinger): "It seems we must pass through a period in which we recognize difference, we celebrate difference, we turn the spotlight on the inadequacies in the integration of our minorities in our past and present, and we raise up for special consideration the achievements of our minorities and their putative ancestors. All this is premised on our failure to integrate blacks. Others are included in this process; but it is the response to blacks, their different condition, their different perspective, that sets the model."[64]

---

[60] Gitlin, *Twilight*, 27, 103, 228-29.

[61] Nathan Glazer, *We Are All Multiculturalists Now* (Cambridge, MA: Harvard University Press, 1997), 51.

[62] Glazer, *We Are All*, 95, 121, cf. 17, 110.

[63] Glazer, *We Are All*, 61-62, 147, cf. 155, 157-61.

[64] Glazer, *We Are All*, 159.

Impressive and powerful as Glazer's moral commitment to redressing the negative effects of a history of discrimination against blacks is, his plea for acknowledging the demands of "multiculturalism" in this special case raises a more general problem. Clearly, he sets out to save the (Enlightenment) universalist ideal of the American Republic and regards "multiculturalism" as a kind of separatist ideology that is *only* justified in the case of African Americans and only *temporally* justified, and therefore only a "passing phase in the complex history of the making of an American nation from many strands," as he puts it in the final sentence of his book. Multiculturalism is not conceived of as a challenge that forces Americans to reconsider the very foundations of their universalist model of culture and society. Yet, he takes up the responsibility systematically to overcome the distortions of rights and social equality concerning black Americans that have crippled society, politics, and culture in the United States.[65] In this sense, "we" are all, and have to be, "multiculturalists now."

Lawrence W. Levine's book *The Opening of the American Mind: Canons, Culture, and History* (1996) is a devastating critique of the conservatives' polemical and "apocalyptic" denouncement of the recent efforts to revise the writing and teaching of American history by openly engaging in its multicultural past and present. Levine points out that "the United States has always been a multicultural, multiethnic, multiracial society," which has only become increasingly difficult to ignore in our own time. And he shows in graphic detail that the seemingly universal and transhistorical truths of the Western canon the conservatives have tried to defend against its "relativistic" detractors were only implemented after World War I and that the so-called immutable canon has always been changing with the politics and the society of the time.[66] He also exposes the contradictions and parochial and reductionist assumptions of the "defenders" of Western civilization who, ironically, have not even studied with any care the history of university education in the U.S. they claim to defend. But what is most crucial about Levine's argument is his insistence on the inescapable "complexity" and "ambiguity" of American history, past, present, and future, that any version of American history that wants to do any justice to its subject matter has to recognize and explore and on the fundamental social changes that have affected all institutions in 20th century America and produced a much greater heterogeneity on the campuses.[67] What is attacked by the conservatives as the result of leftist multicultural ideologues has to be recognized as the consequence of a radical transformation of the American economy and society: "[F]orms of fragmentation—social, ethnic, racial, religious, regional, economic—have been endemic in the United States from the outset. In our own time this historic fragmentation has been exacerbated because a significant part of our population has been removed from the economy and turned into a permanent underclass with no ladders leading out of its predicament and consequently little hope."[68] Also, if the conservative critics claim

---

[65] Glazer, *We Are All*, 161.
[66] Lawrence W. Levine, *The Opening of the American Mind: Canons, Culture, and History* (Boston: Beacon Press, 1996), xviii, xiv-xvi.
[67] Levine, *Opening*, xvii, 28, cf. 18, 32, 64-65, 112, 155, 160, 163, 171.
[68] Levine, *Opening*, 32.

to defend the canon of classic (white) American literature against the dilution through the inclusion of minority writers, they fail to realize that this narrow white male "classic" canon was institutionalized only after World War II, whereas pre-War anthologies (mainly of the 1930s) had given considerable attention to writings by several minority groups (such as Blacks, Native Americans, immigrant writers) and to various traditions of oral and folk culture.[69]

Levine emphasizes the "dynamics and complexity of cultural syncretism" of American identity and defines American culture as the continually changing product of the "*interaction* of the various ethnic and racial groups." It is through "fragmentation" and "difference" that American culture and society have constituted and reconstituted their "identity": "Diversity, pluralism, multiculturalism have been present throughout our history and have acted not merely as the germs of friction and division but as the lines of continuity, the sources for the creation of an indigenous culture, and the roots of a distinctive American identity."[70] American history has not been the history of a dominant (white) core culture and the periphery of a number of "ethnic and racial groups interacting singly on a one-to-one basis with the central 'Anglo-American' culture."[71] Instead, it has been a much more complex and dynamic process in which the "center" was transformed all the time (there never has been anything like a homogeneous "Western culture" or "the West"), in which groups were never monolithic or exclusive, in which they were "simultaneously the products amd the agents of change." Group identities have always been, here Levine quotes Glazer and Moynihan's *Beyond the Melting Pot*, "patterns of choice as well as of heritage; of new creation in a new country, as well as of the maintenance of old values and forms." Or, one could add, American culture has always been, as anthropologist Ulf Hannerz has put it, an open-ended process of transculturation in which many different cultures have creolized each other as well as the culture at large.[72] Levine asks historians finally to recognize that multiculturalism is not a challenge by some outsider groups that has to be placated and "therapeutically" acknowledged. Instead, for historians it is simply a matter of "*understanding* the nature and complexity of American culture and the processes by which it came, and continues to come, into being" and to *explore* the dynamics of the *existing* interactions, negotiations, and conflicts between the various dimensions of cultural difference and study the "intricacies of race, ethnicity, and gender" in a comparative, transnational framework and horizon.[73]

---

[69] Levine, *Opening*, 94-96.
[70] Levine, *Opening*, 112, 119-20.
[71] Levine, *Opening*, 137.
[72] Levine, *Opening*, 136-38, 140.
[73] Levine, *Opening*, 160, 165.

Writing/Narrating American Multicultural History

Questions: If there is something like a viable version of a critical multiculturalism in the United States? How can historians *write* the history of multicultural America? What kind of narrative strategies are available? What is the meaning of "text" and "context" in multicultural historical discourse? What role do the de- and reconstructive analytical strategies in the critical discourses of race, gender, ethnicity, and class worked out in poststructuralist, postmodernist, and postcolonial or minority literary and cultural studies play in American historians' efforts of rewriting the history of their country as a multicultural narrative? Which discursive strategies and concepts in cultural studies that explicitly explore and dramatize inter- or transdisciplinary and dialogic processes of intercultural differences and cross-cultural encounters can be taken up by historians in their projects of writing multicultural histories of the United States that transcend the common parochial limitations of the American multiculturalism debate and place it in an international, global context?

In the "Prologue" to *The Opening of the American Mind*, Lawrence Levine writes: "Because the quest to understand the past and the present in their full complexities and ambiguity can be discomforting and even threatening, there has been opposition to the attempts to seek and articulate multidimensional explanations in such areas as the forging of American identity, the significance of American culture, the nature of the American people, and the role of diverse groups in shaping American consciousness and society."[74] To *articulate* multidimensional explanations and to *write* a multicultural history of the United States is the great challenge American historians face today. Near the end of his book, Levine refers to the late black historian Nathan Huggins' essay "The Deforming Mirror of Truth" (publ. 1991) in which he called for a new structural understanding of American history in which blacks and whites, slavery and freedom are seen and analyzed in their inextricable interrelationship. Huggins rejects the old "master narrative" of American history (or of American historians) as a "conspiracy of myth, history, and chauvinism" that excluded slavery and racism from a dominant teleological white narrative of an inexorable process, or progress, of the development of "free institutions and the expansion of political liberty to the broadest possible public," a narrative that saw slavery and racial oppression as historical accidents to be corrected.[75] In his perceptive account of the historiography of slavery, Huggins also rejects more recent efforts somehow to "incorporate" blacks and other minorities into the master narrative, including the efforts by black historians to recover and affirm the strength of the "slave community," as this still misses its fundamental structural distortion of the history of American society and culture since before the founding of the republic and the specific meaning of slavery in the United States as "social death" (Orlando Patterson). The thesis first ventured by Oscar and Mary Handlin in 1950 that the

---

[74] Levine, *Opening*, xvii.
[75] Nathan I. Huggins, "The Deforming Mirror of Truth: Slavery and the Master Narrative of American History," *Radical History Review*, 49 (1991), 25-48;25.

particularly brutal and systemic form of chattel slavery and racial discrimination, as practiced in the American South were *not* some kind of legacy taken over from the Old World, but were *invented, created* due to unique historical circumstances *in the United States* was, finally, elaborated in its consequences for the writing of American history in Edmund Morgan's study *American Slavery, American Freedom* (1975). Morgan argued that "American freedom itself is the creation of slavery," making "slavery (and unfreedom) a formative and necessary part of the story," which forces American historians to discard their old master narrative and see racial slavery and freedom, Huggins writes with his typical sense of the subtleties of irony, as "inseparably a single, though paradoxical phenomenon": "The challenge of the paradox is that there can be no white history or black history, nor can their be an integrated history which does not begin to comprehend that slavery and freedom, white and black, are joined at the hip."[76]

It is the urgency of this challenge to the old ideological master narrative that convinced Huggins that only a *new* master narrative would do, "new myths and a renewed master narrative which better inspires and reflects upon our true conditions," as he put it at the end of his essay, without addressing the question *if* and *how* such a new "master narrative" could still be *conceived* and *written*.[77] Lawrence Levine extends the scope of Huggins' arguments—but also in some way disperses the power of his radical challenge—by explicitly reinscribing other "dimensions" in the paradoxical revisionary history of the United States, referring to "workers, immigrants, women, and other social and ethnic groups"[78] In the same vein, Vincent G. Harding, a black historian like Huggins, elaborates these reflections on a history of multicultural America and poses more explicitly the question of *how* this new kind of history could be written. He engages in a critical discussion of the pioneering book by the Asian American historian Ronald Takaki, *A Different Mirror: A History of Multicultural America* (1993), that tells the American story from the specific vantage-points of six different groups—African Americans, Irish Americans, Asian Americans, Mexican Americans, Native Americans, and Jewish Americans (also giving some attention to the early English settles of the Atlantic Coast)—, but he looks at these groups from a "multicultural perspective" in order to develop an understanding of their "differences and similarities."[79] Harding writes: "This bold decision to create a multicultural national sampler as a basis for our new history suggests one logical way to engage the steadily rising tide of American consciousness of our multiracial and multicultural roots."[80]

---

[76] Huggins, "Deforming Mirror," 33-35, 37, 38.

[77] Cf. Huggins' different version of the essay published as the new Introduction to a reissue of *Black Odyssey: The Afro-American Ordeal in Slavery* (New York: Pantheon Books, 1990), and David W. Blight's commemorative essay on Huggins' work as a historian "Nathan Irvin Huggins, the Art of History, and the Irony of the American Dream," *Reviews in American History*, 22 (1994), 174-90.

[78] Levine, *Opening*, 168.

[79] Ronald Takaki, *A Different Mirror: A History of Multicultural America* (Boston: Little, Brown, 1993), 10.

[80] Vincent G. Harding, "Healing at the Razor's Edge: Reflections on a History of Multicultural America," *Journal of American History*, 81 (Sept. 1994), 571-84; 573.

What is important about Takaki's history of the multicultural United States is that it reminds us that American history is not simply a multiplicity of separate group histories, but that they have been intertwined in many ways in the common project of creating a new democratic nation in which they have participated, however, under very different circumstances in terms of power, including slavery and racial discrimination. Therefore, American history as the history of the interactions among the different groups and their transformations and "crossing[s] in the making of multicultural America" has to be studied from a "comparative perspective."[81] Obviously, Takaki could not cover all ethnic groups in his book, and his selection of six groups as well as the emphases he has put in portraying the history and culture of these groups in the United States necessarily have neglected other groups and aspects of cultures that other critics may find more crucial for understanding American history. In this sense, Takaki's history of multicultural America is experimental, "a suggestive, experimental history of an experimental nation," as Harding puts it, of the process of the "building of the nation [that] is still going on." Like Takaki Harding continues to envision the recreation, the remaking, the rewriting of a "new master narrative" of American history that brings the different and conflicting histories together,[82] but it can no longer be the task of the individual historian to write single-handedly the total history of multicultural America.

If the public role of the historian, as Harding sees it, is potentially a "healing" or a "therapeutic one" in the contemporary context of the demise of the old white, male, Anglo-Saxon master narrative and of culture wars, this can only be realized in a "collective effort" in which in a "cross-diciplinary, cross-cultural fusing of our energies" the different voices, experiences, perspectives, and questions are combined and interrelated *without* forcing them into *one* new master narrative of multicultural America. Harding hesitates to accept the conclusion that this great challenge "cannot possibly be met in any cohesive form of a new master narrative," as he hopes that historians can, in a collaborative effort, "create methods that allow us to work and act together."[83] He provides some suggestions how this collaborative "reconstruction of our common history" might proceed, experimental efforts of developing "individual group stories of the ways in which we have lived the American experience," extended by the "empathic imagination" of other stories. These other stories would originate with "creative witnesses from within each cohort to tell the[ir] story of how the larger nation may have looked" and in the resources of the literary imagination. These joint efforts would enable historians, finally, to "grope toward what might become at least the proposed outline for a new master narrative, perhaps even a new 'holy history'—one that would immediately be challenged by a generation now in waiting."[84] Harding is self-critical enough to question his—the historians'—longing for a "new master narrative" as possibly just a reconfirmation of the "hegemomic domination" of the older

---

[81] Takaki, *Different Mirror*, 7-10, 375.
[82] Harding, "Healing," 574, 577-59.
[83] Harding, "Healing," 574, 579.
[84] Harding, "Healing," 580-581.

version of a "holy" American history based on the suppression of other stories, but he believes that the notion of a "provisional" history of a common past is crucial for a possible common future. In seeing American history as a multicultural, unfinished, and ongoing *project*, in exploring the idea of America as "an experience in liminality [in Victor Turner's sense], in borderline or 'threshold' existence, in the transitional time of unknown passages and ambiguous identities," Harding as well as Takaki, whom he refers to, hope to find the means of building what Harding calls, in an explicitly tentative and "poetic" manner, "some razor-thin, democratically constructed, provisional place to stand in order to survey and create a usable past and future," or in Takaki's final sentence of his book, a quote from Walt Whitman: "Of every hue and caste am I, I resist any thing better than my own diversity."[85]

Nathan Huggins, Ronald Takaki, and Vincent Harding have not only reassessed and redefined the important role the historian of a *multicultural* United States could and should play in the democratic public culture, but they also have begun to address and pursue in their work the crucial questions of *how* this history can be written, which kinds of comparative, analytical and narrative strategies historians can use and develop in their work, and how the collective project can be undertaken in a collaborative way. Clearly, their proposals were tentative and often fragmentary, still guided by the vision of one new master narrative of American history. By far the most sophisticated and penetrating critical account of these discursive questions is Robert F. Berkhofer, Jr.'s book *Beyond the Great Story: History as Text and Discourse* (1995). Berkhofer analyzes in a comprehensive, systematic manner all the philosophical and methodological challenges to the traditional ways of writing history, or History as the Great Story, the implications of the "linguistic turn" in philosophy, the postmodern crisis of the "grand narratives," poststructuralism, cultural studies, deconstruction, multiculturalism and the multiplicity of various separate group histories have been posing to the practice of the re-writing of history. His metatheoretical study is inspired by the paradox that "[p]oststructuralist and postmodernist theories question the possibility of writing history at the very time that such historicization has become a way of grounding literary studies and the social sciences." Berkhofer's explanation of what this "new historicization" involves and of how it could be argued in its discursive consequences proceeds in a pronouncedly interdisciplinary way, employing a kind of "dialogic presentation of the tensions between modernist and postmodernist orientations and between textualist and contextualist methods" in an attempt "to translate across interpretive and discursive communities even if it cannot reconcile them." He sets out "to present a vision of what new forms historical discourse might take," primarily American history writing done in the United States, and he situates his efforts in the context of the current demands directed at professional American historians to make their publications and their teaching "multicultural, self-reflective, and self-critical."[86] If Elizabeth Fox-Genovese had

---

[85] Harding, "Healing," 583; Takaki, *Different Mirror*, 428.
[86] Robert F. Berkhofer, Jr., *Beyond the Great Story: History as Text and Discourse* (Cambridge, MA: Harvard University Press, 1995), ix-xi.

brought the new "literary studies of race and gender" to the attention of her fellow-historians, Berkhofer widens the scope and engages in a brilliant analysis of the interplay between the literary theorists' turn to historicization and an exploration of the "textualism" in its repercussions and potential for the practice of historians. In his account he draws on the competing interrelations and meanings of "text" and "context" he had provocatively discussed in an earlier article in *American Quarterly*.[87] He examines histories as forms of representation (making use of Hayden White's work) and the contextualization of histories as texts and analyzes historians as a professional community from the perspective of the politics and sociology of historical knowledge and authority. As Berkhofer's reflections are too wide-ranging and complex to be discussed adequately in a few paragraphs, I want to focus on the chapter (ch. 7) in which he explicitly deals with the "implications of multiculturalism for the selection of viewpoint as well as voices in a historical text by focusing on the problems involved in representing otherness."[88]

Near the beginning of the chapter Berkhofer defines the fundamental challenge of the current debate on multiculturalism to authorizing and writing American histories today:

> Multiculturalism challenges both the viewpoint basic to normal history and in turn its authority. Multiculturalism highlights, first, the whole question of the relation between the author's voice and viewpoint and those supposedly represented in any given text. For whom in the end does this text speak, and from what viewpoint and by what authority? Second, multiculturalism challenges the whole idea of a single best or right Great Story, especially if told from an omniscient viewpoint. In questioning a single viewpoint as best for the Great Story and Great Past, multiculturalism undermines the foundation of historical authority used traditionally to justify the discipline. In line with this challenge to traditional authority, multculturalism poses fundamental questions about how politics are embodied in the paradigm of normal historical practice itself through voice and viewpoint. Last, it poses the challenge of how to incorporate multiple viewpoints into historical texts, be they partial histories or Great Stories, or especially the Great Past.[89]

Berkhofer takes up these questions in a close reading of a number of recent historical studies that attempt to write multicultural histories of some period of the U.S. American past. Most of these perceptive and innovative works cover new ground and rediscover or reclaim several competing perspectives, but these multicultural histories do not "transform the presuppositions of the normal history paradigm so much as ... expand their application to untraditional subject matter." A representation of specific otherness, not "Otherness" in general, must negotiate between the extremes of ethnocentrism and of relativism, between degrees of difference and sameness. It must solve the problem of how to represent, in the double sense of the word, "self-representations" of "other groups," such as oral histories, in the writing of histories without falling victim to essentializing, and thereby neutralizing the impact of, the new revisionist group histories

---

[87] Robert F. Berkhofer, Jr., "A New Context for a New American Studies?," *American Quarterly*, 41 (1989), 588-613.
[88] Berkhofer, *Beyond the Great Story*, xii.
[89] Berkhofer, *Beyond the Great Story*, 171-72.

and marginalizing them once more again. That is, the multiculturalist historian who wants to represent different voices and viewpoints from the past must also represent, or "incorporate," the competing and conflicting voices of the present in his or her historical discourse, which can only be achieved in a dialogic manner:

> Such a view of the dialogue about multiculturalism within the present requires distinguishing between polyvocality and multiple viewpoints in professional and political debates over the focus and nature of historical discourse today as opposed to what is aimed for and achieved in any one discourse as a text as a result of this debate. Should commitment to multiculturalist ideals therefore require that any discourse as text exemplify in explicit practice what the tensions in the present make implicit in professional discourse? Should not the diversity of views about achieving multiculturalism in historical discourse be part of the polyvocal dialogue represented in the main body of textual discourses themselves (as opposed to the notes or other paratext)?[90]

The contemporary debates on the ideal of multiculturalism and the dialogic structure of multiculturalist discourse ask the historian to combine in any given historical text multiple viewpoints and different voices, Berkhofer concludes, "(1) from within the represented world of the past, (2) from outside the represented world of the past in light of subsequent events and ideas, and (3) from the conflicting or at least diverse viewpoints existing in the present. In each case we must ask who is represented, and how."[91]

In analyzing a theoretical essay written in this vein by Joan W. Scott and an explicitly multicultural, polyvocal historical study, Patricia Limerick's *The Legacy of Conquest: The Unbroken Past of the American West* (1987), Berkhofer shows that no convincing model has been found as yet that does overcome the conflict or contradiction between multiplicity in *story* and *argument* and the *narrating* and *writing* of history from a single, integrative viewpoint. Then, (how) can historians develop writing strategies that incorporate multiple viewpoints into a multicultural history text? And (how) can these multiple, different narrative viewpoints be interrelated in a dialogic manner, transcending the ideal of a closed, all-encompassing history text, and represent the multicultural dynamics of history as drama and contested debate, like in Thomas Bender's notion of public culture?

Berkhofer takes up recent developments in postmodern anthropology, the writing culture debate in a self-reflective ethnography as cultural critique (James Clifford, George Marcus, Michael Fischer, et al.). These recent approaches propose a revisionary notion of culture as always hybrid, heterogeneous, discontinuous, and intercultural, demanding an ethnographic discourse and cultural analysis in which the voice of the Western anthropologist is decentered and articulated in a dialogue with the voices of "other cultures" in processes of mutual transculturation and contested transactions embedded in the wider context of "global movements of difference and power" (Clifford). Again, Berkhofer senses the danger of "reflexivity appropriat[ing] the other in the name of cross-cultural understanding." The danger is real, but there *are* examples

---

[90] Berkhofer, *Beyond the Great Story*, 176, 182-83.
[91] Berkhofer, *Beyond the Great Story*, 183.

of reflexive dialogue between representatives of different cultures, and there is also the danger of preempting the authority of articulation of "other" cultures about themselves by arguing that "self-reflexivity" or cultural "theory," as they characterize anthropology, are "inherently" features of *Western* academic discourse or cultures. Berkhofer, responding to R.S. Khare's work, puts it quite succinctly: "genuine reciprocity, in short, demands negotiated dialogues about what is known and how it is known, about how it is to be represented and then textualized as a discourse."[92] He remains skeptical about the possibility of achieving this dialogical ideal, yet, I think, the seemingly aporetic situation of having to realize at the same time a "non-violent," "non-coercive," or "non-appropriative" mutual understanding of cultures as other *and* as in some ways sharing the potential of a dialogic interaction *can* be redefined and resolved in cultural practices that acknowledge that the absolute opposition constructed, especially the absolutism of "non-violent" or "non-appropriative" understanding, is an artificial, disabling one.

Berkhofer makes it quite clear that the challenge of multiculturalism and that of the dialogical ideal to history writing have to be seen as inseparably interrelated. In isolation they can be, and have been, absorbed and reappropriated by the old monologically constituted narratives in the vein of the Great Story through multiple strategies of incorporating additional voices or viewpoints into the narrative text without projecting a "new vision of historical authority."[93] The multicultural, dialogical history envisioned has to dramatize and to inscribe the multiple tensions of past and present societies, of conflicting viewpoints and voices, into the modes of textualization in history writing. Berkhofer finds this ideal realized only in part in the—very different—historical-theoretical studies of the new ("postmodern") anthropology or models of a revisionary history. The most radical experiments resolve the formidable problem of writing a multicultural and dialogic history by collage or pastiche, by collecting different outlooks and visions in one volume. However, the question has to be asked if Berkhofer's ideal of "a single text" does not limit the options and modes of dialogic, multicultural representation in an unnecessary way. Also, his critical comment on the book he finds closest to a realization of his ideal, (anthropologist) Richard Price's *Alabi's World* (1990), that "although all voices and viewpoints are supposedly equal, his own prevails in the end,"[94] should, on the contrary, remind us of the insight that it is crucial for the historian, particularly in writing, or dramatizing and representing, a multicultural, polyvocal history, *to take up and articulate responsibility*, also in the sense of answerability, and self-reflexive, necessarily limited "authority" in his or her work.

Therefore, the question of *how* to write a multicultural, dialogic history, of *how* to assemble multiple voices and viewpoints into "a coherent, interrelated structure," the challenge of the new historical methodology, have to be *contextualized* in a "politics of historical viewpoint," in an exploration of *discourse as a social practice*, as "part of a

---

[92] Berkhofer, *Beyond the Great Story*, 195-96.
[93] Berkhofer, *Beyond the Great Story*, 197.
[94] Berkhofer, *Beyond the Great Story*, 198, 200-201.

larger scholarly and political world."[95] Berkhofer confronts the dynamics of the politics of historical representation and of professional practice and paradigms, of power in and of discourse, of the multiple multicultural differentials in "situated knowledges" (Donna Haraway), of the revisionary notions of "ideology" and "hegemony" (Stuart Hall), of the versions and vicissitudes of "radical history," and the "politics of authority" in the next chapter of his book in all their complexity. His analysis leads him to the new historicized cultural studies that are based on a conflictual model of society and politics that grounds its work on the kind of "new contextualism" Berkhofer had critically discussed in recent American history writing (observing a radical political message embodied in a very traditional form of historical contextualization). The question he pursues in the final chapter of *Beyond the Great Story*, "Reflexive (Con)Textualization," therefore is, if the new cultural studies—and here he explicitly moves again beyond the boundaries of the discipline of history—can or will "create new varieties of historicization to match its efforts to resolve the seeming contradictions of the poetics of context." How can a "reflexive contextualization" relate "the various constitutions of context(ualization) ... to one another in a text" on the levels of rhetoric, genre, institutions, politics, history, and ethics, and which kinds or notions of "theory" are intertwined with historical representation and discursive practice?[96]

Berkhofer's concluding thoughts about the discursive strategies of "new historicizations" in cultural studies and historiography sum up again the formidable challenges of the manifold crises of historical representation the historian (and cultural critic) have to face. He cannot, and does not try to, offer any model how a reflexive, dialogic multicultural (con)textualization "beyond the Great Story" should look like. In self-critically positioning himself in his theoretical discourses Berkhofer acknowledges the *pastness* of the (unified and unifying) Great Story as well as a *(re-)visionary utopian perspective* (*not* an ideal to be "realized") all historians have been, and continue to be, after. His penetrating analyses and reflections throughout his book have elaborated and cogently dramatized the highly complex interrelations and tensions between the various theoretical dimensions and discursive practices that historiography and cultural studies are forced to reflect, negotiate, and to re-present in their work, if they want to meet the challenges of the present and the future in the multicultural United States. In its arguments, revisions, and counterrevisions, Berkhofer's study *enacts* the writing of history as a self-reflective, multilayered, and multiperspectival *open-ended process*. The fact that the book is written by one historian does *not* invalidate its revisionary theoretical, multicultural thrust. Instead, it provides *one* important and, in the literal sense of the word, pro-vocative text that invites responses and further elaborations and revisions and asks for dialogues. It testifies to the sincerity and "authority" of Berkhofer's study that he closes with an appeal to his colleagues or partners in the project of history writing "beyond the Great Story": "Only further textual experimentation will answer the question. Only openness to such experimentation will allow

---

[95] Berkhofer, *Beyond the Great Story*, 201-202.
[96] Berkhofer, *Beyond the Great Story*, 242, 244.

the answers to be interesting. What might be the goals of any historic turn or drive to historicize should therefore not be judged by what has been practiced so far in the profession or produced up to this point as discourse. Rather the goals themselves should be part of the experiment."[97]

Conclusion: Internationalizing American Multicultural History

Let me, finally, indicate some—interrelated—conclusions the wide-ranging and challenging debates on the meaning and the repercussions of multiculturalism among American historians suggest. They will return our reflections to the question of the notion and the project of a democratic public culture and the issue of the public role of the historian as well as the understanding of multiculturalism as the social and political organization of cultural heterogeneity and difference. Or, to the understanding of contemporary cultures as cultures of difference that have to be articulated in critical historical discourses that are inherently intra- and crosscultural.

The first conclusion, or critical project, is the need to theorize, in a historical perspective, multiculturalism as the social and political constitution and organization of various, often competing and conflicting dimensions of *intra*cultural differences. This understanding of multiculturalism implies that "culture" is seen as an open, discontinuous, and conflictual process of the construction, deconstruction, and reconstruction of cultural identities (*qua* identifications) and communities (in the sense of provisional affiliations), a process articulated from different positions of unequal power and status. The awareness of the complex dynamics of intracultural differences, this is a second demand, must lead historians to engage more widely and more radically with writing strategies of the different *border discourses* of contact zones, hybridity, creolization, transculturation, *mestizaje*, and diaspora, as they have been worked out by minority critics and critics writing from the margins of, or in opposition to, white male dominant culture.[98] This "engagement" of historians "with" border discourses, however, and this is my third point, must be conceived of as a *dialogic* engagement of differently positioned historians and cultural critics speaking and writing in different traditions and voices, *not* as a "monological" all-inclusive incorporation of other historical and cultural discourses. This multifocal and multivocal dialogue is not an abstract theoretical debate, but has to take place—my fourth point—in the context of political, social, and cultural

---

[97] Berkhofer, *Beyond the Great Story*, 283. For a first debate about the book see the contributions by Michael C. Coleman, Saul Cornell, Betsy Erkkila, and Berkhofer's response in *American Quarterly* 50 (1998), 340-75. A detailed review of *Beyond the Great Story* was written by Thomas L. Haskell who points out a number of problems in Berkhofer's reflections (thus taking up his call at the end of the book). He misconstrues, however, the open, hybrid, dialogical, and (self-)reflexive discursive thrust of Berkhofer's argument by claiming that he is driven by a "hunger for transparency, systematicity, and indubitability," "perfectionism," or a "once and for all" solution to historians' modes of inquiry. Cf. Thomas L. Haskell, "Review of Robert F. Berkhofer, Jr., *Beyond the Great Story*," *History and Theory* 37 (1998), pp. 347-69; 352f., 355.

[98] See my essay "Transnational American Culture Studies."

structures and institutions, in what Thomas Bender has suggestively described, particularly in his more recent essays, as the realm and arena of *public culture* in which the *role of history and the historian* can be debated in all their controversial repercussions. It is this debate that can help to recreate and reconstitute what public culture can mean in an age of postmodernity, multiculturalism, and globalization that is also an age of the revolution in communication technologies and the new technoculture of what Mark Poster in his pertinent essays has called the "Second Media Age,"[99] a challenge rarely taken up by historians as yet. If the concept of culture in multicultural discourse is defined as inescapably characterized by *intra*cultural differences, as inherently "hybrid" (Homi Bhabha) or "creolized" (Ulf Hannerz), it is necessarily also permeated by *inter*cultural differences. The exploration of these *intercultural* or *crosscultural* interrelations and interactions—my fifth and final observation—must lead U.S. American historians to a much more clearly articulated *comparative* and *transnational* approach to the writing of American history, an issue not fully developed in Berkhofer's *Beyond the Great Story*.[100] The terms "comparative" and "transnational" do *not* mean, however, simply to compare the United States with other countries as fixed nation-states according to supposedly objective or universal standards in order to overcome the dubious legacy of the claims of "American uniquenesss" or "exceptionalism," important as this is, as this approach often reintroduces the "Great Story," now on a vaster scale, through the backdoor. It must mean, instead, to resituate the history of the United States in the dynamics of global developments, to *internationalize* American history by explicitly engaging in dialogues with historians from other parts of the world who see the United States and its powerful impact on other countries from very different perspectives.

The profession or discipline of American history (or historiography) has taken important steps in this direction. David Thelen, editor of the *Journal of American History*, has dedicated his unrelenting energy to turning the journal more and more pronouncedly into a forum and arena for an "internationalized American history" that offers space for contributions by non-American historians, reviews their historical studies, even if written in languages other than English, and organizes Round Table Discussions among historians from different nations that discuss issues or periods in American history in a comparative, cross-cultural, international perspective. His own programmatic essay, "Of Audiences, Borderlands, and Comparisons: Toward the Internationalization of American History," though it was already published in the early 1990s, addresses, as the title indicates, some of the critical concerns I just defined as crucial for future work in rewriting the history of the United States and reconceptualizing the objectives of history as a discipline (or transdisciplinary project).

---

[99] Mark Poster, *The Second Media Age* (Cambridge: Polity Press, 1995); for multiculturalism see esp. 40-42 and 52-56.

[100] For his discussion of "comparative history" cf. esp. ch. 2 of *Beyond the Great Story*.

Thelen's desire to draw "foreign scholars and their work into the everyday activities of the *Journal of American History*"[101] is based on the conviction that they by definition introduce, and have to introduce, a *comparative* perspective and *foreign audiences* into the discussion of American history and that they are positioned in "borderlands" that ask for "translation," for exploring the ways ideas, materials from the other culture are transculturated in the borderlands between the cultures. He sees the reason for the loss of audience, for the decline in the public role of the historian in professional over-specialization and narrowness of perspective (that also ignores the understanding of history the majority of the population has). He hopes to overcome this parochialism through exposing American historians and the American audience to the complex transformative responses to the impact of the United States on countries in other parts of the world, especially after World War II, as they have been studied and introduced into the analysis of American history by foreign scholars who invite Americans to see their own particular history in a wider frame. Thelen takes up what he calls the "image" or the "metaphor of borderlands" in order to conceptualize the manifold *intra*cultural and *inter*cultural *encounters* between "people, ideas, and institutions" that interact and are articulated in processes of "translation" and transculturation, processes that help us see, to give an example, charges of "Americanization" and of "American cultural imperialism" in a different light. He argues: "If capital, labor, people, ideas, diseases, environmental destruction, and television programs move across borders rather than having rooted national identities, the question becomes how individuals constructed multinational and transnational historical processes as they met everyday needs in borderlands between cultures."[102]

Internationaliz*ing* American history—and here the progressive form is crucial—means studying "what happens in history's many borderlands." Thelen refers to a remarkable number of case studies defined from differently positioned experiences in "borderlands" of intercultural encounters within and beyond the borders of the United States. They range from Mexican-United States borderland communities, interactions between Native Americans and European immigrant groups over the centuries, the conflictual negotiations of various new immigrant groups with the dominant Anglo-Saxon mainstream culture as well as other immigrant groups in the U.S. or the "creation" of borderlands by Americans traveling or living abroad. Clearly, Thelen stretches the "metaphor of borderlands" to its limits when he, quite rightly, points out that "most American cities contain dozens, even hundreds, of moving borderlands when people from one culture encounter those from another."[103] A careful attention to the different potential of the various border discourses mentioned above could place the manifold case studies in a clearer relief.

---

[101] David Thelen, "Of Audiences, Borderlands, and Comparisons: Toward the Internationalization of American History," *Journal of American History*, 79 (Sept. 1992), 432-62; 432.

[102] Thelen, "Of Audiences," 436, 438, 444.

[103] Thelen, "Of Audiences," 437-38.

But Thelen's essay shows convincingly how the metaphor of borderlands can help to transcend the *one-directional* and *monological* approach to trans- or international history by emphasizing the need for seeing processes of negotiation in cultural encounters from *both* sides, from the perspectives of *both* sides of the "border." Therefore, in some sense, American historians, or historians in general, are "borderline scholars" and have to become, in the contemporary world, experts in "cultural brokerage," and they can learn a lot from studying "interpreters, brokers, smugglers, and mediators" between cultures. They study "peoples on the move," "people in transnational motion," the effects of global migrations like the "black diaspora," and the creation and reinvention of "transnational" ethnic, foreign, or "American identities." He writes: "In focusing on what people do in borderlands between cultures, an internationalized American history will explore how different readers have interpreted 'texts,' both written works and other cultural products."[104] In studying the worldwide diffusion of products of American popular culture historians learn not only how differently the have been received and transculturated, but also how cultural traditions and idioms have "crossed," how they have been "fused" into something else and something new. They learn how contemporary cultures on a global scale have increasingly become more hybridized than ever before, but hybridized also as creative acts of reestablishing local cultural meanings and practices. In exploring these intercultural processes in critical dialogues between American and non-American historians, an internationalizing American history will be asked to explore these interactions with a special attention to issues of political, economic, and interpretative power: "A borderland approach spurs us to explore how individuals negotiate the asymmetrical and unequal relationship that accompanies them into any encounter with individuals from different cultures (or classes, or genders)."[105]

In writing of "borderlands between cultures," of "how much of history happens in spaces between cultures,"[106] Thelen might be taken as still subscribing to the traditional notion of comparisons (the third section of his essay) between cultures seen as stable and unified that, in a kind of secondary move, then encounter and affect one another, but his own examples clearly point in the direction of a more dynamic, dialogical, and conflictual understanding of cultures as multi- and intercultural processes. In his remarks on the role of comparative studies in "internationalized American history," he emphasizes the two dimensions of comparisons, the diachronic and the synchronic, and sees the potential of a comparative dialogue with foreign scholars in "depen[ing] our sense of alternatives in the present era," in confronting Americans with "other pasts."[107] This dialogue with foreign scholars of American history would also provide the chance really to decenter, historicize, deconstruct, and transcend the still unregenerate vision of United States exceptionalism that, as Louis Hartz cogently pointed out more than four decades

---

[104] Thelen, "Of Audiences," 440-41.
[105] Thelen, "Of Audiences," 442-44.
[106] Thelen, "Of Audiences," 436, 444, cf. 439, 441.
[107] Thelen, "Of Audiences," 444.

ago, implicitly asks for a radically comparative analysis instead of making it superfluous. Thelen defines his vision of the future format and objectives of the *Journal of American History* as making "this sense of alternatives in the present" a living reality in the work of comparative historians, in their dialogues on topics such as the "negotiations over class, race, and ethnicity," "slavery and race relations," or "multiculturalism" and models of "multiethnic and multiracial societies," and in newly conceived collective, comparative, transnational research projects. His hope is that in turning the journal into a forum for public, intercultural, international debate it can reach a wider audience, can encourage innovative ways of presenting history to the general public and make historians' insights available to the practice of public policy makers. In this way the journal can at least in some way contribute to rebuilding a democratic public culture and to re-establishing and reaffirming the "responsibility"—in the literal as well as in the political and moral sense—of American historians in the public sphere.[108] Historians are not asked to replace "American history" by world history or global studies, but to resituate and rearticulate developments in the United States in a dialogic and polyvocal perspective.

David Thelen's program of "internationalizing American history" has to be complemented by Robert Berkhofer's reflections on "history as text and discourse," on the writing strategies of a self-reflective, multiperspectival, dialogical multicultural history as well as by Thomas Bender's wide-ranging theoretical reflections on the implications of the concept of public culture and its practical organization and institutionalization as a principle and a forum for combining the u-topian vision of a "new synthesis" in American history and a redefinition of its public role. Seen in this way, the debate among historians in the United States about multiculturalism and history/historiography and their special role and responsibility in the public culture at large does not only define the challeneges and the prospects for the discipline of American history, but also, in different ways, for the future work in cultural studies and multicultural critique in the globalizing (and relocalizing) world of the use of new media in communication and of increasingly complex intercultural interdependencies. Yet in taking up David Thelen's emphasis on borderlands, comparisons, and audiences and his explorations of internationalizing American history European scholars can also offer their own response from the other side of the Atlantic and return the debate on multiculturalism to the pro-vocations of the different preconditions, potential, and directions

---

[108] Thelen, "Of Audiences," 444-45, 447, 451. In addition to the contributions by foreign scholars from various countries collected in the same issue of the journal the essay by Maurizio Vaudagna, "American History at Home and Abroad," *Journal of American History*, 81 (Dec. 1994), 1157-68, is particularly pertinent as a European response to Thelen's project. For the more general debate on "comparative" and/or "transnational" history see the excellent essay by George M. Fredrickson, "From Exceptionalism to Variability: Recent Developments in Cross-National Comparative History," *Journal of American History*, 82 (Sept. 1995), 587-604; also Peter Kolchin, "Comparing American History," *Reviews in American History*, 10 (Dec. 1982), 64-81; Akira Iriye, "The Internationalization of History," *American Historical Review*, 94 (1989), 1-10; Ian Tyrrell, "American Exceptionalism in an Age of International History," *American Historical Review*, 96 (1991), 1031-55, and the response by Michael McGeer, "The Price of the 'New Transnational History,'" in the same issue, 1056-67.

of the discourses on multiculturalism in Europe. "Historicizing" the discourse on multiculturalism in the complex ways elaborated in this essay on the work of American historians could help to revitalize the *Multikulturalismusdebatte* in Germany and other European countries and redefine the issues of "exotic cultural diversity," the integration of foreigners, the nation-state, and citizenship.[109]

---

[109] For an elaboration of the objectives, problems, and the potential of internationalizing American Studies see my essay "Toward a Dialogics of International American Culture Studies: Transnationality, Border Discourses, and Public Culture(s)," *Amerikastudien/American Studies*, 44 (1999), 5-23.

Part II.
Visions of America in/and Europe—
Ambivalent Images and the Role of Intellectuals

AMERICA AND THE EUROPEAN SENSE OF HISTORY

Rob Kroes

The ways in which Europeans have tried to make sense of America constitute a special chapter in the European history of ideas. At first glance what strikes us in the bewildering variety of European readings of America is the recurring attempt at formulating the critical differences that set America apart from the historical experience and cultural conventions of European nations. America is never seen as purely *sui generis*, as constituting an alien entity to be fathomed in terms of an inner logic wholly its own. There is always the sense of America being a stray member of a larger family, a descendant from Europe. If it belongs to the *genus proximum* of Western civilization, the point then is to define the *differentia specifica* according to an almost Linnaean taxonomy. European conventions have always served as the yardstick, implied or explicit, in European attempts at uncovering the rules of transformation that had cut America adrift from the European mainstream. Hardly ever, though, is this intellectual quest for the crucial difference entirely disinterested. Rather than merely being an academic exercise, more often than not there is an existential urgency involved in the exploration of the American difference. If Europe serves as the standard for measuring difference, the outcome of such measurement is always geared to a discussion of its potential impact on Europe. In other words, there is always a triangulation going on, in the sense that the reflection on America as a counterpoint to European conventions functions within a larger reflection on Europe's history and destiny.

If this may seem unduly to intellectualize the repertoire of European views of America, I hasten to say that in addition to the more intellectually articulate versions there are vernacular, or popular, versions. Widely shared and informing everyday conversations, they may seem more like unreflected stereotypes, providing ready answers to those trying to make sense of the many Americas that reach them in their daily lives through the modern means of mass communication. Yet we should not exaggerate the difference between the intellectual and the vernacular views of America. At both levels a similar triangulation takes place, less articulate perhaps at the vernacular level, yet similar in so far as people make sense of America in ways that are meaningful to their own lives. Their constructions of America, shared with peer groups, focus on American counterpoints which then help them develop individual and group identities different from models and standards prevailing in their home setting.

There are yet other ways in which we can explore the similarities underlying the European views of America. If we look at them as so many narrative accounts of perceived differences, they appear as repertoires of metaphors. Again, the metaphors are many, yet a deep structure underlies them of much greater simplicity. In a recent publication[1] I have proposed the reduction of these repertoires to essentially three underlying dimensions which are remarkably stable irrespective of time, national culture, or class. Always these three main dimensions served to structure a discourse of cultural difference, of " Us"—people in Europe—versus "Them"—the Americans. Of these three main dimensions one is spatial, contrasting an America seen as flat, reducing European verticality, hierarchy, the sense of high versus low, of cultural heights and the feeling of depth, to purely horizontal vectors playing themselves out on the surface, exteriorizing what to Europeans is the inner life of the soul. The second dimension is temporal, having to do with a contrast that casts Americans as lacking the European sense of the past as a living presence. The third dimension represents all those views that see American culture as lacking the European sense of holism, of organic cohesion; Americans in this view are never loath to take the European cultural heritage apart, dissecting it into component parts and recombining them in total irreverence to what has grown in historic and spatial specificity. These three dimensions form the discursive formation of Europe's "occidentalism," the underlying structure of meanings, as Raymond Williams called it, capable of spawning an endless number of meaningful sentences and individual utterances ranging from the highly subtle and nuanced to the coarsely stereotypical. Yet in spite of all variation at the level of explicit statements, it is my point that the motifs they use are resonant of repertoires that are more widely shared among the larger public and are of remarkable historical stability.

Three further points need making here. Often the metaphorical repertoires of European occidentalism were used to reject America and its culture, but not always. When European intellectuals elevated America as an example for Europeans to emulate, the same metaphors could serve their expressions of praise. Similarly, at the vernacular level, readings of American culture as a counterpoint to established European cultural modes have used the same metaphorical dimensions for the representation of America, yet at the same time the general appreciation changed from rejection to reception. Developments in Cultural Studies during the last fifteen years or so have helped to shed light on the processes of the transmission and reception of popular/mass culture, and on the way that American culture has influenced the processes of identity formation among younger generations elsewhere. These generations, during our century, rather than meekly reproducing their national cultures, or at least parental cultures as imposed on them, more often than not selectively appropriated American popular culture for acts of cultural rebellion and resistance. What needs further exploration in this context is the way in which European constructions of America were a dialectical exercise in which the real discussion among those at the receiving end was about the national identity of their home country, in the larger context of a debate about Europe. When national elites or non-elite groups use references to "America," or to "Europe" for that matter, we have to see them in the light of infra-national discussions concerning the contours of the national identity, French, German, British, and so on.

---

[1] Rob Kroes, *If You've Seen One, You've Seen the Mall: Europeans and American Mass Culture* (Urbana/Chicago: University of Illinois Press, 1996).

As a second point I should remind the reader that given my focus on Europe in this chapter I may seem to imply that the narrative constructions of "America" by Europeans are in some way typically European. This is certainly not the point of my exercise in exploring the deep structure of views of outsiders who find themselves confronted with the challenges posed by an expansive American civilization. As I argued more at length elsewhere,[2] the three-dimensional underlying structure of meanings would seem to hold for any views of rival cultures seen as overbearing, yet alien. All defensive explorations of the authentic core values of cultures threatened by vigorous rivals have a logic to them that casts the rival civilization as lacking depth and authenticity, as being an exterior veneer, without historical rootedness and legitimacy. Whether the case was that of an emerging German bourgeoisie in the late eighteenth century fending off the appeal of French civilization, or of African intellectuals exploring their Africanness, their *négritude*, in the face of an overbearing European mode of civilization, or of Latin-Americans confronted with the inroads of an American civilization radiating from the United States, the same deep structure of cultural defense and indictment can be discovered. The defensive quest for authenticity seems always to hinge on a diagnosis of the rival culture as lacking depth and soul, as being devoid of a sense of historical growth and of organic wholeness and integrity. I should also point out, that the Europe emerging in my text, is a Europe as imagined by intellectuals in countries that I studied in relative depth, countries such as France, Italy, Germany, England, the Netherlands. I am insufficiently knowledgeable about Europes dreamed up by intellectuals in Eastern-European settings in their reflections on the American difference. It may well be the case, though, that in fact it was Western Europe that was more directly confronted with the American challenge, and felt more directly urged to respond to it.

Thirdly, I should emphasize that for all the stability of the discursive formation of European views concerning America, it is like a dormant resource. Clearly in the continuing European/American encounter some moments are more likely to trigger a European interpretative response than others. Thus, for instance, the 1920s was not just like any other preceding decade in the way that America forced itself upon the European consciousness. In the wake of World War I the United States had, literally if not physically, become a presence in Europe, inducing Europeans to a renewed and urgent reflection upon the American identity. America's intervention in the war, the presence of its armies in Europe, the massive advent of its mass culture in following years, allow us to look at World War I as a watershed. The war forced Europeans to reconsider their traditions, their economic, social and political plight, in short their collective destinies, but they could no longer do this without making the case of America a constituent part of their reflections. If there are continuities in the ways that Europeans have made sense of America, history has also known abrupt leaps in the relative distance that Europeans have felt towards America, like floodgates opening.

In the following I propose to take this argument further and to highlight the intricate interrelations between these distinct levels of response to the cultural difference

---

[2] Kroes, *If You've Seen One*.

presented by America, but perceived and given meaning by Europeans. The way I shall do this is by focussing on one critical period first—the Interbellum—analyzing ways in which European intellectuals used America in their critical reflections on the plight of Europe and of their respective nation states. I shall then change perspective, moving in time towards the post-World War II period, focusing not on the elite but on the way in which America affected non-elite groups in their sense of self and of history.

The Interbellum—Anguished European intellectuals and their views of America

"I confess that in America I have wished to see more than just America. I wanted to find an image there of democracy itself, of its inclinations, its character, its prejudices, its passions; I wanted to get to know it, if only at least to find out what hopes or fears it holds for us." These words from Tocqueville's preface to his *Democracy in America* aptly summarize an attitude that is more generally characteristic of European observers of the American scene. Whether their interest was cultural, political, economic, or social, their observations more often than not were inspired by a sense, anguished or hopeful, that America provided Europeans with a view of what the future held in store for them. This sense was made more acute by the intimation that not only did America offer a glimpse of Europe's future, to be perceived by merely juxtaposing American settings to conditions in Europe, the country was also seen as the historic agent of Europe's future. Even those observers who in their more lucid and detached moments were willing to grant that both the United States and Europe were set on a parallel course of social and cultural transformation, with America being further advanced along that road, often assumed that America would already have left its typical imprint on the forms of the future before these would reach Europe. All the more reason, then, for those of this cast of mind, to watch American developments closely in order better to be able to fend off the threat of Europe's Americanization, and to prepare strategies of cultural resistance.

Many were the voices in Europe during the interwar years calling for a defense of Europe's cultural heritage, defined either in terms of national identities or of a larger entity called "Europe." As I have argued elsewhere,[3] the line dividing both levels of argument was never neat. Clearly the need for defense in the face of a challenge as massive as the one posed by America, called for a canvass equally large: Europe. In that sense European critics of American culture may ironically have much to thank the Americans for. If indeed the American challenge led them to argue their defensive case in terms of a larger construct, called Europe, the idea of Europe and Europeanism appeared like the dialectical mirror image of their views of America and reinforced the reflection by Europeans on the contours of their own larger frame of identification and affiliation. Even so, however, if European intellectuals did not argue their case in terms

---

[3] Kroes, *If You've Seen One*, 82-84.

of clearly national contours, rising to the defense of national cultures and national identities, a discourse cast in terms of national concerns and modes of reflection was never far below the surface. Thus, various Europes transpired in their arguments, appearing as thinly veiled versions of hallowed national identities. While French critics of American culture and civilization elevated a view of Europe that showed the typically French preoccupations with individual creativity and craftmanship, German critics tended to favor a view of Europe in a more collectivist vein, of the *Volk* seen as the carrier of a collective *Kultur*.

Not only do we see how the image of "Europe" is often cast in characteristically national terms, more generally we can say that "Europe" often served as no more than a flimsy rhetorical veneer. More often than not it could hardly paper over the fault lines between the various national cultures. An amusing example of this can be found in André Siegfried's writings. In 1927 he wrote the preface to a study by André Philip about labor conditions in America—*Le problème ouvrier aux Etats Unis*. It is a study about the place of the worker in an industry that had become organized around the tenets of Fordism, of Taylorism, of standardization, of mass production, and above all of "le machinisme." Siegfried lauds Philip as a "bon européen" (a good European) who had set out to measure American labor conditions by a European yardstick of humanist values. He remembers how he himself had only become aware in America of "le monde européen comme un ensemble." (the European world as a whole). Only in America "on prend conscience d'une réalité qui nous échappe ici, c'est qu'il existe un esprit européen, dont l'esprit américain est souvent la parfaite antithèse."(one becomes aware of a reality that escapes us here, namely that a European spirit does exist, to which the American spirit often stands as the perfect opposite). From a moral point of view America, new as it is, has been cut off from our twenty centuries' old traditions by the hiatus of emigration across the ocean; it no longer shares much with the old Europe that is still in direct communion with Rome, with Greece and even with India. Clearly up to this point Siegfried conceives of Europe "comme un ensemble," as a integral whole. But it isn't long before he begins to add individual detail to his picture: "Parmi les peuples européens, le français est celui qui a eu, le plus, la conscience de ce qu'est un individu, un homme ..." (among the European nations, the French is the one that has had the clearest sense of what it means to be an individual, a Man ...). France clearly takes pride of place in the European ensemble, embodying some of the core values of Europeanism. But Siegfried does not leave it at that. He goes on to single out one other country from the European whole, describing it as an America in Europe: Germany. "Les Allemands, si semblables à tant d'égards aux Américains modernes, se sont jetés dans la standardisation avec une sorte de passion, comme ils font toutes choses. Il n'est point d'Allemand, aujourd'hui, qui ne chante avec conviction l'hymne de la 'rationalisation'; celle-ci répond évidemment à leur génie de discipline, avouons-le aussi, à leur manque de personnalité." (The Germans, so similar in so many ways to the modern Americans, have hurled themselves on to a course of standardization with a kind of passion, as they always do. There is no German, today, that does not with conviction sing the praise of 'rationalization'; the latter clearly accords with their mind for discipline, and, let us admit it, their lack of personality). So much for the European ensemble.[4]

Unsubtle as Siegfried may have been in this passage, it is a good example of the kind of triangulation that I am exploring. Gauging the nature of American culture with a view to resisting it more successfully, European critics were torn between defensive positions centering either on their national cultural setting or on a larger European frame of reference. In smaller European countries like the Netherlands the latter point of orientation may have come more naturally to the minds of critics of American culture, yet even in their case the plight of their national culture was always at least an implied concern. The Dutch historian Johan Huizinga may be a good case in point. For one thing, in his reflections on America, he was never solely the historian in his Olympian role of detached observer. He was rather a historian in the role of intellectual, aware of his public calling to probe and make sense of historical trends as these affected the life of his contemporaries. But also, and this is a point of direct relevance to my argument, he was a man who throughout his work performed a continuing triangulation. When he wrote about Dutch culture, he explored it as a variant of European culture, trying to define its specificity. When he evoked life in Europe on the eve of the Renaissance, he did it with a view to producing a picture of European culture that European countries had moved away from since under the impact of larger forces of modernization. When he wrote about America, either as a historian or as an astute observer of its contemporary scene, he did it with European or Dutch culture at the back of his mind. Finally, in his later, darker musings on contemporary history losing form, America is the unnamed site where he had earlier seen these forces of entropy at work. In the following paragraphs let me explore a little more in depth the uses that Huizinga made of America in what were truly reflections on the plight of European culture in the interwar years.

Huizinga's triangulations

Upon his return from his only visit to the United States, Huizinga expressed himself thus: "Strange: among us Europeans who were travelling together in America ... there rose up repeatedly this pharisaical feeling: we all have something that you lack; we admire your strength but we do not envy you. Your instrument of civilisation and progress, your big cities and your perfect organisation, only make us nostalgic for what is old and quiet, and sometimes your life seems hardly to be worth living, not to speak of your future"[5]—a statement in which we hear resonating the ominous foreboding that "your future" might well read as "our future." For indeed, what was only implied here

---

[4] The quotations are from André Siegfried's preface to: A. Philip, *Le problème ouvrier aux Etats-Unis* (Paris: Librairie Félix Alcan, 1927), xi, xv.

[5] J. H. Huizinga, *Amerika levend en denkend: Losse opmerkingen* (Haarlem: H.D. Tjeenk Willink, 1927), 126. The translation is by Herbert H. Rowen, published as *America: A Dutch Historian's Vision, From Afar and Near* (New York: Harper and Row, 1972), 312.

would come out more clearly in Huizinga's more pessimistic later writings, when America became a mere piece of evidence in his case against contemporary history losing form. Thus, in 1935, in his *The Shadows of Tomorrow*, there is the following sweeping indictment: "The number, so it was said, washed across the individual; the mass dragged the individual along, defenseless, and lowered him to a level that always was the largest common denominator of the more simple and coarser features, while levelling and washing away the more complex and 'higher' expressions of the individual. New regimes could stimulate these coarsening trends and use for their own purposes such negative feelings like rancour, vengefulness and cruelty."[6] Still later, in an essay written when World War II already raged across Europe, he would once again connect this more general sense of cultural decline to America: "... the modern world is becoming more and more accustomed to thinking in numbers. America has hitherto been more addicted to this, perhaps, than Europe ... Only the number counts, only the number expresses thought."[7]

Huizinga may have inveighed against an obnoxious Americanism, against an "America" in quotation marks, yet he could not be mistaken as a mouth-piece for a vulgar anti-Americanism. He was too subtle-minded for that, forever aware of the counter-argument, of ambiguity; he was also too open to the real America, as an historical given, to relinquish the mental reserve of the quotation mark. The Huizinga quotation from his book of travel observations, which already was full of ambivalence, continues: "And yet, it is *we* that have to be the Pharisees, for theirs is the love and the confidence. Things must be different than we think." What strikes us in this rejection of what Europe was wont to call Americanism, is the intellectual sense of wonder, of admiration even, and of an affinity with and appreciation of that other variety of Americanism, that heritage of highminded ideals that had inspired so much of American history. Thus, in his 1935 essay on the Dutch cast of mind,[8] he did ponder the onslaught of ominous trends of a machine-like organization of social and political life—of the mechanization of life, as he called it—trends which he had earlier seen as typifying life in America; yet at the same time he saw a countervailing force in Dutch virtues of tolerance and a sense of liberty which had formed the nation around its myth of origin in a historic struggle for freedom and independence. It had set the nation apart as a "noble part of Western Europe," finding its center of gravitation across the sea. It found its partners in the Atlantic world, where freedom was still preserved. In its westward orientation "lay the strength and *raison d'être* of our existence," as Huizinga saw it.[9]

Yet, in Huizinga's attempts at triangulation, casting America as the pure type representing more general forces of social transformation, we easily recognize the repertoire of metaphors that were current among critics of American culture during the

---

[6] J.H. Huizinga, *In de schaduwen van morgen* [1935], reprinted in the *Collected Works* (Haarlem: H.D. Tjeenk Willink, 1950), Vol. VII, 313-424.

[7] J.H. Huizinga, *Over vormverandering der geschiedenis* [1941]), reprinted in the *Collected Works*, Vol. VII, 192-207.

[8] J.H. Huizinga, *Nederland's geestesmerk* [1935], reprinted in the *Collected works*, Vol. VII, 279-313.

[9] Huizinga, *Geestesmerk*, 312.

Interbellum. If from that perspective we judge Huizinga by the company he kept, he did in fact use language that others put in the service of a more facile anti-Americanism. In the above quotations we already have clear examples of the metaphoric deep structure of a European discourse casting America as the counterpoint to European cultural traditions. When in America Huizinga longed for "things old and quiet," the triangulation may well have implied the monastic, medieval Europe that Huizinga affiliated with so strongly. In the Europe of his time he may well have felt similarly estranged, yet there was more of a living past, a sense of connection to the forms of earlier European history, which America could never provide. In his 1926 collection of travel observations there is one such moment of epiphany, reminiscent—ironically—of Henry Adams's affiliation with the European Middle Ages. While ranting about the banality of the cultural forms that Americans used to shape their cultural consumption, Huizinga pauses to reminisce on a few hours spent in Cologne, in between trains. Contemporary Cologne aggravated him. The holy city on the Rhine had become ugly and banal (not unlike, Huizinga seems to imply, the America of his day). But leaving the indifferent street life behind him, in the semi-darkness of a church where mass was being celebrated, Huizinga suddenly realised what a true ritual is, what it represents as a cultural value and a cultural form. It was like an act of communion with a past in which these things to all were the essence of life.[10]

Observations like these, it may be clear, we can group among a repertoire of metaphors that all have to do with time, casting an America that critically lacks a sense of the past as the antithesis to a Europe where the present is meaningfully related to life in the past. The other Huizinga remarks that we quoted above, rather illustrate a second metaphorical dimension, one that contrasts America and Europe in terms of spatial images. America is typically seen as the country eroding European cultural heights and sense of depth. It typically does so by reducing quality to quantity, intrinsic value to exchange value, individual difference to the uniformity of numbers. Huizinga's observation that, in America and increasingly in the Old World as well, only the number is seen as capable of expressing thought, is in a sense a mild form of the more pejorative European view that Americans reduce everything to dollars. Other variations in this second, spatial repertoire point to the exteriority of life in America, as a life literally on the surface, shallow, lacking depth, devoid of the European sense of the tragic.

Huizinga's contemporary, Oswald Spengler, in his *Jahre der Entscheidung*, argued along similar lines, only with greater dramatic emphasis. Highlighting the European sense of *Tiefe* (depth) and *Seele* (soul), as well as the element of true historical tragedy, he actually merged two metaphorical dimensions, the spatial and the temporal, into one: he connects the shallowness of life in America to its lacking a sense of true *historical* tragedy. Others, following a later world war, would have a similar hunch. Albert Camus, following his 1946 visit to the United States, had this observation: "The afternoon with students. They don't feel the real problem; however their nostalgia is evident. In this country where everything is done to prove that life isn't tragic, they feel something is

---

[10] Huizinga, *Amerika levend en denkend*, 165/6.

missing. The great effort is pathetic, but one must reject the tragic *after* having looked at it, not before."[11] Jean-Paul Sartre at about the same time had similar observations on the absence of a tragic sense of life in America. The country, for all its blithe optimism, struck him as tragic in a rather pathetic way, due precisely to this absence. In his early postwar study of European views of America, André Visson, an expatriate Frenchman, already commented on the ironies of this peculiar complaint by European intellectuals. There is indeed a strange psychological mechanism at work among European intellectuals who tend to pride themselves on their tragic sense of life rather than admitting to feelings of collective guilt about Europe's suicidal orgies in two world wars. They turned feelings of envy and inferiority towards America, as the country that had twice saved Europe from its worst excesses, into a sense of intellectual superiority. The contrast indeed between the splendor of life in a victorious America and the miseries of war-torn Europe may have been too much to confront directly. Only rarely do we come across an unmediated expression of this contrast. Camus comes close to putting it into words: "... I am literally stupefied by the circus of lights. I am just coming out of five years of night, and this orgy of violent lights gives me for the first time the impression of a new continent. An enormous, 50-foot-high Camel billboard: a G.I. with his mouth wide open blows enormous puffs of *real* smoke."[12] According to Visson, Sartre like many other European intellectuals seems convinced that Americans are fundamentally unhappy. Sartre—and Visson quotes him—met Americans who, "though conventionally happy, suffer from an obscure *malaise* to which no name can be given, who are tragic through fear of being so, through that local absence of the tragic in them and around them."[13] But clearly, the perception of Americans as a people essentially unhappy, because unable to rise above their collective mad dash for happiness, is as old as Tocqueville's observations on "the sentiments of Americans."[14] Equally clearly, it is an ineradicable habit among observers of cultural difference to translate their experience of outsidership—after all: they are the outsiders trying to look in—into the language of quasi-inside reports. Small wonder, then, that never having been on the inside, they tend to report on voids and absences. Never having probed much beyond the surface, all they find worth mentioning is that the "other" culture has nothing but surface to offer. In all such cases, observations *from* the outside are no more than observations *of* the outside.

At times Huizinga seemed aware of the metaphorical quality of his exercise in measuring the difference between America and Europe along dimensions of polar opposites. Thus, in the diary he kept while traveling in the Unites States, published posthumously, there is this observation, made almost literally in passing: "In the morning from Philadelphia to Baltimore. The landscape has something light, something *ingénu, sans conséquence*, lacking depth, *as if one dimension were missing* [my Italics]. At times everything here makes that impression. As if, orbiting in a sphere around the

---

[11] Albert Camus, *American Journal* (London: Sphere Books, 1990), 42.
[12] Camus, *American Journal*, 32.
[13] A. Visson, *As Others See Us* (Garden City, N.Y.: Doubleday, 1948), 149.
[14] A. de Tocqueville, *De la démocratie en Amérique* (Paris: Librairie de Charles Gosselin, 1930/40), Vol. III, 272 ff.

essence of things, one is suddenly moved out to a more distant, wider sphere, at higher speed but more remote." Simply watching a landscape from a train, he must have become aware of the deeper logic underlying his attempts at ordering his observations of critical differences and contrasts between America and Europe. Otherwise his hunch that in American landscapes a vertical dimension is missing, when taken literally, does not make much sense. Yet he was never fully aware of the full range of dimensions he used in making sense of the American difference.

So far, we have recognised two dimensions in Huizinga's order of observations, the spatial and the temporal. These two may well be the ones most commonly found in European constructions of America, triggered more in the way that stereotypes are, like ready-made categories of observation and interpretation. They are, as we argued above, an indication more of the facile leap of outsiders who try to pose as vicarious insiders than the result of any imaginative attempt at interpreting differences in terms of the inner logic of the other society, the one under intrigued scrutiny. Things may well be different with the third dimension of metaphors, conceiving of America as lacking the European sense of the organic cohesion of cultural forms and styles. Not only do Americans tend to discard the established European hierarchies, ranking cultural forms in terms of high versus low, not only do they irreverently recycle the European repertoires, blurring high culture and mass culture, in their production, distribution, appreciation and consumption of culture. Also, at every level, whether in the adoption by Americans of European forms and styles of high art, or in more technical areas of production for the market, a spirit of blithe and irreverent bricolage is at work, which does not shrink from taking things apart and putting them together again in different forms, put to different purposes.

Huizinga may have been at his most astute in exploring this difference in the mental and cultural habitus of the Americans. At times his appreciation of the difference could be highly positive, as in his attempts at accounting for the radically American nature of authors he liked, such as Emerson and Whitman. As he argued, they had to differ from European standards; there was no way they could hope to rival European authors by trying to emulate the artistic forms developed in Europe. These forms had grown in Europe, in temporal and spatial specificity, and could be of no use for an expression of American thought and creativity. Formlessness was what innovating American authors had to experiment with. At other moments, though, similar perceptions led Huizinga to make more critical judgments inspired by an over-all sense of a cultural degeneration and loss in America of things valued highly in Europe. Particularly in his more anguished perceptions, of course, Huizinga was never solely the detached observer. Europe was always foremost on his mind, as the cultural domain likely to be tainted by trends observed in America.

These concerns were more central to his second than to his first book about America. Examples abound. American journalism, for instance, typified this fragmenting approach to the news, cutting its meaningful links to a larger history unfolding. The fragmenting of the news, the separation of current events from their historical context, the reduction of the news to, as Huizinga put it, "Slogan, the brief, catchy phrase," all constituted, as he saw it, "a regression of culture." They all resulted from

America's being a mass democracy and would therefore, in due course, come to other mass democracies as well, a case, clearly, of parallel developments, with Europe following closely on the heels of America. Yet, interestingly, Huizinga also connected these trends, as observed in America, to a strictly American background factor, the "anti-metaphysical cast of mind" in America. This mentality was the lasting heritage of an Enlightenment rationalism that had more firmly entrenched itself in America than anywhere else. "Do we not feel as if placed back in the eighteenth century?," Huizinga wondered. And, he continued, "the anti-metaphysical cast of mind naturally implies an anti-historical one. In spite of a flourishing and superbly organized practice of history [as an academic endeavor] America's mind is thoroughly anti-historical. A historiography that in the march of humankind wants to see purely the theodicee of progress, is not the true kind." Or, as he put it elsewhere, the American is directed towards the present and the future too much to be open to the mystery of the past.[15]

Whoever lives totally in the present, has no sense of historic meaning and context. Nor will such a person have a sense of organic cohesion. For indeed, anything that can be conceived in terms of internal coherence has a historical dimension, or, shall we say, a historicist specificity in its configuration of constituent elements. As a general theme it can be taken as indicative of the third metaphorical repertoire used by Europeans to give expression to American cultural defects, as they saw them. Once again Huizinga provides us with a telling example. When introduced to the Dewey Decimal System, the system for the systematic filing of library holdings as recently adopted in America, he recognized a quintessentially American impulse at work. As he saw it, time and time again living organic connections in the body of human knowledge were sacrificed to the need for classification. The human mind had been made subservient to the tyranny of the decimal system. It confirmed his intimations concerning the anti-metaphysical bent of the Americans and their inclination toward subjecting the spiritual realm to the dictates of technical organization.[16]

Clearly, then, in his attempts at making sense of America as a cultural counterpoint to Europe Huizinga used the repertoire of Europe's language of "occidentalism." His reflections were geared in part toward gauging the inner logic, the cultural *modus operandi*, of a civilization intriguingly at odds with European conventions and habits of mind. Yet his more central concern, particularly in his later writings, was with the portent of his reading of American culture for Europe's destiny. Typically, in his musings on American civilization we see Huizinga taking this larger view. He perceives in America the first signs of a process of civilization that is much more general in portent: "Organization becomes mechanization; that is the fatal moment of the modern history of civilization."[17] His broader view, however, does not make his mood of cultural demise any less acute. Yet he is aware that without mechanization there will be no

---

[15] Huizinga, *Amerika Levend en denkend*, 175.

[16] Interestingly, this observation is from Huizinga's first book on America: *Mensch en menigte in Amerika* [1918], reprinted in the *Collected Works*, 332/3.

[17] For Huizinga's views on the mechanization of contemporary life, see his *Mensch en menigte in Amerika* (Haarlem: Tjeenk Willink, 1918), chapter II, and his *Denkend Mensch en Menigte*, 14 ff.

civilization at all: "The process of refining culture is inseparable from that of instrumentalization." The process, however, has two distinct effects; it has a power-to-bind and a power-to-liberate. And it would appear ("taking America as the most perfect example") as if the balance tends too much towards the first, toward the subservience and bondedness of the individual, rather than towards setting him free. Huizinga goes on to ponder the possibility of whether the instrumentalization of life in America might not work out differently than in Europe: "Organization in the sense of standardization means the establishing of a uniform and well-defined technical nomenclature ... to the American it constitutes not only an individual need rather than a necessary evil, it also constitutes a cultural ideal ... Everyone familiar with their sense of conformity and collective identity will realize this. The American *wants* to be equal to his neighbor. He feels spiritually safe only in the normatively ordained, not to mention the fact that the latter also implies 'efficiency'." Typically, Huizinga is wavering here between two modes of interpretation. We recognize a distancing strategy when he tries to link the more ominous implications of the trend towards mechanization to character traits that he deems typically American. Yet at the same time he reminds the reader that he is taking America "as the most perfect example," implying that his cultural critique applies more generally.

There is a similar ambivalence in Huizinga's reading of another ominous cultural trend perceived in America, yet again of more general portent: the shift away from a culture centering on the word towards one centering on the image. Huizinga's views on film are a good case in point. They reflect the mixed feelings he had about America. At one point in his 1927 collection of travel impressions he went so far as to accept film as an art form, for which a new Muse or patron saint would have to be found. But he instantly qualified this position, pointing out that the "Movies"—as he put it in his Dutch text—are a mere illustration, albeit the most important, of an ominous shift in our civilization—away from reading to watching, away from the printed word toward "ideographic" information. Yet again Huizinga was ambivalent. Pondering the impact of film as he had witnessed it in America, he was aware of its democratic potential. Film was Whitmanesque in its capacity to restore a democratic vista, allowing people a comprehensive, if vicarious view of the variety of life in their society. Yet, at the same time, Huizinga's more pessimistic views of the mechanization of contemporary culture qualified these high hopes. As one of the new mass media, film, like radio, aimed at a mass audience, catering to its average taste. Film tended to simplify and stereotype its message. It might widen people's views of society, but only spuriously so, through a flattening of the social and cultural landscape. "[Film] habituates the nation from high to low to one common view of life. Due to its limited means of expression, its highlighting of what is external, and the need to appeal to a general audience, film shuts off entire areas of spiritual activity. It imposes a limited number of standard views of life that will eventually become the mass view."[18] Thus, film was one of the contemporary forces of cultural erosion that were at work in America. As an art form, visual though

---

[18] Huizinga, *Amerika levend en denkend*, 28.

it might be, it would never create lasting, self-contained forms, like sculpture or painting. In its narrative flow film, to him, was more like literature or drama. Yet again, geared as film was to a mass market, like radio, it could catch the attention of its audience compellingly, yet only transiently, for fleeting moments. Unlike drama or literature, it could never cause the audience to pause and reflect.

Yet, mixed as Huizinga's feelings about film may have been, he managed astutely to define the inner force of a medium in a way that inspires the critical reflection upon film until the present day. Even today the academic study of film is centrally involved with the intriguing exchange between the imaginary world of the silver screen and the sense of identity of the individuals watching it. A process of identification with the shadows on the screen occurs that leads the audience to step outside itself. Huizinga made the following, perceptive observation: "[Film] shows the urban dweller country life, or at least an image of it, it shows the countryman urban life, it gives the poor a view of luxury and the rich one of misery, all highly stylized so as to make it easy to appropriate. Thus film rather works to conciliate than to sharpen class resentment. The repeated illusion of the life of the rich affords the poor a certain communion with luxury and refinement; its fantasy image becomes a part of their daily existence. In the hero the audience exalts itself, and, beyond this, film stars off the screen offer it a new model for emulation, a novel assurance of options open to everyone ..."[19]

Interestingly, in these musings concerning film as one modern medium for the mechanical reproduction of culture, and as such an illustration of the wider trend of the mechanization of contemporary civilization, we see Huizinga perceiving a tension between the promise of a democratic art and its fake realization as mass culture. Not only is he torn between two modes of appreciation of American culture, or two forms of Americanism we might say, capable of experimenting with new forms of a democratic culture, while at the same time subverting them through a subservience to the dictates of a mass market for cultural consumption. He also, in passages like these on film, shows an awareness of the media of transmission of American cultural influences to audiences elsewhere. It is one thing to declare in writing that America holds forth an image of Europe's future, as so many of Huizinga's fellow critics of America's culture argued, it is quite a different intellectual challenge actually to explore the ways in which these dismal trends would be transmitted to Europe.

Huizinga had a keen and open eye for the ways in which the early forms of American mass culture worked to produce virtual phantasy worlds. In addition to film he was aware of the role that advertising began to play in the 1920s. In his travel notes, which would be the basis for his 1926 collection of essays, there is this observation from the streets of Chicago: "Looked at the advertisements. Rosy-cheeked boy with a smile and three packets of cereal: For that million dollar boy of *yours*. Puffed wheat. —Speculation on the love for children, health and the sense of dollars.—The advertisements, taken together, very clearly show an ideal, an ideal of no great reach. —Girls being offered a camel by an enamored boy, surf-riding girls with sun blisters.

---

[19] Huizinga, *Amerika levend en denkend*, 28.

The girl on the telephone. Remember! Keep that schoolgirl complexion. Palmolive. Always the half-sentimental type, presented as pure and healthy, a variation and refinement of what Ch. Dana Gibson launched thirty years ago. The public constantly sees a model of refinement far beyond its purse, ken and heart. Does it imitate this? Does it adapt itself to this?"[20] Apposite questions indeed. As in his reflections on processes of identification among film audiences, Huizinga again is aware of the problem of reception of the virtual worlds constantly spued forth by a relentless commercial mass culture. More generally, in these musings, Huizinga touched on the problem of the effect that media of cultural transmission, like film and advertising, would have on audiences not just in America but elsewhere as well. In these more general terms, the problem then becomes one of the way in which non-American audiences would read the phantasy worlds that an American imagination had produced and which showed all the characteristics of an American way with culture so vehemently indicted by European critics.

In conclusion to this section, let me point out one cruel irony. If in his later writings Huizinga would dwell on the problem of contemporary history changing, if not actually losing, form, under the combined impact of forces of mechanization, industrialization, and the advent of mass society, he may, in spite of his sophistication and open-mindedness, have missed one crucial way in which people's sense of history was changing. Under the impact of precisely those media of mass communication that Huizinga had subtly explored, rather than ignoring or rejecting them out of hand as so many of his fellow cultural critics were wont to do, the mass of his contemporaries were beginning to furnish their historical imaginations with the ingredients of virtual phantasy worlds rather than the stuff that history used to be made of. What to Huizinga and other like-minded intellectuals may have been a mere epiphenomenon, hiding real historical forces from view, would provide the markers of history to generations growing up in the second half of our century.

American mass culture and our changing sense of history

Three vignettes to set the stage for our discussion. All three are taken from European films. Each represents a formative moment, if not an epiphany, in the lives of the films' protagonists. In each, it is America that provides the ingredients for these moments of revelation. Dramatically, these moments serve as epic concentrations, condensing into a single moment what normally is a continuing process of identity formation. The first example is from Jacques Tati's 1949 film, *Jour de fête*, the second from Alan Parker's *The Commitments*, released in 1991, and the third from Bernard Tavernier's *Around Midnight*, which came out in 1986.

---

[20] J. Huizinga, *Amerika Dagboek: 14 April—19 June, 1926* (Amsterdam: Uitgeverij Contact, 1993), 93.

In *Jour de fête* Tati satirized the modern obsession with speed, presenting it as a peculiarly American obsession, but one which was highly contagious. In later work, like *Mon oncle*, he would satirize other American infatuations, like the love of gadgets, labor-saving devices, automation and remote control. There he would show it as it had already invaded France, providing French appetites for a life of ostentation and invidious distinction with the snob value of American contraptions. Interestingly, in his *Jour de fête*, he would show us the moment of contagion. The protagonist of the film, a French provincial postman, at one point is shown peeking through a crevice in the canvass of a big tent. Inside a film is shown dealing with speedy American postal techniques involving virtuoso time-saving feats. The feats themselves are satirically transformed into nonsensical dare-devil acts of motorized mail delivery men jumping through hoops of fire, and of airplanes dropping mailbags which are picked up by postmen on motorbikes driving at full speed. Never mind. Many of the propaganda films shown in Europe under Marshall aid auspices and meant to instill a sense of American efficiency in the minds of Europeans, may well have been perceived and remembered as equally fantastic. In fact, what we see we see vicariously, as if through the eyes of our astounded postman. The images shown to us may well be the product of his eager imagination rather than conveying anything in the actual documentary film. Later hilarious sequences then show the way in which Tati's postman has creatively adopted the American model, adapting his bicycle delivery act, while experiencing a new mail (male?) identity.

The other two film vignettes are variations on this theme of Europeans looking in from the outside, undergoing a culture shock, while experiencing it as a moment of conversion. In Bertrand Tavernier's film it is the encounter of a young Frenchman with American jazz in the late 1940s. Unable to afford the price of admission to a Paris jazz club where one of his cultural heroes is playing, we see him hunched outside a window, literally eavesdropping on a world of meaningful sounds, coded messages from an enticing, but far-away culture. As it happens, he manages to get in touch with the revered musician, recasting his own life into a mission of support and protection of the drug-ravaged career of his tragic hero. In Alan Parker's *The Commitments* another musical encounter makes for a moment of epiphany. A group of poor Irish boys is casting about for a musical form that would allow them to express their working-class sense of themselves. Much of the American pop music that blared from radios in Ireland they critically rejected as irrelevant to their quest. But at one point, early in the story, they are watching James Brown on television do his trade-mark soul act. When the show is over the leader of this small group instantly translates the experience into terms relevant to the lives they lead in Ireland. "We have to become like him. He is like us. The Irish are the blacks of Europe, the Dubliners are the blacks of Ireland,and we Northenders are the blacks of Dublin. Say it once and say it loud: we are black and we are proud." In disbelief his friends silently repeat the last words, their lips moving to form the words of the punch line. We are black and we are proud. Slowly the message sinks in. Yet another appropriation of American culture has taken place, affecting the sense of identity of these youngsters. They are cast in the role of celebrants in a ritual of cultural conversion.

These moments of voluntary affiliation with American life styles and cultural models are a recurring feature of postwar European cultural production, in film, on television, and in literature. The three examples that I gave should be seen as only a sample of this larger body. A more comprehensive study would be of interest for two reasons. They would give us a sense of the many settings in which these critical encounters with American culture took place. They are like moments of remembrance as everyone growing up in postwar Europe will have them. They are the condensed memorable versions of the more continuing exposure to American culture that Europeans have all experienced. When taken together they are like an album of vignettes vividly illustrating the ongoing process not only of the forms of reception of American culture, but also of its selective appropriation, which is to say of the ways in which American culture was redefined and made to serve the cultural needs of Europeans. Settings of reception, defined in such terms as class, age, gender, or ethnicity, then become the crucial focus for analysis.

Whatever the precise setting, it was always a matter of people finding themselves relatively at the margin of established mainstream cultural modes and molds, people who were not, or not yet, fully integrated into these dominant conventional forms. American culture, as they read it, provided them with alternatives of non-conventionality, informality, and a sense of freedom of choice, all in marked contrast to cultural conventions they were expected to make their own.

If this would be one reason to create our album of vignettes, there is a second one. In cultural studies the exploration of the process of reception, or of cultural consumption, is a nut devilishly hard to crack. Whatever area of mass cultural production one takes, whether it is world's fairs, film, television soap operas, or literary forms like the romance, we are always dealing with mass audiences consuming these products. It is one thing to explore the programmatic strategies of the organizers and producers of such forms of mass culture, it is a totally different thing actually to gauge what the audience chooses to get out of them. Interesting response studies have been done in these areas, such as of housewives watching soaps, or of readers reading romances. But the larger the issue becomes, as in the case of the European postwar reception of American mass culture, the more formidable are the problems of how to study the process of reception. That is where a study of vignettes as I have suggested them above might play a role.

After all, as narrative moments in stories told by Europeans, they are like second-order evidence of the reception of American culture. They tell stories of reception. They are recycled, or reconstructed, moments meant to convey remembrances of critical encounters with American culture. In that sense they are explicit indications of a process of reception. As such they are more open to research than questions of first-order reception. It is harder to see someone eating a Hamburger in Paris as making a cultural statement, expressing an identity challenging established conventions, than it would be to interpret a narrative passage, in a film or a book, presenting Hamburger consumption in precisely the light of a cultural peripety, wilfully subverting European conventions of eating out. Or, for that matter, it would be harder to find proof of a direct, first-order American influence in Alan Parker's style of film-making than it would be to trace his awareness of such influences taking place. After all, he turns them into the stuff of narration himself. This much may be clear, then: if moments of the reception of American culture, presented in the dramatic light of moments of epiphany, have become a recurrent feature of European story-telling, they testify to a degree of self-conscious awareness of the American cultural impact which it would be unwise to neglect.

Condensed into single moments, points in time serving as *lieux de mémoire*, to use Pierre Nora's felicitous phrase, all vignettes of the reception of American culture in Europe highlight what has truly been an ongoing process. Whatever conversion moments Europeans may vividly remember, they have all been more continuously exposed to an environment of free-floating cultural signifiers made in America. Confronted with an ongoing stream of vistas of the good life, as carried by media such as film, advertisements, television, music videos, they have walked through a duplicate world of images as a continuing accompaniment to their lives. They never walked alone. Highly private as the consumption of American culture may have been, eavesdropping on AFN broadcasts late at night and against parental wishes, watching a Hollywood movie, or shutting out one's environment through the use of a Walkman, yet the cultural products that made for such private moments were at the same time consumed by many others, constituting a mass audience. These private moments, then, may well be seen as forms of collective behavior typical of contemporary mass societies. The very fact that the private consumption of mass culture is necessarily shared with many others gives mass culture its paradoxical quality of setting the public stage, giving an era its particular cultural flavor. Reminiscing, individual people become aware that they share similar cultural memories with others. They are able to reconstruct the feel of years past, evoking moments of cultural consumption that it turns out they shared with others. Everyone knows the exhilarating moments discovering that others enjoyed the same film or rock song one thought one had enjoyed privately. There is the sudden sense of a joint return to a past that briefly comes to life again. That is why we now find Archie Bunker's chair, the throne of a world that he so masterfully commanded, exhibited in the Museum of American History. Taken from the fictional world of a television series, it has entered the real world of historical artefacts. It serves as a trigger to awaken the historical experience of a generation that collectively enjoyed, and vicariously spent part of their lives, in a world entirely imaginary.

In that sense modern mass culture, much of it in an American mold, has given our sense of history a particular coating. If Huizinga bemoaned the fact that history as he conceived of it was losing form, and escaped his capacity to recognize patterns of coherence and meaning, he must have been unaware of contemporary mass culture giving our sense of history this new coat. As a shared repertoire of recollections, allowing people to call forth an image of their own collective past, the mass cultural mold of an era is certainly a new form that history has assumed. It serves people as a switch that allows them to connect private memories with public memories. More importantly, as in neural networks, such recollections often connect to historical events of a more traditional nature. If, for instance, in the years following World War II, most strongly so in the 1950s, there was a marked reconstitution of the domestic sphere, in the context of the rapid sub-urbanization of the United States, these were large-scale, and anonymous forcesof social change that it would be hard for historians to render in vivid forms of historical narrative. Huizinga, for one, would have felt at a loss, using the traditional tools of his craft, to come up with narrative forms tellingly catching these processes. Yet, as he himself surmised in some of his musings concerning mass culture, the story of America's return to domesticity found its narrative forms precisely at that level. As it is, the process of social change was accompanied, if not actively promoted, by a host of Hollywood movies and television productions centering on the family home, presented as the "natural" setting for the way that Americans structured their private lives. Collectively they set the cultural tone and gave the cultural feel to an era. To the extent that Americans now remember the era, it is by means of these mass-cultural representations. To the extent that Europeans remember the era, it is doubly vicarious: not only did these films and television programs allow them to look in on American family life, they also provided European audiences with views of the good life, of single family homes, cars in the drive-way, "American kitchens," and of husbands happily returning to the family fold. "Honey, I'm home!"

We all, it is my contention, remember such historical configurations through the images that the mass media brought right to our homes, and which are now the stuff of our historical memory. But there are additional ways in which mass culture mediates and shapes contemporary history. It is not only a matter of fictional representations, as in film or television sitcoms, that imaginatively reflect and capture the social and cultural trends of an era. Much of what actually happens in terms of the day-to-day events that make up the daily news, and that are conventioally seen as the real stuff of history, now reach us almost instantly through the modern mass media, in the form of newspaper photographs, or television news flashes. Some of these images gain an iconic status, recapitulating an event in ways that leave an indelible imprint on our minds, as if on an etcher's plate. Often such images start leading their own lives, serving as summary recapitulations of recent history. And given America's centrality in the history of the post-World War II world, given also its central position in communication networks spanning the globe, America not only was centrally involved in many events making up recent history, it was also a central provider of images representing these events. To the extent that they acquire iconic status, they pop up time and time again. There is, to give just one example, the case of Nick Ut's photograph of napalmed Vietnamese children running in terror towards the eye of his camera. Many, in the United States and Europe, vividly remember the photograph. And interestingly, not unlike Archie Bunker's chair coming home to a museum of history, the photograph was able to spawn its own afterlife as a factor of newsworthy history. Having become an emblem of the atrocities of the Vietnam War, it remained at the same time the picture of an individual girl in pain, creating an interest in her individual fate. In the Fall of 1996, on Veteran's Day, the public's reading of the photograph suddenly moved from the emblematic to the personal. The girl in the photograph re-appeared on the stage of history as a woman of flesh and blood, individualized, no longer solely an icon. On Veteran's Day she came to a ritual of remembrance at the Vietnam War monument in Washington, DC, offering forgiveness.[21] A new meaning was added to an icon of mass culture that had long allowed us to give shape and form to our understanding of the Vietnam War. Yet, as a bitter irony, our empathy with this one victim of the war would never have been awakened, had she not first led the life in our collective memories as an emblem, through the mediating role of an iconic photograph. Many like her, similarly victims of the war, will forever remain faceless and nameless, and will never draw our collective attention.

There are yet other ways in which the coat of mass cultural memory is used to recreate the past. They resemble the ways in which the reception of American mass culture is recycled into individual vignettes, into those single moments of conversion that I talked about before. They are like a second-order, conscious use of the mass-cultural coat of history for the reconstruction of historical events. Again, the Vietnam War may offer apposite illustrations of what I have in mind. Surely, Vietnam War movies in their own right are mass-cultural products adding to the sediment that mass culture leaves on our sense of history. Trying to evoke images of the Vietnam War, we often do so with the help of Hollywood's attempts at rendering the war. Nor does Hollywood shrink from adding iconic heroes to our store of recollections, for instance in the form of Rambo as a latter-day raging Roland. Yet the very way in which many of these films go about taking us back to the historical event is through the use of collectively remembered mass-cultural products of the era. The music of the Rolling Stones and the Doors in Francis Ford Coppola's *Apocalypse Now* trigger historical connections in the minds of contemporary audiences. Similarly, the heart-rending finale of Michael Cimino's *The Deerhunter* has the remaining protagonists join in the singing, with voices wavering, of Irving Berlin's *God Bless America*. For the re-assertion of their mutual bonds, grieving over those they have lost, they use a popular song richly evocative of their larger bonds with America. Yet, tellingly, European audiences were strongly moved as well because they vicariously shared the musical repertoire and its associative force. Barry Levinson, in his *Good Morning, Vietnam,* made this connecting strategy the central ploy of his narrative. The high point of his film, of a wellnigh transcendent force, is his combined use of various tools from the realm of mass culture. In a sequence following Robin Williams's announcement of just another song in his radio program for the American forces in Vietnam, we hear the voice of Louis Armstrong singing "What a wonderful world." Accompanying the lyrics there is a jumble of images of the Vietnam war as any prime-time television news from Vietnam would show these. Yet the structural logic of the sequence does not only resemble television news flashes. It is at the same time structurally similar to the standard music video, more often than not equally a jumble of images made coherent only by the accompanying sound track. Ironically, the clip from the film became a hit as a music

---

[21] See the report by Jan Scruggs, "A child of war forgives ... "*New York Times*, November 11, 1996.

video, following the release of the film, and disseminated worldwide through MTV, an American pop music channel. Merging the evocative force of Armstrong's voice with the hodge-podge logic of television footage into something which clearly appeals to our familiarity with music videos, Levinson manages to use all these mass-cultural triggers to produce a moment of transcendence, a bitter comment on the horror of the war. It makes us sit back and reflect, in spite of what prewar critics of American mass culture had argued in their mood of cultural pessimism.

Were these critics alive today, what would they have to say to these new forms that now play a role in shaping our sense of the past? Many undoubtedly would have seen it as the ultimate victory of a cultural inversion they had been the first to see as typically American, an inversion that replaces reality with its fake representations. From Georges Duhamel and Simone de Beauvoir to more recent observers of American culture like Jean Baudrillard and Umberto Eco the language may have changed from the straightforward invective to more esoteric formulae like *simulacrum* or *hyperreality*, the diagnosis remains essentially the same. They all come up with their own variations on the old Marxian theme of false consciousness. A man like Huizinga too might have been reluctant to see present-day forms of historical awareness as worthy replacements of the historiographic forms whose decline and ultimate demise he observed or foresaw. Yet he may have come closest to an historiographic perspective that has been gaining adherence in recent decades. His almost sociological sense of the role and function of rituals, ceremonies, and public spectacles in late medieval Europe, his keen sense also of the role that modern mass media played in providing frameworks for identification and self-definition to mass audiences, took him to the threshold of an epistemological seachange in the historiography of collective consciousness. Huizinga would have had no quarrel with a current relativism that sees collective identities, of nations, of ethnic groups, of regional cultures, as just so many constructions. Precisely the invented rituals of celebrating and memorializing such identities he would have recognized as dramatic forms of history that he himself had studied. Yet he may have disagreed as to the implied voluntarism of this perspective and its attribution of historic agency. In Huizinga's case in fact the agency rested with historians. It was they who shaped history into larger narrative forms. Much current historiography, however, places the agency in history itself and explores it in terms of group strategies, struggles for cultural hegemony, and the invention of rituals meant to rally people around strategic readings of their collective identity.

This takes us back to a problem I raised earlier. Exploring the strategic agency behind the formation of group identities and frameworks for identification is one thing. But there is always the further question as to why, at the level of individual reception and appropriation of the rival constructions, people opt for particular readings of their collective identity. How do we explore the meanings and significance, at the point of reception, of such rival appeals? What messages and representations of reality do people store and digest to render meaningful life histories? As I argued before, the mass cultural setting of our contemporary life is a powerful ingredient in these individual constructions. Yet at the same time, as a setting that individuals have shared with countless others, it also provides them with a language of remembrance that they share with others. If, to quote Carl Becker, everyone is his own historian, we have to go down to the level of individual historical awareness and try to fathom the sense of meaningful history at that level. It may be highly private, yet at the same time as a private construction it draws on repertoires widely shared with contemporaries.

If indeed mass cultural products, produced and disseminated under American auspices, do function as the markers of time and the moulders of the collective historical recollections not only of Americans but of Europeans as well, we need to make one further point. The sense of history as I have explored it here is necessarily of a transient nature. It applies only to history as a shared experience, remembered collectively. As generations succeed each other on the stage of history, there is unavoidably a point in the past beyond which this repertoire of shared memories cannot stretch, a point following them like a ship's back wash. A century hence none of the markers of time and triggers of historical recollection, as I have explored them here, will be operative any more. Does that mean that our history for future historians will be just like any other and older stage of history? Undoubtedly, the feel that our recent history has to us who lived through it will be beyond retrieval. Yet the mass-cultural coating of our age will be there for later historians as a necessary resource. Much like cultural historians of our day and age they can return to films, recorded television programs, music, with a view to exploring their force in moulding and reflecting collective identities.

Today, at any rate, the challenge to study the mass-cultural coat of our age is eagerly taken on by contemporary historians. When they are involved in the production of television documentaries about recent historic episodes they consciously draw on the repertoires of mass culture produced at the time. Thus, in the celebrated PBS/BBC series on the Great Depression, historic footage of farmers losing their farms is followed by a clip of Betty Boop, with the narrator reminding us: "Even Betty Boop lost her farm." The soundtrack sets the tone for recollection playing the iconic musical reflection of the mood of the time: "Brother, can you spare a dime?" Other footage shows us Busby Berkeley choreographies, such as the celebrated "Remember my forgotten man." Not only do these ingredients take us back to mass culture popular at the time, more specifically it makes us aware that mass culture at its best is able to reflect the pressing concerns of a period. There are many more instances of this increased awareness among historians of the mass cultural forms of history. In search of audiences that want to see their personal histories displayed, books, special exhibits, and, yes, entire museums are now devoted to the everyday lives of common people, showing the advent of mass cultural products into their homes, work, leisure time pursuits, and so on. If mass culture has provided people with the rituals and ceremonies for the public display of their collective identities, its time has now come to be displayed in its own right.

LOCALIZING THE SUBLIME:
CONCEPTS OF CULTURE IN GERMANY AND THE UNITED STATES

Klaus J. Milich

I

Some years ago, *San Francisco Chronicle* columnist Gerald Nachman wondered why American opera fans would put up with a libretto as "silly and sentimental" as Rossini's *Barber of Seville*. Nachman concluded "that it must be the American reverence for all things European and our tendency to take for granted all things quintessentially American. I thought we were over that but it's too ingrained; we're patriotic about everything but our art." Lawrence Levine furthered Nachman's argument "that Americans, long after they declared their political independence, retained a colonial mentality in matters of culture and intellect."[1]

Reiterating the long tradition of laments about the supposedly impoverished soil of American culture, Levine's and Nachman's notion of America's "colonial mentality" and "reverence for all things European" builds upon a binary opposition that designates Europe as the universal subject of culture, intellect and critical reason while the United States is seen as a cultural desert prone to philistine utilitarianism and mere operational thought. This dichotomy could be translated into the more scholarly distinction between culture and civilization. In his "Remarks on a Redefinition of Culture" Herbert Marcuse revisited this polarity, according to which "culture" refers to some higher dimensions of human autonomy and fulfillment, while "civilization" designates the realm of necessity, of socially necessary work and behavior, where man is not really himself and in his own element but is subject to heteronomy, to external conditions and needs. [...] In its prevailing form and direction, progress of this civilization calls for operational and behavioral modes of thought, for acceptance of the productive rationality of the given social systems, for their defense and improvement, but not for their negation. And the content [...] of the higher culture was to a great extent precisely this negation: indictment of the institutionalized destruction of human potentialities, commitment to a hope which the established civilization denounced as "utopian." To be sure, the higher culture always had an affirmative character inasmuch as it was divorced from the toil and misery of those who by their labor reproduced the society whose culture it was--and to that degree it became the ideology of the society. But as ideology, it was also dissociated

---

[1] Gerald Nachman, "Take All You Want off the Top, Figaro," *San Francisco Chronicle Datebook*, October 4, 1987, quoted in Lawrence W. Levine, *Highbrow/Lowbrow. The Emergence of Cultural Hierarchy in America* (Cambridge/London: Harvard UP, 1986), 1.

from the society, and in this dissociation it was free to communicate the contradiction, the indictment, and the refusal.[2]

In his famous study on *The Civilizing Process*, Norbert Elias describes both spheres in a similar way, though with less contempt for civilization. For Elias, the concept expresses the self-consciousness of the West. In its overall meaning it sums up everything in which Western society believes itself superior to earlier or "primitive" contemporary societies, or what constitutes the West's special character and what it is proud of: "the level of *its* technology, the nature of *its* manners, the development of *its* scientific knowledge or view of the world." Insofar, however, as Elias differentiates between the English and French use of the word, on the one hand, and the German meaning of civilization, on the other, the culture-civilization dichotomy not only becomes a relevant issue in comparing the Anglo-American and German concepts of culture. It seems worthwhile to discern the impact of the different meanings of culture and civilization upon our notions of culture defined as either modern or postmodern.

According to Elias, in English and French "civilization" sums up in a single term the pride in the significance of national contributions to the progress of the West and of mankind, whereas in Germany "*Zivilisation* means something which is indeed useful, but nevertheless only a value of the second rank, comprising only the outer appearance of human beings, the surface of human existence."[3]

The French and English concept of civilization can refer to political or economic, religious or technical, moral or social facts. The German concept of *Kultur* refers essentially to intellectual, artistic, and religious facts, and has a tendency to draw a sharp dividing line between facts of this sort, on the one side, and political, economic, and social facts, on the other. To a certain extent, the concept of civilization plays down the national differences between peoples; it emphasizes what is common to all human beings or—in the view of its bearers—should be. It expresses the self-assurance of peoples whose national boundaries and national identity have for centuries been so fully established that they have ceased to be the subject of any particular discussion, peoples which have long expanded outside their borders and colonized beyond them. In contrast, the German concept of *Kultur* places special stress on national differences and the particular identity of groups; primarily by virtue of this, it has acquired in such fields as ethnological and anthropological research a significance far beyond the German linguistic area and the situation in which the concept originated. But that situation is the situation of a people which, by Western standards, arrived at political unification and consolidation only very late, and from whose boundaries, for centuries and even down to the present, territories have again and again crumbled away or threatened to crumble away. Whereas the concept of civilization has the function of giving expression to the continuously expansionist tendency of colonizing groups, the concept of *Kultur* mirrors the self-consciousness of a nation which had constantly to seek out and constitute its boundaries anew, in a political as well as a spiritual sense, and again and again had to

---

[2] Herbert Marcuse, "Remarks on a Redefinition of Culture," *Deadalus*, 1 (1965), 190-207; 192-193.
[3] Norbert Elias, *The Civilizing Process. The History of Manners* (1936) (New York: Urizen, 1978), 4.

ask itself: "What is really our identity?" The orientation of the German concept of culture, with its tendency toward demarcation and the emphasis on and detailing of differences between groups, corresponds to this historical process. The questions "What is really French? What is really English?" have long since ceased to be a matter of much discussion for the French and English. But for centuries the question "What is really German?" has not been laid to rest. One answer to this question—one among others— lies in a particular aspect of the concept of *Kultur*.[4]

Since the Enlightenment the culture-civilization dichotomy has been the basis of an inherent antagonism that splits modernity into a cultural sphere of modernism and the social and technological process of modernization. Arising from this polarity, modernity's intrinsic discord was not only echoed in the split between the humanities and the natural sciences known as the "two cultures controversy"; it also served as a geopolitical unconscious which engendered each other's notions on both sides of the Atlantic: Europe, and Germany in particular, as the place of culture and modernism; the United States as the place of civilization and modernization, which in a way sounds as if the "two cultures debate" between C.P. Snow and F.R. Leavis or T.H. Huxley and M. Arnold has been put on the national agenda.[5]

The emphasis on American civilization and modernization and the denial of a distinctive American culture has been compensated by a discourse of the sublime that cloaked manual work, operational thought, social progress and technological innovation with divine sanction. The natural resources and historical conditions under which the exalting process of civilization and modernization could flourish in the United States helped solidify and circulate the notion of an "exceptionalism" that not only seemed to indemnify the United States in matters of culture and intellect, but conveyed a collective sentiment of ultimate emancipation from and even superiority over Europe in a variety of fields. Although the American sublime drew heavily on European ideas in the fine arts, in literature and philosophy, it acquired a specific function of legitimizing America's historical uniqueness and moral superiority which in the end was not more than a European-American contest of culture versus civilization. Since American postmodernity tried to overcome this very dichotomy upon which the idea of an American sublime was based, it seems pertinent to discern both the specific function of the sublime and the particularities of American postmodernity.

Within the discourse of postmodernity, geopolitical parameters engendering transatlantic cultural differences arising from deviating meanings and historical

---

[4] Elias, 4-6.

[5] For the "two cultures controversy" cf. Charles Percy Snow, "The Two Cultures and the Scientific Revolution" (1959). *The Two Cultures and a Second Look*. Rede Lecture, Cambridge University. 5. ed.. (New York: New American Library: 1963); Frank Raymond Leavis, "Two Cultures? The Significance of C.P. Snow." *Richmond Lectures* (London: Chatto und Windus: 1962); Lionel Trilling, "The Leavis-Snow Controversy" (1962). *Beyond Culture. Essays on Literature and Learning* (New York: Viking, 1968); Matthew Arnold, "Literature and Science" (1882). *Philistinism in England and America. Complete Prose Works of Matthew Arnold*, ed. by Robert Henry Super. Vol. 10. (Ann Arbor: University of Michigan Press, 1974)

functions of terms like culture, civilization, modernity or the sublime seem to disappear in the sphere of an encompassing postmodern global economy. Rob Wilson, for example, claims that the American sublime "will have to be refigured, within a postmodern economy, to imagine forth and represent America as an entity of transnational cyberspace that 'knows no national boundaries, feels no geographic constraints'." Wilson argues that globalization will happen at the superstructural level of cultural production,

> as transnational corporations emerge, amalgamate, transform, flow, and exchange signs and profits across tired nation-state boundaries and grow oblivious to cultural or ideological distinctions that once inspired allegiance. Passing out of nation-state modernity and Fordist modes of massive industrial accumulation, the United States is fast entering a more fluid world of transnational incorporation.[6]

Wilson quotes Jacques Attali's model of totalizing postmodernization, arguing that "the world is becoming an ideologically homogeneous market where life is being organized around common consumer desires, whether or not those desires can be fulfilled."[7] Assuming, however, that any "given" or "natural" characteristics would already legitimize labels like postmodernity or modernity as descriptive terms, I would argue with Niklas Luhmann that essentialist uses of the terms are misleading:

> The discussion about modern or postmodern society operates on the semantic level. In it, we find many references to itself, many descriptions of descriptions, but hardly any attempt to take realities into account on the operational and structural level of social communications. Were we to care for realities, we would not see any sharp break between a modern and a postmodern society ...
> We may call this modern or postmodern society. The question is rather whether it makes any sense to use a historical distinction to mark the problem. The distinction of before and after will not prove to be very helpful. Like the rhetorical scheme of *antiqui/moderni* in the Middle Ages and the Renaissance, it is a scheme to organize second-order descriptions. It shares the weakness of all indications and distinctions so far. Society can describe itself as modern or as postmodern, but if it does so, what is the information? What is the difference that makes the difference?[8]

Elaborating on the premise that cultural terminology operates within the dialectics of global and local connotations, and hence unfolds different semantic fields according to the historical, social and political contexts in which specific terms appear, I would argue that the notion of postmodern globalization cannot do away with national discourses inscribed in cultural concepts and engendering the specific meanings and functions of terms like postmodernity, modernity and the romantic concept of the sublime. Against the common perception of the world as a postmodern global village, my basic argument here is that while Europe, and in particular German culture, defines itself along modern ideas, U.S. American culture has come into its own by discarding modern paradigms.

---

[6] Rob Wilson, "Techno-euphoria and the Discourse of the American Sublime," *National Identities and Post-Americanist Narratives*, ed. by Donald E. Pease (Durham/ London: Duke UP, 1994), 209.

[7] Jacques Attali, "The European Bank for Reconstruction and Development," *Vital Speech*, 57 (May 1, 1991), 422.

[8] Niklas Luhmann, "Why Does Society Describe Itself as Postmodern?" *Cultural Critique*, 30 (Spring 1995), 171, 183.

I will argue that with the emergence of postmodernity in the 1960s, the United States developed a concept of culture which by contesting European notions of modernity has begun to critically account for the specific course of American history. This critique, which in the course of postmodernity initially concerned itself with debates over high versus popular culture as part of modernity's inherent antagonism, has now extended to more contemporary clashes about the asymmetries between national and cultural identity in the context of the multicultural or postcolonial debate, feminism and cultural difference in general.

Thus, since I understand postmodernity as a historical signifier which in the United States has replaced a specific concept of modernity through which particularly German culture has tried to come to terms with *its* political, social, historical and philosophical traditions, I want to address postmodernity not as a universal term meant to overcome modernity as an equally global and totalizing category, but as a marker, by which the United States has gradually set itself off against "continental" conceptions of culture.

II

The American sublime has long operated under three key emblems which fostered the notion of American civilization and modernization: nature, technology, and democracy. To David Nye, the North American continent alone (not to speak of technological innovation or social and political progress) already

> possesses every feature that a theory of the natural sublime might require, including mountains, deserts, frozen wastes, endless swamps, vast plains, the Great Lakes, and hundreds of unusual sights, notably Yellowstone, Mammoth Cave, Niagara Falls, and the Grand Canyon. Likewise, its tornadoes, hurricanes, floods, and other natural disasters are among the most terrifying phenomena one could encounter anywhere. It would be tempting to say that had no theory of the sublime existed, Americans would have been forced to invent one.[9]

Hence, throughout the eighteenth and nineteenth century the sublime centered around a particular representation of landscape which identified and accommodated the emergence of the United States as a geopolitical power of international status. As a foundational scene of American appropriation and continental expansion the landscape widely circulated among painters of the Hudson River School and served—though often with great ambivalence—as a leitmotif in the literature of the American Renaissance.[10] But the landscape not only provided the "neutral territory" of romance that Nathaniel Hawthorne made emblematic of American literature.[11] The vast spectacle of nature also

---

[9] David E. Nye, *American Technological Sublime* (Cambridge/London: MIT Press, 1994), 1

[10] Bob Wilson, "Techno-euphoria and the Discourse of the American Sublime," *National Identities and Post-Americanist Narratives*, edited by Donald E. Pease, Durham/ (London: Duke UP, 1994), 205.

[11] Hawthorne opens his Preface to *The House of the Seven Gables* (1851) by saying that "when a writer calls his work a Romance, it need hardly be observed that he wishes to claim a certain latitude, both as to its fashion and material, which he would not have felt himself entitled to assume, had he professed to be

induced politicians to turn the cultivation of the wilderness into a sublime national task that would account for the superiority of America's progressive civilization which distinguished the United States from Europe. In 1847 George Perkins Marsh, for example, declared before the Rutland Country Agricultural Society that America was "the first example of the struggle between civilized man and barbarous uncultivated nature." While elsewhere the earth was subdued slowly, he continued, in America for the first time "the full energies of advanced European civilization, stimulated by its artificial wants and guided by its accumulated intelligence, were brought to bear at once on a desert continent."[12]

The landscape, which according to Leo Marx has for a long time functioned "as a master image embodying American hopes" to ground manifest destiny in the immanence of nature, was soon succeeded by another "fulcrum of national power." Against the backdrop of the United States's transformation from an agricultural community into an industrial society, the "rhetoric of the technological sublime" replaced the pastoral image.[13] Not nature itself, but the cultivation and exploitation of nature became the source of value which by the end of the nineteenth century advanced the belief that "the seat of energy has migrated from Europe to America." "The labors of successive generations of scientific men," Brooks Adams wrote in 1902, "have established a control over nature which has enabled the United States to construct a new industrial mechanism, with processes surpassingly perfect. Nothing has ever equaled in economy and energy the administration of the great American corporations."[14] What is striking is not only the control which man has acquired over nature through science, but also the control which America has gained over the world through economy:

> The West Indies drift toward us; the Republic of Mexico hardly longer has an independent life; and the city of Mexico is an American town. With the completion of the Panama Canal all Central America will become a part of our system. We have expanded into Asia, we have attracted the fragments of the Spanish dominions, and reaching out into China we have checked the advance of Russia and Germany, in territory which, until yesterday, had been supposed to be beyond our sphere. We are penetrating into Europe, and Great Britain especially is gradually assuming the position of a dependency, which must rely on us as the base from which she draws her food in peace and without which she could not stand in war.[15]

---

writing a Novel." Accordingly, Hawthorne asks his readers not "to assign an actual locality to the imaginary events of this narrative [and] trusts not to be considered as unpardonably offending, by laying out a street that infringes upon nobody's private rights, and appropriating a lot of land which had no visible owner, and building a house, of materials long in use for constructing castles in the air."

[12] George Perkins Marsh, quoted in Leo Marx, *The Machine in the Garden. Technology and the Pastoral Ideal in America* (London/New York: Oxford UP, 1964), 203f.

[13] Leo Marx, *The Machine in the Garden*, 159, 155. See also Howard Horwitz, "Sublime Possession, American Landscape," *By the Law of Nature: Form and Value in Nineteenth Century America* (London/New York: Oxford UP, 1991), 55.

[14] Brooks Adams, *The New Empire*, New York: Macmillan, 1902, quoted in Daniel Bell, "The End of American Exceptionalism," *The Winding Passage: Essays and Sociological Journeys, 1960-1980* (Cambridge: Cambridge UP, 1980), 247.

[15] Adams quoted in Bell, 248.

If Brooks Adams conceived of nature intertwined with applied science as the ultimate source for America's geopolitical and economic supremacy, it was particularly the steam-engine and the railroad which symbolized both territorial and industrial expansion in conjunction with economic and scientific progress. If "fear haunts the building railroad," Ralph Waldo Emerson already noted in September 1843, he left no doubt that it also "will be American power and beauty when it is done." Inflating the transformation of the pastoral into the technological sublime, Emerson helped soften the threat of capitalism and the deprivations of industrialization that the railroad workers had to endure by alluding to the exemplary course of history that distinguished America from other nations. In the case of the Irish immigrant labor he saw their "stern day's work of fifteen or sixteen hours, though deplored by all the humanity of the neighborhood" as a healthy antidote to rebellion: "These peaceful shovels," he continued, "are better than the pikes in the hands of these Kernes."[16]

The land has not only been a shaping element for pastoral and technological icons but has also been constitutive for the development of the third emblem of the American sublime: democracy. From de Tocqueville to Fredrick Jackson Turner, it was strongly believed that the providential wealth of a virgin continent not only evoked unsurpassed technical and economic progress, but also social progress that made the United States exceptional among the world's nations. The "errand into wilderness" seems to have recompensated America with a democratic system that grew out of a confrontation with and cultivation of nature. Reiterating his famous frontier thesis, Fredrick Jackson Turner wrote in 1903 that "American democracy was born of no theorist's dream ... [but] came out of the forest and it gained strength each time it touched a new frontier." For Turner, American democracy was the product of the physical environment inasmuch as he conceived of the frontier as the shaping element of the American character. For him, frontier democracy was as natural to America as liberalism was for Louis Hartz. The United States, which did not have to endure a democratic revolution, has "presented the world with the peculiar phenomenon, not of a frustrated middle class, but of a 'frustrated aristocracy'," as Hartz opens his list of historical factors and ideologies underlying the myth of American exceptionalism: "The nonfeudal world in which Americans lived shaped every aspect of their social thought: it gave them a frame of mind that cannot be found anywhere in the eighteenth century, or in the wider history of modern revolutions." A society, which began with and Americanized Locke, remains faithful to him by virtue of an absolute and irrational attachment and "becomes indifferent to the challenge of socialism in the later era as it was unfamiliar with the heritage of feudalism in the earlier one." Socialism, as Hartz defines it, "is largely an ideological phenomenon, arising out of the principles of class and the revolutionary liberal revolt against them which the old European order inspired. It is not accidental that America which has uniquely lacked a feudal tradition has uniquely lacked also a socialist tradition. The hidden origin of socialist thought everywhere in the West is to be found in the feudal

---

[16] Ralph Waldo Emerson, *Selections from Ralph Waldo Emerson*, ed. by Stephen E. Whicher, (Boston: Houghton Mifflin, 1957, 1960), 221.

ethos. The *ancien régime* inspires Rousseau; both inspire Marx."[17] But no matter whether American democracy grew out of nature or—as an act of will—emerged from a "revolution that never had to happen," as Richard Hofstadter once put it,[18] American democracy has been considered exceptional and unique and thus been able to become a sublime image that affected American culture in a variety of fields.

Differentiating between the "European novel" and an "American romance," for example, literary critics turned the discourse of uniqueness and the sublime into a distinctive feature of American literature. While Henry James, for instance, still complained about the lack of a "complex social machinery to set a writer in motion," Richard Chase, Lionel Trilling, and many other proponents of the romance thesis thought[19] that the ostensible cultural deficiency "has proved most fertile to the American imagination," as Amy Kaplan phrased it:

> In the richly textured social world of the European novel, Chase argued, characters develop in relation to entrenched institutions and the struggle between classes. The isolated hero of the American romance, in contrast, embarks on melodramatic relations and unfettered by the pressure of social restraints. As his title suggests, Chase was deliberately establishing a national alternative to F.R. Leavis's *The Great Tradition* of English novelists from Jane Austen to George Eliot, Henry James, and Joseph Conrad. Where the 'great tradition' seeks order through the reconciliation of the individual and society, the American tradition, from *Wieland* to *The Sound of the Fury*, explores the open-ended states of individual alienation and cosmic disorder.[20]

But not only Americans fueled the imagination of the sublime. The early European middle classes also contributed substantially to exalting American civilization and modernization. "In imagining a 'New World' that was better than the European 'Old World'," David Noble writes, they "created an 'America' in which *their* modern values of limitless economic resources and individual political liberty could be fulfilled."[21] These material aspirations were not only accompanied by intangible desires and hopes of those writers, artists and intellectuals who sought refuge in the United States against totalitarian political persecution; Donald Pease reminds us that "instead of experiencing American life as if it were an unsuccessful effort to remember Europe's past achievements," D.H. Lawrence "described Europe as a dying civilization in need of America's spirit of renewal:"

> By migrating to America Lawrence is only following in the steps of the great spirit of Western civilization itself, as it progressed from Rome to Europe then to America. By studying the classics in American literature, Lawrence aspired to embody the spirit of Europe's past in its living form. [...] So instead of emigrating to the Old World of Europe's past, as did his contemporaries Eliot and Pound,

---

[17] Louis Hartz, *The Liberal Tradition in America* (New York: Hartcourt Brace Jovanovich, 1955), 8, 6, 39.

[18] Richard Hofstadter, *The Progressive Historians* (New York: Alfred Knopf, 1968), 445.

[19] Richard Chase, *The American Novel and Its Tradition* (New York: Doubleday, 1957).

[20] Amy Kaplan, *The Social Construction of American Realism* (Chicago: Chicago University Press, 1988), 2.

[21] David Noble, "Revocation of the Anglo-Protestant Monopoly: Aesthetic Authority and the American Landscape," *Soundings* (Spring/Summer 1996), 149.

he migrated to a new world, the America that Europe had dreamed of in the past when her spirit needed revival but that had not yet been turned into a living reality.²²

Whereas the American transcendentalists and writers of the American Renaissance helped to circulate and solidify the pastoral and technological sublime, one could argue that the technological and democratic sublime—though again with great ambivalence— had its literary bards in writers of American realism. According to Winfried Fluck the realist novel served as a cultivating instrument by negotiating and circulating exemplary social practices appropriate to the Gilded Age. In accordance with Norbert Elias's definition of "civilization," Fluck reminds us that the American use of the term not only contains the idea of economic and technical progress but also moral progress. Compared to the rapid economic and technical expansion of nineteenth century America, however, "'civilization' in terms of an encompassing moral refinement" was still to come.²³ It was in the sphere of civilization, Fluck continues, that the realist novel both as cultural strategy and discursive practice had its primary function as moral regeneration. In contrast to the American Renaissance, which promoted eccentric figures living at the periphery of society, the realist novel focused on representative social characters. Insofar as Chase's romance thesis grew "full-blown out of the American soil to define the exceptional nature of American culture," and thus was based on the profoundly historical myth of "America as a classless society without internal ideological conflicts," Kaplan and Fluck object to the idea that "Americans do not write social fiction [...] which makes realism an anomaly" and thus "in effect, un-American."²⁴ Their theories of literary realism, therefore, have to be located in the wider context of a critique of American exceptionalism.

While indigenous American Studies since the 1930s have constructed a narrative which furthered and celebrated American exceptionalism and uniqueness, David Noble has argued, scholars in American Studies²⁵ were only able to construct this narrative by repressing the institution of slavery, the expulsion and expatriation of Native Americans, and the usurpation of the Northern half of Mexico in 1846.²⁶ While Noble directs his criticism on *early* American Studies, Günter Lenz reproaches the so-called "*new*

---

²² Donald E. Pease, *Visionary Compacts. American Renaissance Writings in Cultural Context*, (Madison: University of Wisconsin Press, 1987), 3-5. Pease refers to D.H. Lawrence's *Studies in Classic American Literature* (1923).

²³ Winfried Fluck, *Inszenierte Wirklichkeit: Der amerikanische Realismus 1865-1900*, (München: Wilhelm Fink Verlag, 1992), 78-79; my translation.

²⁴ Kaplan, *The Social Construction of American Realism*, 3-4.

²⁵ Noble mentions Perry Miller, F.O. Matthiessen, Henry Nash Smith, R.W.B. Lewis and Leo Marx.

²⁶ Noble draws on Amy Kaplan's essay "Left alone with America: The Absence of Empire in the Study of American Culture," *Cultures of the United States: Imperialism*, ed. Amy Kaplan and Donald Pease (Durham: Duke University Press, 1993) and her reading of Perry Miller's *Errand into Wilderness*. He argues that "by continuing to imagine an 'America' culturally separate from Europe many recent scholars in the United States have [not only] been able to ignore the ways in which post-colonial cultural theory can be used to illuminate the imperialism of the dominant culture in the United States," but sustain and further the myth of "American" exceptionalism and innocence as well as a bourgeois nationalism.

American Studies" with what he criticized as a "*new* exceptionalism."[27] Lenz argues that after the crisis of American studies in the 1960s and the productive decomposition of the field into a multiplicity of interdisciplinary programs like Women's and Ethnic studies,[28] even politically progressive scholars would now call again for a "new synthesis."

In contrast to the innovative and resourceful disintegration of American studies and its transformation into American culture studies, now with a focus on the multicultural dimensions of and cultural differences within U.S. American society, Lenz suggests that this call for a "new synthesis" entails not only a revival of totalizing perspectives, but also a sophisticated exceptionalism, which is sustained by two basic strategies:[29]

1. The sanitation of American history by redefining conflicting issues as mere rhetorics, as a civil war of competing discourses, diminishing the often habitual but nonetheless crucial triad race, class and gender to mere episodes of regionalism. These episodes are considered insignificant to the project of 'America' as a whole and hence non-constitutive to American cultural critique.
2. Sustaining the assumed uniqueness of United States history, critics of the 'New American Studies' insist that European critical theory and philosophy is inapplicable and thus superfluous to the analysis of the specific features of American society. Instead, their reappropriation of the Emersonian tradition is celebrated as the transcendence and unique accomplishment of European anti-systematic thinking.[30]

Both strategies, Lenz maintains, that is the deployment of transcendental philosophy to the secular predicaments of contemporary America and the transformation of conflicting issues into mere rhetorics, share a consonant dehistoricization and depoliticization of American culture and society.

---

[27] Günter H. Lenz, "Multicultural Critique and the New American Studies." Hans Bak, ed. *Multiculturalism and the Canon of American Culture*. Amsterdam: VU University Press, 1993. For a critique of a "new American exceptionalism" see also Günter H. Lenz and Heinz Ickstadt, "After Poststructuralism and Deconstruction. A New American Exceptionalism." Gerhard Hoffmann and Alfred Hornung, ed. *Affirmation and Negation in Contemporary American Culture* (Heidelberg: C. Einter, 1994). The term "New American Studies" has been coined by Philip Fisher, ed. *The New American Studies: Essays from Representations* (Berkelely: University of California Press, 1991).

[28] I. e. African-, Asian-, Hispanic-, Native-American studies.

[29] Lenz mentions philosopher Stanley Cavell, political scientist George Kateb and literary scholars like Sacvan Bercovitch, Walter Benn Michaels, Richard Poirier, and Phil Fisher, among others, who advocate this sophisticated American exceptionalism; cf. Stanley Cavell, *This New Yet Unapproachable America. Lectures After Emerson After Wittgenstein* (Albuquerque: Living Batch Press, 1989) and *Conditions Handsome and Unhandsome. The Constitution of Emersonian Perfectionism* (LaSalle: Open Court, 1990); George Kateb, "Thinking about Human Extinction (I). Nietzsche and Heidegger," *Raritan*, 6 (Fall 1986) and "Thinking about Human Extinction (II). Emerson and Whitman," *Raritan* 6. (Winter 1986); Richard Poirier, *The Renewal of Literature. Emersonian Reflections* (New York: Random House, 1987); Walter Benn Michaels, *The Gold Standard and the Logic of Naturalism* (Berkeley: University of California Press, 1987).

[30] Nietzsche, for example.

III

The transformation from modernity to postmodernity has been diagnosed in a variety of symptoms[31] and manifests itself in a plethora of post-plus compounds starting with post-avant-garde via post-Fordist, post-industrial, to post-Marxist, post-national, post-historical, post-feminist, and post-structuralist, to name only a few. The repertoire of reproaches that have been used, especially in Germany, to characterize postmodernity includes contradictory attributes such as anti-Enlightenment and radical-democratic as well as conservative and anarchist. Misusing Paul Feyerabend's plea for a greater variety of theories, the concept of postmodernity is often misunderstood not only in the sense of promoting an "anything goes" attitude. "Postmodernity" seems to be a useful "buzzword" (Dick Hebdige) or "passepartout-concept" (Wolfgang Welsch) for anything that has not yet been named but appears as a possible answer to the crisis of modernity and that has only been integrated into the journalistic and scientific vocabulary through traces of similarity.

The multiplicity of meanings arising from the semantics of the various academic and public discourses partaking in defining postmodernity also manifests itself in the origination of the term, a history which cannot be limited to mere etymology. Do the roots of postmodernity lie in German and French philosophy, for example with Nietzsche, Heidegger, or poststructuralism, or should they be sought in American literary criticism? The answer not only involves different disciplines, but also different geopolitical and cultural-historical contexts. Granting the fact that a variety of disciplines participate in the discourse of the postmodern, what are the criteria available for defining the term if all disciplines write their own history with its own specific breaks and epochs on the basis of the objects, methods, concepts, language, and correspondingly the episodes available to them. What ordering principles can act as the basis for an epoch that puts the catagories of its own historicity into question? What is the status of cultural and historical concepts in a time when the search for an Archimedean point from which the constant evolution of history and with it the break between the modern and the postmodern could be fixed is dismissed as being dated? What authority do such terms have in a time when modern meaning-producing discourses—often dismissed by postmodern critics as "arbitrary" fixings—have been dissolved and replaced by an apparent "postmodern randomness"–as modern critics argue?

In order to avoid confusion and arbitrariness in defining postmodernity, it has repeatedly been postulated that it must be made clear to which modernity the new term refers, especially since in the work of even a single author, a number of different concepts of modernity can be found. Lyotard sometimes construes modernity as the period beginning with the European Renaissance around 1500, that is with the shift from the ontological to the mental paradigm and thus from a philosophy of being to one of

---

[31] Cf. for example the long list of so-called postmodern symptoms which Dick Hebdige provides in his book *Hiding in the Light* (London: Comedia, 1988), 181-182.

consciousness. With this change, the existential legitimization of human beings was no longer grounded in metaphysics (that is, as God's creation), but instead grounded within man himself and his ability to think and doubt, and legitimated by his ability to control nature. In his programmatic work *The Postmodern Condition*, however, Lyotard defines the modern as the eighteenth century production of metanarratives (on the emancipation of mankind through science, rationality and reason in the *Enlightenment*; the teleology of mind and the hermeneutics of meaning in *Idealism*; the liberation from capitalist oppression through *Marxism*, and the promise of wealth and prosperity under *Capitalism*). His most well-known opponent in the debate, Jürgen Habermas, posits postmodernity as a turn away from the project of modernity, i. e. from Enlightenment ideals, especially a turn against the consensus-building and cathartic effect of reason which Habermas finds endangered by the alignment of "young conservative" anti-modernist theorists such as Derrida and Foucault with "old conservatives" and "new conservatives." "Old-conservative pre-modernists" such as Leo Strauss, Hans Jonas, and Robert Spaemann never caught on to cultural modernism, while "neo-conservative postmodernists" such as Daniel Bell and Arnold Gehlen greeted the development of modern science, if only to spur technological progress, capitalist growth and a rational administration, i.e. a one-sided technological-economic modernization. Through the eyes of Baudelaire and avant-garde art, Theodor W. Adorno saw the beginning of modernism in 1850. Grounded in Adorno's ideas, Hans Robert Jauß understood the postmodern as an attempt to break with aesthetic modernism of the nineteenth century. In contrast, the English architect Charles Jencks reads this break in opposition to the modernism of the twentieth century.[32] In the face of this long and diverse genealogy of the modern, Habermas introduced his vehement critique of postmodernity with the following, in Germany widely accepted summary of its predecessor:

> The word 'modern' in its Latin form 'modernus' was used for the first time in the late fifth century in order to distinguish the present, which had become officially Christian, from the Roman and pagan past. With varying content, the term 'modern' again and again expresses the consciousness of an epoch that relates itself to the past of antiquity, in order to view itself as the result of a transition from the old to the new.
> Some writers restrict this concept of 'modernity' to the Renaissance, but this is historically too narrow. People considered themselves modern during the period of Charlemagne in the twelfth century, as well as in France of the late seventeenth century at the time of the famous 'Querelle des Anciens et des Modernes.' That is to say, the term 'modern' appeared and reappeared exactly during those periods in Europe when the consciousness of a new epoch formed itself through a renewed relationship to the ancients—whenever, moreover, antiquity was considered a model to be recovered through some kind of imitation.
> The spell which the classics of the ancient world cast upon the spirit of later times was first dissolved with the ideals of the French Enlightenment. Specifically, the idea of being 'modern' by looking back to the ancients changed with the belief, inspired by modern science, in the infinite progress of knowledge and in the infinite advance towards social and moral betterment. Another form of modernist consciousness was formed in the wake of this change. The romantic modernist sought to oppose the antique ideals of the classicists; he looked for a new historical epoch and found it in the idealized Middle Ages. However, this new ideal age, established early in the nineteenth century, did not remain

---

[32] Cf. also Wolfgang Welsch, *Unsere postmoderne Moderne* (Weinheim: Acta humaniora, 1988), 47.

> a fixed ideal. In the course of the nineteenth century, there emerged out of this romantic spirit that radicalized consciousness of modernity which freed itself from all specific historical ties. This most recent modernism simply makes an abstract opposition between tradition and the present; and we are, in a way, still the contemporaries of that kind of aesthetic modernity which first appeared in the midst of the nineteenth century. Since then, the distinguishing mark of works which count as modern is 'the new' which will be overcome and made obsolete through the novelty of the next style.[33]

At the beginning of the twentieth century the historical distance between the modern and its respective predecessors had shrunk so dramatically that not only the modern concept itself became "classical"; the conceptualization of time reversed itself from a backward orientation into an "orientation toward the future," the "anticipation of an uncertain future," and the upgrading of "the transitory, the elusive and the ephemeral"—a change of perspective that expressed itself in the spatial metaphor of the vanguard or in an avant-garde venturing into unexplored areas.[34]

The manifold history of the concept of modernity shows that it can hardly serve as a point of reference for postmodernity. Nor does it make sense to distinguish the postmodern from the modern along political lines in terms of understanding literary modernism as a homogeneous phenomenon against postmodernism. Authors from a wide political spectrum such as Bertolt Brecht, Heinrich Mann and Henry Roth, but also Thomas Mann, William Faulkner and T.S. Eliot, are not comparable to the fascist and antisemitic affinities of Ezra Pound, Wyndham Lewis, Knut Hamsun and Gottfried Benn. Thus, the common attempt to distinguish the postmodern from the modern by a "right-left" schema is questionable insofar as it eventually turns against literary modernism itself.[35]

A further fracturing of modernism is apparent in the various categorizations of the relationship between modernism and the avant-garde. While both are commonly used in the United States as a synonym for progressive or experimental literature of the twentieth century, Peter Bürger limits the avant-garde to expressionism, dadaism, surrealism, Russian constructivism, futurism, and agitprop. For him, these already historical movements are not primarily identifiable by formal elements such as stream of consciousness, interior monologue, symbolism and irony, but rather through an immanent critique of modernism that was no longer a critical reflection on the social and technological developments following from modernization, but remained locked in a self-referentiality in terms of the *l'art pour l'art* movement. In Marcel Duchamp's "Urinoir" and other ready-mades, and in Breton's demand to "practice poetry," Bürger sees the avant-garde intention to bring art back into the realm of everyday life and thus to do away with the autonomy of art and the separation between producers and

---

[33] Jürgen Habermas, "Modernity—An Incomplete Project." Hal Foster, ed. *The Anti-Aesthetic. Essays on Postmodern Culture* (Port Townsend, WA: Bay Press, 1983), 3-4.

[34] Habermas, "Modernity—An Incomplete Project," 5.

[35] Cf. Andreas Huyssen, "The Search for Tradition: Avantgarde and Postmodernism in the 1970s" (1981), *After the Great Divide: Modernism, Mass Culture, Postmodernism* (Bloomington/Indianapolis: Indiana University Press: 1986), 163, and Daniel Bell, *The Cultural Contradictions of Capitalism* (New York: Basic Books: 1976), 51.

consumers of art. While Bürger confines the avant-garde to a specific historical moment, it can be placed into a concept of modernity that begins with the Enlightenment and includes romanticism, impressionism, realism, and naturalism. In the American context, however, modernity (synonymously used with modernism) is usually understood as a unique style or movement limited to the decade following World War I and marking a break with both romanticism and realism. If modern art had its grand entry in 1913 with the New York "Armory Show," then it was above all writers such as T.S. Eliot, Ezra Pound, Gertrude Stein, William Faulkner, and William Carlos Williams as well as African-American authors, musicians, and artists of the Harlem Renaissance such as Langston Hughes, Zora Neale Hurston and Claude McKay who established the literature and art of American modernism and the avant-garde.

The inability to differentiate between the two terminologies would lead to the problematic conflation of Thomas Mann and William Faulkner with dadaism, or Proust with surrealism, or Breton and Rilke with Russian constructivism. Because the avant-garde is understood in the American context as a style that is not historically limited, the problem is doubled in so far as the term is not only used as a synonym for modernism but is also often used to connote postmodernism. As a result, no basis is available for developing a meaningful distinction in terms of epoch and style between Gertrude Stein's modernist or avant-garde style and Pynchon's postmodern writing strategies, or between Duchamp's avant-garde ready-mades and Warhol's postmodern silk screens, or the paintings and sculptures of other Pop artists.

Reducing modernism, the avant-garde, and the postmodern to stylistic phenomena, therefore, entails very inexact and thus inadequate categorizations, particularly because the aesthetic innovations attributed to postmodernism, e.g. moving beyond mimetic representation, and the emphasis on self-reflexive modes of writing and painting or irony and parody, are characteristics which were already essential to the experimental canon of stylistic elements and strategies in modernism and the historical avant-garde. Further, eclecticism and pastiche are not new to either modernism or postmodernism. The history of art and architecture contains numerous examples of stylistic reiterations, from antiquity to the historicism of the nineteenth century, and the Renaissance, the Baroque, Mannerism, neo-classicism and neo-gothic are themselves in part or altogether imitations of earlier styles. In other words, the danger of fixating the debate on stylistic elements of these three terms is that postmodernism can only be distinguished from modernism and the avant-garde by nuances so subtle that it can hardly be justified as a historical category of analysis.

This lack of definition results in part from the fact that the term modern is not well defined in the United States, in contrast to the history of this term in Germany, where it entered cultural and social theory via the work of Max Weber and was then developed further in the context of the Frankfurt School's critical theory.

In his foreword to *The Protestant Ethic* (1920), Weber asks if scientific, artistic, political, and economic developments outside "modern European culture" have not been forced into the rational categories that are particular to the occident's own self-understanding. The Enlightenment set in motion a process of demystification that allowed modernism to develop a profane culture out of the remnants of a religious world-view. In this process, art became not only autonomous, but it profited as well from a rationalized economy and in particular from the technological and administrative advances. Weber points to, for example, advances in music such as counterpoint and tonal harmony, the rational use of gothic arches as a method of distributing weight, newspapers and magazines as a type of literature created specifically for and only possible in a print culture, as well as a rational and systematic professionalization of the sciences. On the other hand, the rationalization as an integral part of modernity set into motion a process by which Western capitalism was characterized by a great number of technological potentialities and the calculability of its factors. In the course of this development, the natural sciences—being mathematically and experimentally exact and rationally grounded and because of their economic usability—received important impulses from capitalism. Both these systems of rationalization were functionally interrelated and resulted in a form of modernity, which differentiated and polarized the sphere of cultural and aesthetic modernism from social and technological modernization under the rubric of the terms culture and civilization. Although Weber's theory of a split modernity is applicable not only to Germany but to all Western capitalist societies, his analysis of the inherent antagonism of modernity did not resonate in the United States.

Framing the relation between modernism and modernization and respectively postmodernism and postmodernization, Jochen Schulte-Sasse drew attention to the fact that American politicians often use the culturally defined term "modernism" not to designate either a distinct literary movement between 1850 and 1950, or the entire cultural sphere since the Enlightenment, but employ it for their particular "martial arts." In the context of the Reagan administration's arms deal with Iran, for instance, "former CIA head William Colby held that the ultimate aim of U.S. foreign policy toward Iran is that country's 'return to modernism and civilized international relations." *Los Angeles Times* columnist William Pfaff criticized the Reagan administration for its political agenda regarding modernism: "They do not acknowledge that the Iranian revolution is driven by the rejection of exactly that modernism–and that it is a profound movement, encompassing elites as well as the masses."[36] Accordingly, Schulte-Sasse wondered whether we are "to think that the political agenda of an imperial power like the U.S. is motivated by the desire to convert the population of another country into an -ism?" He suggested that the term modernization should refer "solely to the social dimensions of modern society and a separate one that refers to the cultural movements within these societies."[37]

Although a distinction between postmodernization and postmodernisim would not make any sense insofar as postmodernity—at least in its early decade—had just tried to overcome this very dichotomy, Jochen Schulte-Sasse called attention to another important aspect often negelcted in the modern-postmodern discourse. No matter how

---

[36] Quoted in Jochen Schulte-Sasse, "Modernity and Modernism, Postmodernity and Postmodernism: Framing the Issue," *Cultural Critique*, 5 (Winter 1986/7), 5.
[37] Schulte-Sasse, 6.

the terms are employed, he continued, "they should be used as *analytical* categories apprehending features of and differences between societies and cultures. Such a usage would prevent a lot of confusion if commonly accepted."[38]

Taking up his suggestion to use "modernity" and "postmodernity" as categories to discern cultural differences between certain cultures and societies, Schulte-Sasse does not answer the question why the United States has never felt the need for distinguishing between the cultural realm of modernism and the technical process of modernization. Would such a split at all fit in with the historical and political self-definition and -perception of U.S. American culture?

But before pursuing this question let me first conclude with Wolfgang Welsch that the dividing line is not between modernity and postmodernity, but between various notions of modernity itself. Though necessary, it is not enough, however, to demand a distinction between the many notions of modernity in order to determine which one is pertinent—in terms of chronology, content, sector and function—to defining postmodernity. This would only displace the need for grounding and differentiation from postmodernity back onto notions of modernity, and thus not ultimately solve the problem. In order to come closer to an understanding of postmodernity, it is rather a matter of considering the relationship between any one notion of modernity and its corresponding notion of postmodernity and their compounds. This would not only avoid overgeneralizing the universal notion of modernism and postmodernism; it would also create a repertoire of concepts in which it becomes clear that neither modernity nor postmodernity are ahistorical and stable but changing and heterogeneous terms.

This type of a semantic perspective offers an answer to the question of why, despite similar cultural, technological, and economic developments, the postmodern has become a dominant form of cultural and historical self-definition in the United States but not in Europe, where it remains an inessential and limited term for a style rather than an epoch. The problematic then becomes no longer a question of defining the universal relationship between postmodernism, modernism, and the avant-garde. Instead, postmodernism must be seen within a context of geopolitical borders, if not nations and their institutions as well as their cultural-historical and ideological backgrounds in which the specific uses of the term have developed.

Despite sporadic and unsystematic references in Great Britain, Germany, and Spain since the end of the nineteenth century, the term postmodernity never became indigenous to European cultures. In fact, the occasional references remained inconsequential and the term disappeared in the 1930s. Due to the idea promoted by the Frankfurt School that the immanent contradictions between culture and civilization, or modernism and modernization could be resolved within modernity itself, and especially because modern culture had been considered the last bastion to take refuge against fascist and Stalinist barbarianism, the term postmodernity had not been taken up and furthered after World War II.

---

[38] Schulte-Sasse, 6f.

In the United States, however, the discussion around postmodernity only began in the early 1950s[39] and leading up to a paradigm shift in cultural debates by the end of the decade. In 1959 two significant references to postmodernity were published which indicate that postmodern discourse took on a particular American dimension by merging the general debate about the crisis of modernity with that of the suitability and applicability of the European, or better German logic of modernity manifesting itself in the antagonism and dialectics of its two spheres. The first reference was made by literary critic Irving Howe in his by now classical essay "Mass Society and Post-Modern Fiction"; the second was made by the English writer, politician and physicist Charles Percy Snow in his lecture on "The Two Cultures and the Scientific Revolution."[40]

Although Snow did not explicitly mention postmodernity in his lecture, he set up the polemical opposition between scientific-technological and literary-intellectual thinking that was to become the framework for the paradigm in the first phase of postmodernity.

It was above all German and American intellectuals who took part in what became an international debate, and it was they who played a decisive role in discussions of the transition from modernism to postmodernism. Those often mentioned in this context were Irving Howe, Susan Sontag, Leslie Fiedler, as well as Lionel Trilling, Herbert Marcuse, Theodor W. Adorno, Max Horkheimer, and Jürgen Habermas. But what remained unrecognized was the fact that the discussion centered on these figures and thus limited the modern/ postmodern debate to Marxist literary and cultural critics of the New York Intellectuals and the Frankfurt School. In this context it was less a matter of universal, formal-aesthetic characteristics of literary texts, which the New Critics had placed in the center of an internationally recognized notion of modernism. It was rather a matter of the function of literature, art, the humanities, and their relationship to the process of social, economic, and technical modernization and the disciplines that reflected these.

Even though the New York and the Frankfurt intellectuals made similar critiques of the myth of technical and economic progress since the 1930s, the discussion of the crisis of modernity took a different turn in Germany than in the United States. Although the historical avant-garde movements had already failed to reunite art with everyday life, and although it became clear in the examples of National Socialism and Stalinism that the proletariat could not be the sole addressee of theories of emancipation, the Frankfurt School held on to a principle of reason, tempered by self-critique and revision and still

---

[39] The American origin of the term goes back to Randolph Bourne, who in 1916 mentioned postmodernism once in connection with questions of cultural assimilation in his article "Transnational America." In the early 1950s Charles Olson after having invited John Cage, Merce Cunningham, and Robert Rauschenberg to participate in improvisations in the summer of 1952 at the Black Mountain College had used the term post-modern in the successive years to designate a break with the obsessive intellectualizing and rationalizing that he attributed to modernism.

[40] Irving Howe, "Mass Society and Post-Modern Fiction." *Partisan Review,* 3 (Sommer, 1959); Charles Percy Snow, "The Two Cultures and the Scientific Revolution." In addition C. Wright Mills published his essay "Culture and Politics," *The Listener* (BBC), März 1959.

had faith in modernism as the incomplete project of the Enlightenment. While Nietzsche's and Heidegger's very different critiques of causal, metaphysical, reason-oriented thinking had remained peripheral, the dialectical-materialist concept of modernism based on Hegel, Marx and Weber was renewed by the Frankfurt School's Critical Theory in the 1960s and became an anchor in the German context.

In comparison, the discussion in the New York circle and their *Partisan Review* coalesced around the question of whether or not the European model of a dualistic modernity and a materialistic dialectic could be an adequate concept for describing and analyzing American cultural and social experience. The inaptitude of many social theories in the US, wrote Daniel Bell in his essays collected under the telltale title of *The End of Ideology*, can be traced back to the uncritical application of European sociological concepts to the vastly different experiences of everyday life in the United States. This is particularly apparent in the theories of mass culture by critics who were themselves mostly from an aristocratic, Catholic, and Existentialist background. For example, "Ortega y Gasset, Paul Tillich, Karl Jaspers, Gabriel Marcel, Emil Lederer, Hannah Arendt, and others–have been concerned less with the general conditions of freedom in society than with the freedom of the *person* and with the possibility, for some few persons, of achieving a sense of individual self in our mechanized society."[41]

Although American modernity also stood on a continuum with the Enlightenment, it was only the translation of the culture-civilization dichotomy into textual categories that created the discourse of modernism in the United States. In this sense Howe, Trilling and other intellectuals of the first generation had honored the critical distance, intellectual seriousness, and the pedagogic effects of modern literature as operative for the United States. In contrast, younger members of the New York circle such as Sontag, and Fiedler criticized the fact that popular culture was discredited by the dichotomies of art vs. technology and aesthetic experience vs. everyday life. While Howe and Trilling defended an autonomous cultural sphere in which critical transgression, opposition, and denial as well as the utopia of an inalienated life could develop, for Sontag and Fiedler the exclusionary boundary between high art and mass culture has proved itself to be idealized and dysfunctional in relation to the permissive reality of the social world. For them the critical distance of the cultural sphere and the autonomy of art was as unconvincing as Snow's one-sided advocacy of technological progress. Instead of rational interpretation and hermeneutics, Sontag supported an "erotics of art," a "new sensibility" in the dialectics between art and everyday life that to her was expressed in the unmediated character of pop art, happenings, and sit-ins. Fiedler defended the passive resistance of authors of the Beat Generation (Jack Kerouac, William Burroughs, Allen Ginsberg) and the counterculture of the 1960s which Howe and Trilling had denigrated as political amnesia. In response, Fiedler called for a move to cross the border between high and popular culture and to close the gap between science fiction or the western and so-called serious literature. Relating Sontags and

---

[41] Daniel Bell, *The End of Ideology. On the Exhaustion of Political Ideas in the Fifties* (Glencoe, Ill.: Free Press, 1960), 21.

Fiedlers concept of postmodernity to the sublime, it seems reasonable to argue that their notions of culture in terms of secularization and immediacy did not comply with the romantic idea of exaltation and eminence.

It does not come as a surprise that Critical Theory was skeptical about the postmodern attack on the autonomy of art and literature. The Frankfurt School could not interpret Fiedler's and Sontag's emphasis on immediacy other than as a *falsche Aufhebung* of art in everyday life. From the German point of view their focus on representing in literature and art what *is* rather than what *could be* was understood as a contamination of the artistic ideal by the utilitarian-materialist perspective and a replacement of critical reflection with operational thinking. If in Germany the process of modernization was often understood in terms of encumbering inalienated life, American postmodernity just seemed to have insisted upon this process as a source of an event culture.

Therefore, at a closer look there was more at stake than just overcoming the inherent contradictions of modernity, the more so as the struggle between the two cultures was also a central theme in Europe, as the Snow debate had shown—a dispute that had a prominent precursor in the quarrel between Matthew Arnold and Thomas H. Huxley in 1882. The Snow debate was only the spectacular high point of the crisis of modernity since industrialization, urbanization, and the transformation of Western societies into late capitalism. One has to ask, however, why in the United States overcoming this crisis of a split modernity was tied to the concept of postmodernity, while in Europe this term could never really gain credence.

The reason for this can in part be found in the often over-looked difference between German and American interpretations of the Enlightenment described by Louis Hartz in 1955 in his book *The Liberal Tradition in America*. According to Hartz the dynamic conflicts between the aristocracy and the bourgeoisie that had brought about the Enlightenment in Europe was absent in American history. The freedoms that had been fought for there, in particular in terms of John Locke's ideas of liberalism, were already present in America's self-understanding from the day of its independence. "It is not accidental that America which has uniquely lacked a feudal tradition has uniquely lacked also a socialist tradition. The hidden origin of socialist thought everywhere in the West is to be found in the feudal ethos. The *ancien régime* inspires Rousseau; both inspire Marx."[42]

What had established itself in Europe as a philosophy of emancipation with artistic blueprints of a better world postponed and transcended into utopian projections, differed substantially from its transatlantic counterpart: the "American dream" as a practically approachable utopia has always been considered a perpetually improvable, but basically fulfilled or potentially satisfiable dream. The higher dimensions of human autonomy and fulfillment, which in Germany served as a cultural leitmotif in art and literature, expressed themselves in immediacy, the quotidian, and material success which was not

---

[42] Louis Hartz, *The Liberal Tradition in America. An Interpretation of American Political Thought Since the Revolution* (New York: Harcourt, Brace & World, 1955, 1991).

only a question of a better standard of living, but also the guarantee for independence. As a result, the notion of a profaned "utopia," a better society and individual freedom is not associated with the sphere of culture but with the process of civilization. While in Germany the goal of self-realization implied more than a mere improvement in the standard of living and indeed constituted a cultural paradigm, the American dream was entrusted to the realm of operational thinking and technical-economic progress–a sphere, which from the perspective of the Frankfurt School has always been suspected to impede critical reflection and autonomous thinking.

Focussing on the production of knowledge, on the homogenizing strategies of modernity and its insistence on closure, unity and meaning, the concept of postmodernity changed with the emergence of poststructuralism, at the beginning of the 70s. In other words, against the ususal identification of poststructuralism and postmodernity it should be noticed that Jacques Derrida's deconstruction of modern epistemology became influential only in this second phase of postmodernity, i.e. after he had introduced his theory upon "La Structure, le signe, et le jeu dans le discours des sciences humaines" at a conference at Johns Hopkins University in October 1966 upon which he was offered a position as guest professor in Baltimore and later in New Haven, where his American disciples Paul de Man and J. Hillis Miller had moved to and founded with Harold Bloom and Geoffrey Hartman the school of *Yale Deconstruction*. Derrida's radical questioning of language as a representation of reality was accompanied by Roland Barthes's provocative thesis of "The Death of the Author"—that is, the end of the romantic ideal of the author as a representative genius of originality and individuality. Derrida and Barthes no longer considered the text as a self-enclosed world but rather as a multidimensional space in which a great number of texts come together —none of them original—as a "tissue of quotations drawn from the innumerable centres of culture."[43] Many authors such as John Barth, Donald Barthelme, Thomas Pynchon, E.L. Doctorow, Ishmael Reed, Walter Abish, Raymond Federman, Robert Coover, Ronald Sukenik have written in a manner analogous to this understanding of the text and applied intertextual references and metafictional strategies which threw into question the notion of the originality of the author and problematized writing as the communication of experience. If such a thing as realism still exists, as Fredric Jameson remarked in 1984 in relation to postmodernity, then it is the recognition that language is a prison house: "It is a 'realism' ... of slowly becoming aware of a new and original historical situation in which we are condemned to seek History by way of our own pop images and simulacra of that history, which itself remains forever out of reach."[44]

In addition to Jameson it was above all Ihab Hassan who contributed significantly to the spread of deconstructivist postmodernism. Hassan, however, understood the concept less in a chronological than in a typological, transhistorical sense. Already in

---

[43] Roland Barthes, "The Death of the Author" (1968), *Image-Music-Text* (New York: Hill and Wang, 1977), 146.

[44] Fredric Jameson, "Culture. The Cultural Logic of Late Capitalism," *Postmodernism or, the Cultural Logic of Late Capitalism* (Durham: Duke University Press, 1991), 25.

the 1960s he had differentiated two currents of literary modernism that went against the model of language as a simple instrument of mimicry: "Both are manners of silence, formal disruptions of the relation between language and reality. It is these two modes ... that account for the development of antiform in modern literature from Kafka to Beckett."[45]

According to Hassan not only postmodern but modern authors such as Franz Kafka, James Joyce, Henry Miller, Jean Genet, and Samuel Beckett already left behind the project of mimesis: "The postmodern spirit lies coiled [already] within the great corpus of modernism ... It is not really a matter of chronology: Sade, Jarry, Breton, Kafka acknowledge that spirit."[46] Thus, Hassan's postmodernism is less defined by a particular body of texts of a certain historical period than by a retrospective recognition that simple mimesis had already been shattered in previous epochs: "Thus, for instance, we perceive now—but did not thirty years ago—postmodern features in [Laurence Sterne's] *Tristram Shandy* precisely because our eyes have learned to recognize postmodern features. And so we propose *Tristram Shandy*, but not *Tom Jones*, as a 'postmodern book'."[47]

Individual literary genres were for Hassan not only partial descriptions of what was otherwise characterized by indeterminacy; like Hans Blumenburg, Hassan argues that epochs cannot be considered as essentially distinct from one another because they inevitably stand in mutual and dynamic relation to one another.

While Hassan's almost ubiquitous "postmodern spirit" undermined the use of the term as a historical category, Fredric Jameson's concept of postmodernity—though engendered by poststructuralist theory—did not lose sight of the Marxist insistence upon representing history. Taking off from Ernest Mandel's three phase theory of capitalist societies, Jameson understood realism and modernism as the cultural representations of market capitalism and monopoly or imperialist capitalism, while postmodernism was the cultural logic of multinational late capitalism, in which capital has expanded into areas that were previously untouched by the market. This logic of late capitalism manifests itself among others in an image-oriented, standardized consumerism, in certain styles of fashion and advertising, in tv, architecture and suburban sprawl. Jameson discerns two primary characteristics of this logic. First, a proliferation of pastiche as the result of a radical fragmentation in which nothing remains except stylistic heterogeneity. Pastiche is for Jameson merely empty parody that has abandoned the original motivation of satire, humor and the hope of something "normal" beyond that which is parodied. The second characteristic of the postmodern logic is described by Jameson as collective schizophrenia (a reference to Lacan's poststructural psychoanalysis) that manifests itself as a breakdown in the chain of signifiers, that is, the dissociation of words and their referents. In as far as language creates order out of the experience of past, present and

---

[45] Ihab Hassan, "The Dismemberment of Orpheus," *American Scholar*, 32 (1963), 474. See also *The Literature of Silence. Henry Miller and Samuel Beckett* (New York: Knopf, 1967).

[46] Ihab Hassan, *The Dismemberment of Orpheus: Toward a Postmodern Literature* (New York: Oxford University Press, 1971), 139.

[47] Ihab Hassan, *The Postmodern Turn: Essays in Postmodern Theory and Culture* (Columbus: Ohio State University Press, 1987), xv-xvi.

future as well as memory and identity, the schizophrenic patient is condemned to living in a never-ending present of meaningless signifiers that lack a context. Applying this to the cultural logic of late capitalism, Jameson understands postmodernism as a transformation of reality into "images" and the fragmentation of time into a series of permanent presence.

Since both Jameson's and Hassan's concept of postmodernity are well known it should suffice to place both theories into the broader history of the term. While Hassan's fusion of literary periods was often criticized for its ahistorical (and thus in a way homogenizing) indeterminacy, Jameson's work had added a political and historical dimension to this debate, which, however shared with Hassan a certain totalizing perspective by focusing on the modes of production as the determining cultural factor. In other words, his theory of a cultural logic of international capitalism was too global to relate the demands of the civil rights and women's movement for recognition of the differences within American society to the postmodern critique of the exclusiveness and elitist perspective of modernity. Although Leslie Fiedler had already in the 1960s favored the iconoclasm of the counter-culture as an attack on the dominance of white-anglo-saxon-protestant-male-heterosexuals in modernism, the theoretical implications and concrete contexts of this critique remained initially apodictic.

Only in the 1980s the term postmodernity entered an alliance with the nascent interdisciplinary cultural studies. Feminist scholars as well as theoreticians of multiculturalism and postcolonialism discovered in the postmodern emphasis on heterogeneity a potential for the voices of those marginalized by modernity to be heard in both public and academic discourse. Demarcating labels such as homogeneity, autonomy, structure, closure and meaning were replaced by relational terms such as heterogeneity, alterity, dialogue or hybridity—terms that transformed the exclusionary borders of modernity from the outside to discursive differences of the inside.

Despite Jacques Derrida's and Roland Barthes's theories of the text, the sign, and the author Michel Foucault's poststructuralist revision of modern power and subjectivity was of decisive importance for this third phase of postmodernity. In his *Archeology of Knowledge* he showed that the production of knowledge and the formation of discourses are not neutral and objective but inseparably bound to power constellations and social institutions. Given that power is dispersive and not contained in one institution or another, theorists from such various branches as feminist theory, gender, gay and lesbian studies, African-, Asian-, Hispanic- and Native-American studies as well as postmodern anthropology and historiography began to expose the engrained strategies of power and representation that shape social discourses. After feminist theory had grounded itself in essential and biologistic positions up until the 1980s, with postmodernity categories such as sexual difference and orientation, race and age were identified as social constructions in the same way that Marxism had already insisted that class identity, though economically determined, was not essential or unchangeable in nature.

Central for the discussion of postmodernity and social marginality was the question of the relationship between Enlightenment philosophy and cultural or social practice, a relationship that manifested itself most prominently in the critique of Enlightenment universalism. While most feminist critics and scholars held on to political, emancipatory ideals such as freedom, equality and justice, they also criticized the universalism implicit to the Enlightenment subject, who supposedly has the freedom of choice and who is inevitably male. "If postmodern-feminist critique must remain 'theoretical'," write Nancy Fraser and Linda Nicholson as representatives of multicultural and postcolonial critique, "not just any kind of theory will do."

Rather, theory here would be explicitly historical, attuned to the cultural specificity of different societies and periods and to that of different groups within societies and periods. Thus, the categories of postmodern-feminist theory would be inflected by temporality, with historically specific institutional categories like "the modern, restricted, male-headed, nuclear family" taking precedence over ahistorical, functionalist categories like reproduction and mothering ... When its focus became cross-cultural or transepochal its mode of attention would be comparativist rather than universalist, attuned to changes and contrasts instead of to "covering laws." Finally, postmodern-feminist theory would dispense with the idea of a subject of history. It would replace unitary notions of "woman" and "feminine gender identity" with plural and complexly constructed conceptions of social identity, treating gender as one relevant strand among others, attending also to class, race, ethnicity, age, and sexual orientation.[48]

IV

With the paradigm shift in dominance from a consensus-oriented and homogenizing social discourse to one that recognizes cultural difference, the United States has not only gained self-consciousness and has come into its own; it has also created a model that can act as an instructive foil for European concepts of culture, in particular the German myth of cultural, ethnic and national unity. While the discussion of cultural alterity in Germany still organizes itself around an "insider/outsider" or "we/them" matrix of *ius sanguinis*, the focus in the American debate is rather on manifold intercultural and transnational relations. If poststructuralism in Europe is still stuck with the stigma of being a grave digger of the Enlightenment, in relation to a multicultural America (however controversial this term is) it has found a social field in which it became possible to think theoretically about cultural and ethnic heterogeneity. Whereas feminist theory and the debate of multiculturalism in the United States profit from the long social practice of cultural difference, the German debate on multiculturalism orients itself around an additive, but not a revisionist perspective and which is more concerned with the state and the social practice of "dealing with the foreigners." In this respect the internal cultural critique of marginalized groups remains outside of the debate, as does the question of the so-called common East and West German cultural heritage.

---

[48] Nancy Fraser and Linda J. Nicholson, "Social criticism without philosophy: an encunter between feminism and postmodernism," in Andrew Ross, ed., *Universal Abandon? The Politics of Postmodernism* (Minneapolis: University of Minnesota Press, 1988), 101.

It is here where the necessity of a historical place for postmodernity in the cultural self-understanding of the United States becomes evident, whereby on the whole a diachronic look at the individual phases reveals a tendency that is common to all versions of American postmodernity: The search for social and historical conditions as well as the specific Enlightenment interpretations of a concept of culture that is appropriate to the United States. With this attempt American postmodernity continues a long tradition of the United States's drive for cultural independence from Europe. It also has thereby developed a notion of culture that carries the mark of multiculturalism that is common to all societies. The different ways in which the Enlightenment ideas have been concretized and put into practice has shown not only why it is understandable that terms such as postmodernity, poststructuralism, or multiculturalism have established themselves in different manners on both sides of the Atlantic. Analogous to Derrida's formulation that "America is Deconstruction,"[49] Germany and the United States are comparable in terms of the matrix modernism-postmodernism.

---

[49] Jacques Derrida, *Memoires for Paul DeMan* (New York/ Oxford: Columbia Uiversity Press, 1986), 18.

BRITAIN, AMERICA AND DANISH MODERNITY

Jens Rahbek Rasmussen

In spite of the rather strict news management in late absolutist Denmark, the news of the American Declaration of Independence could be found in one of the country's leading newspapers on September 2, 1776, almost two months after the event. The delay was of course mainly due to the slow communications of the time, but two other Scandinavian papers had actually carried the news (which they had got from the same German source) four days earlier. It was thus only after some deliberation, and after having removed all derogatory references to kings—which, given the contents of the Declaration, made large parts of the text almost incomprehensible—that the Copenhagen paper trusted itself to publish the momentous news.[1] The news was welcomed by the middle and lower classes, whereas the ruling elite dismissed the "insolent" document of the "rebels." But they did allow it to be published, and it "unleashed neither revolutionary nor critical currents in Danish intellectual circles"—notwithstanding the fact that Denmark had experienced two recent *coup d'états* (in 1770 and 1772).[2] When in 1784, after yet another political coup, a free though regulated public debate was allowed, America soon became a popular topic. One Dane seems in 1785 to have answered the famous prize essay on whether America had benefitted mankind, and when the university of Copenhagen in 1792 announced a rather similar topic, two entries were published.

In an article in 1796 the author accepted that until twenty years ago, America was almost unknown in Denmark except as a theatre of wars between England, France and Spain. But the revolution of 1776 had changed this; now the United States deserved. and increasingly got, the attention of every citizen and the world because it had obtained for its inhabitants that great treasure, civil liberty, and by sage laws fortified it against all attacks, so that America, compared to other Free States, can pride itself on the most unlimited freedom. Admittedly the American citizen is taxed more heavily now than under British rule, but then he can avail himself of so many more, and greater, business opportunities.[3]

The article later also emphasized that people in America "abhorred all restrictions on ... the liberty of religion." All in all, such writings may be considered a sort of

---

[1] Thorkild Kjærgaard, *Denmark gets the News of 1776* (Copenhagen: Danish Ministry of Foreign Affairs, 1976).

[2] Kjærgaard, *Denmark gets the News*, 34.

[3] Quoted in C. Borberg and J. Damm, eds., *Amerika—Utopia? Udvandringen til USA og Amerikaopfattelsen i Danmark 1870-1920* (Varde: Dansklærerforeningen/Skov, 1982), 9.

vicarious protest against the autocratic system at home, albeit without immediate political effect. But the sympathy for the Free States[4] inevitably threw up questions about the country they had rebelled against. The very existence of the United States forced a rethink on England—a rethink which imminent political events would have demanded anyway. The remainder of this paper will discuss how Danes perceived the similarities and differences between Britain, the United States, and Denmark up to 1914. Special consideration will be given to the 1830s as the formative period where surprisingly durable images were created for Danish consumption.

At the time of the American revolution Danish liberals, like their counterparts elsewhere, often looked to England for political and not least technological inspiration. The funeral in 1785 of the engineer and shipbuilder Henrik Gerner, who had studied in England and brought the first steam engine to Denmark, turned into a political demonstration against those civil servants who (it was alleged) had harassed him to death.[5] But by and large Danes knew little of the British Isles. Almost all cultural inspiration came from or via Germany. At least in Copenhagen German was spoken by high and low, though with varying competence (rather as with English today), something which came as a pleasant surprise to German visitors.[6] This obviously did not preclude French or English ideas reaching Denmark; on the contrary the easy access to German texts and translations enjoyed by the bilingual Danish elite probably facilitated contacts, albeit indirect, with European culture. But it did mean that fewer were prepared, or needed, to learn other languages, and among those who did, French was the first choice.

The outbreak of the French Revolution provided Danish liberals and radicals with a new political ideal, more clearly progressive than Britain whose industrial revolution and parliamentary democracy seemed to be at least counterbalanced by the conservative role of the monarchy and the aristocracy, and by the manner in which the British tried to be "a free but conquering people," defending liberty at home while denying it to their colonies in America and elsewhere. The letters from the young liberal historian Frederik Sneedorff, who went abroad in 1792, were clearly less enthusiastic about Britain than about revolutionary France. The articles by Tom Paine published in Danish journals hardly helped improve the image of Britain either as their comparisons of the standard of living and the degree of democracy in America and Britain were highly unflattering to the latter.[7]

---

[4] *Nordamerikas Fristater* (the Free States of North America) competed with the official and directly translated name *Amerikas Forenede Stater* in Danish parlance. As late as 1939, the Danish writer Johannes V. Jensen (of whom more below) chose *Fra Fristaterne* as the title for a travel book.

[5] F.A. Rasmussen, "'Han tænkte dybt og klart som Newton': Henrik Gerner mellem videnskab og teknologi" ["'His mind, like Newton's, was profound and clear': Henrik Gerner between science and technology"], *Den jyske historiker*, no. 61 (Nov. 1992).

[6] Vibeke Winge, *Dänische Deutsche—Deutsche Dänen: Geschichte der deutschen Sprache in Dänemark 1300-1800 mit einem Ausblick auf das 19. Jahrhundert* (Heidelberg: Carl Winter, 1992). Several Danish writers and poets tried to tap a larger and much more lucrative market by writing German versions of their work, though the result seldom impressed native speakers.

[7] Borberg and Damm, eds., *Amerika—Utopia?*, 10.

But political events were soon to stifle the debate on America and, though for unrelated reasons, to create an opinion openly hostile to Britain. In 1799 the liberal experiment was discontinued and censorship came back. In 1801 the British, fed up with Denmark's ever more provocative interpretations of its neutrality, sent their navy under Nelson to Copenhagen. The one-sided battle ended in defeat for the Danes, but it was hailed as a moral victory and came to play an important role in the creation of a Danish national identity;[8] it also led to a more cautious Danish policy of neutrality, which did not prevent large fortunes from being made from trade.

However in 1807 the British came back and launched a preventive strike lest Napoleon avail himself of the (in spite of 1801) far from negligible Danish navy. The loss of the navy, and especially the terror bombardment of Copenhagen carried out by the later Duke of Wellington, led to intense hostility towards the British. A lot of anti-British poetry was written, defiantly before the war, in anger and sorrow after it ("Who gave you [Britain] once your tongue, your life? / Is Denmark not your mother?"). It is hardly a coincidence either that of the few books published in Danish on British history between 1800 and 1814, three dealt with, respectively, the (attempted or successful) invasions of England from the Romans over the Danes to the French; the fate of the Stuart line; and "thoughts and opinions on the miserable conditions the British people will suffer in the future," incidentally a translation of an English publication from 1749. The war of 1807-14 led to the break-up of the Danish-Norwegian monarchy. Norway was dependent on free trade, an open sea and good relations with Britain, and the country suffered grievously from the economic blockade during the war. In 1814 they accepted, however reluctantly, a union with Sweden (set up by the Great Powers for entirely different political purposes) which allowed them to keep their progressive constitution and left them largely free to conduct their own commercial policy. This had certain repercussions for Danish-English relations as well, for Norway's links with Britain had always been much closer than Denmark's. Thus the Danish translation of *Wealth of Nations*, which was published in 1779 (three years after the original), was actually by subscriptions from Norwegian merchants.[9]

The events of 1807-14 obviously influenced the Danish image of Britain, but in a rather complex way. When the British behaviour was criticized by quoting from *Richard II.* (now at long last available in a Danish translation): "That England which was wont to conquer others / hath made a shameful conquest of itself," the point was inadvertently made that English literature was in fact becoming more widely known—as yet only

---

[8] It should be stressed that the national identity at this time was not (exclusively) Danish but a state patriotism where the *patria* was the Danish monarchy, which comprised Norway (until 1814) and Schleswig-Holstein (until 1864). Several of the national poems in 1801 were written in German.

[9] Danish was the only written language used in Norway at this time.—For Scandinavia's involvement in the Napoleonic wars, see H. Arnold Barton, *Scandinavia in a Revolutionary Era, 1760-1815* (Minneapolis: University of Minnesota Press, 1986).

seldom in the original language, and often still in German, but increasingly in Danish translation.[10]

However these cultural contacts went hand in hand with a general dislike and distrust of the English who were seen as dishonourable thieves and robbers. Around 1850 a pupil in a grammar school got into trouble when, in a fight with a boy from the (largely English-speaking) Danish West Indies, he called him "an English thief"; in his defence he pointed out that he had never heard the word "English" used except in connection with "thief." As late as 1884, on her trip to Scandinavia, Oscar Wilde's mother noted that Nelson and Wellington still seemed to be cordially hated in Copenhagen.[11] In this situation the United States was seen as a kind of substitute by the liberal opinion: a dynamic and democratic country without entrenched class differences who, like Denmark, had fought Britain in the recent world war, although the treaty of Ghent was a good deal more favourable to the Americans than that of Kiel was to the Danes. It was almost like a bond between the two countries that the British frigate involved in the episode which triggered the war of 1812-14 was named *Little Belt* and had, as *Lillebælt*, been part of the Danish navy seized by the British in 1807.

It was admittedly an unfortunate start to the new friendship that American sailors were repeatedly attacked by members of the lower classes in Copenhagen, who recognized them as English speakers and drew their own wrong conclusions.[12] Nevertheless American-Danish relations soon grew closer. In 1801—perhaps not incidentally the year of the first Danish-British clash—Denmark established diplomatic relations with the United States. After the wars the increasing economic importance of the United States was recognized by the appointments of more consular officers and the conclusion of a commercial treaty in 1826.

Shortly after the first portraits of America as an Eldorado or a "Land of Cockaigne" appeared in Danish literature.[13] One such treatment, later to become a children's classic, was Christian Winther's *Flugten til Amerika* [The Flight to America] (1833).[14] A boy from a solid middle-class home in a provincial town, who feels dejected because he has been awarded low marks in school, been scolded by his mother, and been let down by a girl he fancies—all in one day—decides that enough is enough. He will go to America, and tries to persuade his little brother to come along. Hesitant at first and not terribly

---

[10] Jørgen Erik Nielsen, *Den engelske litteratur og Danmark 1800-1840*, I-II (Copenhagen: Akademisk Forlag, 1976), with an English summary. The first Danish translation of Shakespeare were to have been published in 1807, but was delayed until 1813. That had nothing to do with hostility to Britain, but several manuscripts had perished under the bombardment, and the war created a paper shortage.
[11] Kjeld Galster, "Læreren i dansk Litteratur," *Vor Ungdom* (1916).
[12] E.C. Werlauff, *Af min Ungdoms Tid* (Copenhagen: Hagerup, 1954), 105.
[13] Thomas Thomsen, *Farvel til Danmark: De danske skillingsvisers syn på Amerika og på udvandringen dertil* (Aarhus: Jysk Selskab for Historie, 1980).
[14] It is available in a much later, but congenial English translation by Danish scientist, inventor and producer of light philosophical verse ("Grooks"), Piet Hein: *Flugten til Amerika / The Flight to America* (Copenhagen 1976). The cultural resonance of the title may be gauged from the fact that it was chosen for the first scholarly book on Danish emigration to the United States, by Kristian Hvidt, in 1971 (English translation 1975).

impressed by hearing about the gold and silver that can be picked up for free, the younger brother proves unable to resist the following description:

> Raisins and almonds and walnuts abound
> and jars full of syrup and honey,
> lollipops cluster on all trees around,
> and nothing costs any money.
>
> Candy for bread comes wherever one goes,
> and in chocolate muffins you wade;
> with sugar pebbles it hails and snows
> and rains with lemonade.
>
> Liberty is what you just are at
> to whatever you ever desire;
> you spit on the floors when you feel like that
> and play with cigars and fire.
>
> You sit all the leisurely day and swing
> in heavenly rocking chairs,
> and going to school or not is a thing
> that depends on whether one cares!

The last argument about the school clinches the case, and with a sugar pretzel and an illustrated Bible as material and spiritual sustenance for the journey, the two are about to set off, when their mother spots them ("With the book in the street, why what's the idea?") and calls them in to the waiting dinner:

> Perplexed did we stop there and wavered and swayed,
> forgetting our journey and all,
> unconsciously turned our feet and obeyed
> the motherly masterful call.
>
> Her sweet mild voice set my mind at ease
> and made my defiance stoop.
> I drowned my worry and found my peace
> deep down in the sago soup.

So Biedermeier Denmark was, after all, preferable to Utopian America.

A strikingly similar idea is found in Hans Christian Andersen's libretto for the light opera *Festen på Kenilworth* (written before 1832). The play itself, based on Walter Scott's novel *Kenilworth*, is deservedly forgotten (in fact it has never been published in its final version), but one song with the refrain "Pity that America / lies so very far away" ("Skade at Amerika / ligge skal så langt herfra") became popular enough to make the refrain a familiar quotation still to be found in Danish Bartletts. Here Andersen, with perhaps more gusto than subtlety, lambasts the popular utopian idea of America's affluence: gold and silver grow in the fields, roast pigeons nest in the woods, and the fountains sprout champagne.[15]

It seems certain that the two songs were written independently. Andersen wrote his in or before 1832, and only published it in 1836. Winther wrote his in 1833 and included it in a volume of poems in 1835; the inspiration came to him when he heard a friend tell how her sister's two boys had planned to run away "and become two Robinsons." It is almost impossible but there should not have been some common inspiration, perhaps a popular book on America published in the early 1830s, but I have been unable to identify it.[16]

Two more serious works on America also appeared. In 1820 C.F. von Schmidt-Phiseldeck, a German who like so many of his educated compatriots had chosen to pursue a career as civil servant in the bilingual Danish monarchy, published his *Europa und Amerika*, which quickly appeared in Danish, English, and other European languages; a second lightly revised edition came out in 1832. Best read in conjunction with his *Der europäische Bund* [The European Union] from 1821, it argued that Europe was in imminent danger of being eclipsed by the American continent (like many of his contemporaries Schmidt-Phiseldeck predicted an even greater future for South America), amd could only be saved by closer co-operation between the European states. His efforts have earned him brief mentions in works dealing with 19th century ideas concerning Europe, America, and Russia, and indeed de Tocqueville may have known of his ideas.[17] His book on America is far from original, though he is too economical with his references to enable his precise sources to be identified; they seem to be predominantly German journals and newspapers. Also he never visited the United States, a fact that his critics were only too happy to emphasize.[18] Even in the second edition of 1832 Schmidt-Phiseldeck saw his pessimism confirmed by the fact that the July Revolution of 1830 seemed to be a repeat performance of 1789. But whereas the book in 1820 had caught the popular pessimistic mood, by now liberals were quietly confident about the future and no longer saw America (now usually referring to the United States alone) as a threat. The dangers to Europe did not come from abroad, but from within, said a Danish reviewer; and they could be averted if (as in Denmark) a wise, listening

---

[15] It is beyond me how Sven H. Rossel can claim that this song should *not* be read as a mockery of popular enthusiasm for America: "The Image of the United States in Danish Literature," *Scandinavica*, 25 (1986), 50-1.

[16] Tove Barfoed Møller, "H.C. Andersens Scott-libretti i samtids- og nutidsbelysning," *Anderseniana* (1996), 11-24, with English summary; Erik Sønderholm, "Hans Christian Andersenals Opernlibrettist. Eine kritische Untersuchung," *Anderseniana* (1996), 25-48; Chr. Winther,*Poetiske Skrifter*, vol. I, ed. Oluf Friis (Copenhagen: Gad 1927, Danmarks Nationallitteratur), 369.

[17] De Tocqueville's *Democratie en Amerique* was never translated into Danish, although extracts of it were published in a journal edited by a leading liberal politician in 1844 (and a full Swedish translation appeared in 1839-46).

[18] E.g. Frances Trollope in her *Domestic Manners of the Americans* from 1832: "Dr. Von Phiseldeck (not Fiddlestick), who is not only a doctor of philosophy but a knight of Dannebrog [the Danish flag] to boot, has never been in America, but he has written a prophesy, showing that the United Stayes must and will govern the whole world[...]." Quoted in Thorkild Kjærgaard's postscript to the reprint of C.F. von Schmidt-Phiseldeck, *Europe and America* (Copenhagen: Rosenkilde og Bagger, 1976), 261 n. 6.

monarch co-operated freely with the people's moderate leaders against the threats of reactionary absolutism on the one hand and revolutionary republicanism on the other.[19]

The ponderous prose of Schmidt-Phiseldeck's book, which is only too recognizable in English translation, must have limited its popular appeal considerably. Far more accessible was Frederik Klee's "historical-statistical" handbook from 1835-7 which set out to provide, in readable form, information on a continent still unknown to most Danes—or so Klee claimed. They tended, he said, to look more to the past than to the present; but their history books had neglected the continent, and the newspapers said little about it.[20] This was in fact not entirely true: the standard textbook in history for grammar schools did deal with America, including recent events, and displayed a sympathy for the country similar to Klee's:

> In no other state is there greater freedom, more flourishing industry, or lower taxes. The country's rich resources, a suitable constitution, and its wise rulers...have contributed to this progress. To this land of liberty fled bands of Europeans made unhappy outcasts through the Old World's revolutions, bringing with them their knowledge, talents, enterprise and capital ...[21]

Klee did however perform a useful service in synthesizing the extensive German literature on America and thus providing the Danish public with what was generally reliable, up-to-date information. In fact Klee is sometimes weiting more as a contemporary journalist: in the first volume there is a reference to President van Buren's inauguration speech in 1837 (taken from a German political journal), and in the second Klee deals at length with the ongoing upheaval in Canada. Like Schmidt-Phiseldeck (whom he fails to mention) Klee dealt with the entire American continent, describing events and conditions in Haiti and Brazil as well as in the United States and Canada.[22]

Klee was in general enthusiastic about the United States. In his opening paragraph he vividly described how, as if by magic, populous and industrious cities appear, canals and railways hundreds of miles long are built, so that with the speed of the wind we can hasten from one end of the vast states to the other, across lakes and rivers, along roads blasted through the rocks, through felled primeval forests, across vast plains—places where but a few years ago only the wild animals or the quick Indians left their hardly perceptible traces.[23]

Fully aware that there were notable differences between the East, West and South, Klee still felt able to picture some national characteristics. First and foremost there was

---

[19] N. David in a review in *Maanedsskrift for Litteratur*, 8 (1832), 156.

[20] Frederik Klee, *Amerika især i den nyeste Tid: En historisk-statistisk Haandbog*, I-II (Copenhagen, 1837-39).

[21] It may however be a sign of the ambivalence towards America that Estrup specifically warned his pupils to emigrate to America, citing the extremely high prices of cattle and horses as proof of the difficulties which emigrants would encounter. Quoted in Erik Helmer Pedersen, *Drømmenom Amerika* (Copenhagen: Politiken, 1985), 44-45.

[22] Another similarity between Klee and Schmidt-Phiseldeck was that Klee too had written on post-1815 Europe before he turned to the New World: Fr. Klee, *Europa siden 1815*, I-II (Copenhagen, 1836-37).

[23] Klee, *Amerika især i den nyeste Tid*, 157.

national pride, based on "their free and certainly in many respects excellent constitution which cancels every difference of rank and makes the poorest workman the President's equal." The Americans were serious and industrious; they toiled unremittingly, almost like machines, and even when they had made a considerable fortune did not allow themselves to slow down. They had a certain sophistication, equally far from rude incivility and the Europeans' polished delicacy. Common sense pervaded state and society. Even women had much practical sense, "and it is quite usual for them to be well acquainted with physics, chemistry and experimental science, which most European women—or even men—know only by name."[24]

But he was far from blind to the country's faults. He dealt at length and with great sympathy with the fate of the Indians, and, as so many European observers, castigated the glaring contrast between the institution of slavery and "the political institutions built on the principles of equality and liberty which banish all hereditary power and do not accept any nobility, any ruling church, or any clergy which acts as a state within the state; which do not know of titles or privileges, nor of a standing army or a secret police."[25]

At other occasions, however, he qualifies his opinions—whether as a consequence of his eclectic use of sources, or because he himself was ambivalent. While the immorality of the treatment of Indians and slaves is not questioned, he allows that there are "not insignificant political considerations which make the Negro slavery on the southern states less odious"—especially the fear that the slaves, if emancipated, may desire to become masters in a part of the world where the climate allows black but not white people to work. This problem does not exist in the North, so that "the Northeners' efforts to free the Negroes are less meritorious in that they themselves will lose little or nothing by the emancipation"; and Klee concludes with a somewhat inaccurate prediction:

> Slavery and the extinction of the Indians are the worst stains on the American national character, hence the fierce clashes between Northern philantropists and Southern egotists; it is however immanent not only in the American constitution, but also in human nature, that these issues are far less important for the survival of the union than those which more directly affect pecuniary interests, such as the questions of banking and customs.[26]

It might be asked why the state censors allowed such praise for a rebel republic. Was there still a lingering "anti-British" sympathy for the United States, even in official circles? Perhaps, but a more likely answer, I suppose, is that the Danish state, like that of the Habsburgs, was absolute but fallible; after all, in 1843 a Danish book, duly approved by the censors, offered a complete blueprint for a utopian communist state!

It was also in the 1830s that two of the most influential intellectuals in 19th-century Denmark came out criticizing both America and Britain for their inhumanity and profit-

---

[24] Klee, *Amerika især i den nyeste Tid*, 217-18.
[25] Klee, *Amerika især i den nyeste Tid*, 157-8.
[26] Klee, *Amerika især i den nyeste Tid*, 221.

seeking. One was N.F.S. Grundtvig (1783-1872), a controversial clergyman, historian, linguist, prolific hymn-writer and, not least, spiritual creator of the Danish Folk High Schools. The other was J.L. Heiberg (1791-1860), a philosopher, poet, playwright and critic in the conservative Hegelian mould who saw British and American thought as aberrations from the European, i.e. Latin and German, tradition. The two could hardly have been further apart in Danish politics, Grundtvig trying to educate the farmers so that they could seize power, both politically and intellectually, from the urban intelligentsia represented by Heiberg. Still they shared the same antipathy to modernity and materialism, in its American or British version.

Grundtvig went to England three times around 1830 to study Anglo-Saxon manuscripts, and came back with a profoundly ambivalent attitude to the country. He was impressed by the energy and dynamism so unimaginably different from the sleepiness of the provincial backwater he had left, and his thinking on questions like theology and education was greatly influenced by what he saw in Britain. But at the same time he (as so many others) was profoundly shocked by a society where men seemed to be mere adjuncts of machines. A conservative populist who only later embraced democratic ideas, Grundtvig preferred the enlightened absolutism at home to the economic liberalism that he encountered in England and America (like Hans Christian Andersen he never visited the latter).

In a book written in 1831 Grundtvig expressed his dislike not only of German thought (a recurrent theme in his writings) and of French democracy (for which he coined the term "Pøbel-Parisisk," or "mob-Parisian"), but also of Anglo-Saxon liberalism which he called "Kræmmer-Amerikansk," or "profit-first-American." He compared the monarchy to an estate run for the common good, democracy to a factory "run solely for the maximum profit of the shareholders, while the labour-force is worn out and discarded with the same carelessness as is the machinery."[27] It is true that Grundtvig repeatedly toyed with the idea that there was a special kind of freedom and enterprise in countries imbued with "Anglo-Saxonism," including the United States which had been peopled from Britain, and (sometimes in the future) Denmark where after all the Angles were supposed to have originated. But he hardly ever discussed this topic without stressing that the social gap between rich and poor created by freedom and enterprise would set off a social revolution.[28]

This view of Britain was inherited by the Grundtvigian folk high school, whose Danish nationalism was always much closer to German ways of thought than they cared to admit, and fairly impervious to Anglo-Saxon ideas. It is true that they became slightly more open towards the United States, where so many Danish emigrants went (often

---

[27] Quoted in V. Wåhlin, "Grundtvig in the 19th century," in *Heritage and Prophecy: Grundtvig and the English-speaking World*, ed. by A.M. Allchin (Aarhus: Aarhus University Press, 1992), 258. "Kræmmer" is a retailer or shopkeeper.

[28] N.F.S. Grundtvig, *Mands Minde 1788-1838* (Copenhagen: Schönberg, 1838), 433. He also described the British parliament as "not the last bulwark of liberty...[but] the chief stronghold of plutocracy, whose walls consist of the people's freehold and whose moats are filled with the blood of the poor."

establishing Grundtvigian churches in the process), but there was never any significant exchange of ideas between the Danes in America and at home.

Now to Heiberg whose main intellectual inspiration came from Germany and France. He had no English and when forced to spend a fortnight in London the only entertainment he could follow was the Italian opera. Rather incidentally he in 1834 had an opportunity to expand on what he and the cultural elite must have felt and thought about Anglo-Saxon modernity. He had been criticized for his Danish version of a (rightly forgotten) English play. In his defence he pointed to differences in national character and sentiment. The Germans were learned, the Spanish religious, the French military; hence the dominating idea in Germany was science, in Spain religion, in France honour. But the important thing was that these were all *ideals*, albeit of different kinds, whereas England was crassly materialistic and commercial. Now Denmark would certainly not take after England:

> for in Denmark the shopkeeper spirit (*Kræmmer-Aanden*) does not predominate; for us the English character is, without doubt, the most incompatible and antipathetic; we sympathize far more with nations directed by ideal principles. It stands to reason, therefore, that we cannot take the same interest as a commercial people may in accounts of the ups and downs of man's earthly fortune; we cannot attach the same importance to mercantile interests as to those either moral, political, or literary; a business going bankrupt moves us less than a state being dissolved; a merchant despairing that he cannot honour his bills is, in our view, different from a hero who succumbs in the struggle for an idea.[29]

That line of criticism obviously applied to America as well, and in his satirical masterpiece *En Sjæl efter Døden* [A Soul after Death] from Heiberg let a narrowminded Copenhagener with a conspicuous lack of spiritual interests express his yearning "to see the country of such boundless force / the country where on freedom's soil you tread / where steam-engines can handle every task."[30] This was how Danish conservatives (like their counterparts on the Continent) came to view America: a country bereft of culture, thinking only of material goods, as one might expect from the kind of people who emigrated there. But Britain was little better and was often coupled with America as crassly materialistic and ruled by a spirit of economic calculation.[31]

Of course one could find more positive attitudes to societies based on commerce and modern technology. One of them was in fact Hans Christian Andersen, whose youthful joke quoted earlier gives no indication of his later attitude to modernity and America. That is conveyed in his story "In a Thousand Years" ("Om Aartusinder") from 1852.[32] Here he predicts that in a thousand years "the young inhabitants of America will

---

[29] J.L. Heiberg, *Om Vaudevillen og andre kritiske Artikler*, ed. by H. Hertel (Copenhagen: Gyldendal, 1968), 212.

[30] See Henning Fenger, *The Heibergs* (New York: Twayte, 1971).

[31] When the Schleswig branch of the Provincial Assemblies (*stænderforsamlinger*) in 1836 held a debate on the rights of Jews, a casual reference was made to "the English-American spirit of speculation" (the point being that the Jews would be less dangerous there than in a peasant society like Denmark).

[32] The story was published in a newspaper in January 1852, It has been translated into English in a number of inaccessible editions. I draw here on an Internet version made available by an Israeli professor of mathematics, Zvi Har'El.

become the visitors of old Europe," arriving on "wings of steam," their number having been telegraphed in advance. The first stop is "the land of Shakespeare, as the educated call it; in the land of politics, the land of machines, as it is called by others." Having seen England and Scotland in one day, "the busy race," armed with their guidebook *How to See all Europe in a Week*, continues its journey through "the tunnel under the English Channel" to France, Spain and Italy, where all that is left of Rome is "a single ruined wall," perhaps the remains of St. Peter's. They also visit Athens and Constantinople, and travel back along the Danube to Germany and Scandinavia, whence they return home, proud to have "done Europe."

Andersen was an indefatigable traveller and greatly enthusiastic about railways and other technology. He found it a "beautiful, interesting moment" when in 1852 he was first shown how a telegraph worked; the year before he had lamented the fact that a letter he wrote to a recipient who was then in America would take weeks to arrive: "if only we had an electromagnetic wire across the ocean," he sighed. That wire of course came seven years later; Andersen's new Utopia was a realistic one.

In 1853 Carsten Hauch (a trained zoologist) published his novel *Robert Fulton*, freely based on G.D. Colden's biography from 1817. Hauch had never been to America either, a fact which in his preface he declared to be immaterial: the writer of historical novels could not be expected to have visited the place of the action any more than to have lived at the time when it took place.[33] Andersen liked the novel, which incidentally opens in 1776, and in a letter he wrote:

> I have daily skirmishes with [his friend and fellow poet] Ingemann regarding the importance of inventions. He sets poetry high above science; I do not. He admits that we live in a great age of inventions, but will only allow them to affect the mechanical and material world; whereas I consider them to be the indispensable support for the spiritual, the branches on which the flower of poetry may blossom. That people draw more closely together, and that countries and cities connected by steam and electromagnetism become one assembly hall, seems to me to be of such spiritual greatness and splendour that the very thought lifts me higher than any poet's song ever could.[34]

Given Ingemann's views on technology and poetry it is hardly surprising that he did not like America either. In a novel from 1852 he referred to the beginning emigration and the California gold-rush. "If I shall become a truly natural human being, I have to go to the country of liberty, where what counts is what you are," one character says, only to be told:

> Do you plan to visit the natives in their forests then? They have probably all been exterminated by the noble conquerors who have usurped their continent. As far as I know the situation in America, you will

---

http://www.math.technion.ac.il/rl/Andersen/thousand.html (16 July 1997).

[33] Carsten Hauch, *Robert Fulton*, I-II, ed. by Poul Schjærff (Copenhagen: Gad, 1928, Danmarks Nationallitteratur), viii. Andersen never visited America either, somewhat surprising in view of the fact that he travelled so widely (including the Ottoman Empire in 1839-40) and was encouraged several times to do so by his friend Henriette Wulff.

[34] Andersen to Henriette Wulff, 5 June 1853, in *H.C. Andersen og Henriette Wulff: en brevveksling*, I-III, ed. by H. Topsøe-Jensen (Odense: Flensted, 1959), vol. II, letter no. 246.

no doubt everywhere find great business acumen and much political progress, but hardly a more elevated spiritual life or interest in the arts than in that venerable cradle of culture and history which you in your dejection now disparage.[35]

Ingemann's view was more widespread among Danish poets (and among Danes as such) than Andersen's. Obviously there were other groups such as businessmen who would like to see more of the spirit of commerce and enterprise in Denmark; in that sense there was the same divide between liberals and conservatives in Denmark as elsewhere. But I would argue that in Denmark the anti-modern conservative criticism of commercial and industrial capitalism, and of Britain and America as the two markers og modernity, became unusually pervasive. The two dominant groups well into the 20th century were farmers and civil servants, whose sharply conflicting views came to dominate politics after a democratic constitution was introduced in 1849. Disagreeing on most issues they were at least united in their extreme reluctance to embrace modernization. After the defeat by Prussia in 1864 and the loss of the duchies of Schleswig and Holstein Denmark was seized by a kind of "mental inwardness" and there was a broad consensus to the effect that Denmark's future lay in agriculture and that it would not (and should not) become an industrialized country. When in 1912 the leading industrialist Alexander Foss with uncanny precision predicted that industry would overtake agriculture in economic importance around 1950, the general tenor of the debate which followed was "perish the thought."

Danish society was perceived as being on a more human scale and more consensual than others, and was firmly believed to be superior even if small and rural—in fact superior *because* it was small and rural. No countries, except possibly the Scandinavian neighbours, were worth imitating. Germany was disliked for political and national reasons; Britain and the United States for social and economic ones. That the two Anglo-Saxon powers were both democracies no longer set them apart from Denmark (though the principle of parliamentarism was in fact only introduced in Denmark in 1901). Even the two main religious tendencies fighting for control of the Danish church—the pietistic Home Mission of cottagers and labourers and Grundtvig's "happy Christianity" which appealed to well-to-do farmers—buried their disagreements faced with the challenge from the "practical" English and American theology.

It is ironical that this parochial attitude evolved at the same time that Danish contacts with both Britain and the United States began to grow rapidly. In the second half of the 19th century Denmark became almost completely dependent on the export of bacon and butter to the urbanised and industrialised Britain; and Danish emigration to the United States, limited to a few thousand before 1850, now took off and by 1914 300,000 Danes had crossed the Atlantic. But the attitude to the two countries taking Denmark's exports and population surplus, respectively, remained curiously distant and aloof. Agrarian capitalism Danish style, was all right, but chiefly because its success (or so it was thought) would help to block the introduction of "real" industrial capitalism.

---

[35] Quoted in Sven H. Rossel, "The Image of the United States," 54; translation slightly altered.

Incidentally, not a few British and American observers—Rider Haggard and the American ambassador Maurice Egan among them—seemed to agree.[36]

As before Danes found that Britain's commercial mentality seemed to taint and corrupt the positive aspects of the country. A headmaster visiting England in 1859 enthused about the textbooks and the teaching, but deeply regretted that the schools' advertisements were "boasting, bragging and full of self-praise"; though how could that be otherwise, he added, "where the spirit of money and calculation is so powerful as in England?"[37] But the political resentment of Britain eventually began to dissolve in the face of German antagonism, and towards 1900 opinions on Britain certainly became more divided. On the one hand its behaviour during the Boer War seemed to mark it as a cynical Great Power whose attitude to subject nations as Ireland and India seemed resembled German policy in Poland, Alsace and Schleswig; on the other the autocratic tendencies in Germany and the repercussions of the Dreyfus affair in France contributed to a fresh appreciation of the virtues of British liberalism. Also Britain attracted a good deal of "know-how" emigration, especially of civil engineers (often with theoretical qualifications that the English lacked), and who often looked beyond Britain to the world; to a Danish newspaper in 1902 "it is with great expectations that we see the many young Danes now being filled by the English spirit."[38]

Yet this English spirit was still not to everyone's liking. When Queen Victoria died in 1901, the Danes had been greatly impressed by the way the nation mourned: everything shut down, and apparently owners of theatres, concert halls and shops took the considerable loss of income in their stride. When it was revealed that these people had long ago taken out insurances precisely against such an eventuality, and thus had suffered no actual (pecuniary) loss, Danish opinion was outraged.[39] That kind of economic activity was morally speaking immeasurably inferior to selling bacon.

Similar criticism was of course later directed at America. When for instance a Danish newspaper in 1907 referred to advertising as "the great awkward Americanism of the twentieth century," this is of course precisely what the headmaster quoted above had, fifty years earlier, thought peculiarly British; and Grundtvig's condemnation of treating workers like cog-wheels in a machine echoes in Henrik Cavling's observations about the American worker: "The worker not only takes care of his machine. He is part of it. He neither thinks nor talks. If he does not understand how to adapt as an obedient tool of the factory, he is unceremoniously thrown out."[40] The unacceptable face of capitalism was now American. Even radicals in favour of thorough political and

---

[36] J.R. Rasmussen, "Socialismen, landbruget og imperiet: Rider Haggard i Danmark 1910," in *Historiens kultur: fortælling, kritik, metode*, eds. N. de Coninck-Smith, M. Rüdiger and M. Thing (Copenhagen: Museum Tusculanum, 1997), 144, 154 (notes 8-10).

[37] E. Manicus, "Det lærde Skolevæsen i England," *Dansk Maanedsskrift* (1859), II, 419-20.

[38] *Politiken*, 27 August 1902.

[39] *Politiken*, 25 February 1901.

[40] Quoted in Niels Thorsen, "The intellectual discovery of America in Denmark," in *Within the US orbit: small cultures vis-à-vis the United States*, ed. by Rob Kroes (Amsterdam: Free University Press, 1991), 104, 112.

intellectual change began to worry about the consequences. When the literary critic Georg Brandes in 1883 used the word "Americanism," in a review of a novel deeply critical of the grammar schools' fossilized classical curriculum, he did so as a warning against what unthinking criticism of traditional European culture might lead to. Brandes disliked the traditional school, but would not want to see it replaced by a purely utilitarian one; a middle way had to be found based on modern languages and culture.[41]

Here Britain seemed to offer the right mix of modernity and tradition. In the years up to 1914 Britain came to be seen as less "commercial" or "enterprising" and more "imperial-aristocratic"—to which the funerals and crownings of 1901-2 and 1910-1, well covered by the Danish newspapers' ace reporters, must surely have contributed. At the same time it was also becoming more "democratic," without however lapsing into American vulgarity. The gap between rich and poor was narrowed by the Liberals' social policy, which surprised many because "England in the general opinion appears as the home of the dogma about the state's non-intervention in the economy."[42]

Conversely the image of the United States became "Americanized" after the turn of the century. Its corrupt and vulgar democracy was no longer the model it had once been. And whereas the emigrants had originally gone to the agrarian Mid-West, with the urbanization and industrialization more of them ended up in cities characterized by everything Denmark was determined to avoid. Given that more than 300,000 Danes left the country in little more than half a century, there was surprisingly little public debate on emigration, as opposed to Sweden (where admittedly a population twice as large produced four times as many emigrants).[43]

And in spite of the lively communications across the Atlantic there was little cultural transfer. People who came back from the States often found the stolidness and moderate pace of Danish life hard to adapt to. The Danish writer Johannes V. Jensen (who actually won the Nobel Prize in 1944) captured this cultural encounter in a story from 1903, "The Golddigger."[44] A man who had left his wife and small child to follow a Mormon missionary to the United States (knowing however that the two would be taken care of by the parish) returns to his village many years later to find out if his son will let him spend his declining years in his house as a sort of pensioner. He meets with a cool reception from his son, and eventually leaves again, presumably for America. But while he is there he demonstrates his strength and abilities in all kinds of work. The locals are impressed and most of them respect him, but at the same time tend to ridicule him: He was good at all kinds of work, if only you could stop him improving and tinkering with all the tools. To him nothing was ever right, nothing ever went quickly enough. He drove manure in a gallop and ploughed so that the sparks flew from the flint;

---

[41] Georg Brandes, *Samlede Skrifter*, vol. III (Copenhagen: Gyldendal, 1901), 442.

[42] *Politiken*, 22 August 1912.

[43] H. Arnold Barton, *A folk divided: homeland Swedes and Swedish Americans, 1840-1940* (Stockholm: Almquist & Wiksell, 1994).

[44] "Guldgraveren," repr. in Borberg and Damm, *Amerika—Utopia?*, 108-12. In 1944 Jensen became one of the probably lesser known Nobel laureates.

he himself always was in a rush as if he came from a fire to fetch the midwife. He specializes in digging for marl, an extremely demanding physical activity:

"Golddigger" was much in demand and made a lot of money. This, it seemed, was his thing; he simply had to dig. But he showed enterprise as well by going partners with three big Swedish scapegraces in a regular marling business. They slaved away for a month. Then Golddigger had a locomobile brought out from the nearest town, some thirty miles away, and they started to transport the marl in dump cars along a track. People were impressed: imagine digging marl on such a scale! But after only one week of using steam power, the bed of marl was found to be depleted, and the locals laughed their heads off! ... That was America for you! Why, if he had stuck to the old way of digging, there would have been marl enough to last him a lifetime!

Only after the Second World War did American culture, technology and management seriously impinge on Denmark. But it was British troops that in 1945 liberated Denmark from German occupation, and Danes turned anglophile with a vengeance. If this operated as something of a brake on the Americanization which followed, it perhaps also facilitated it in the sense that any cultural resistance to learning and speaking English was muted because it was associated with Britain rather than America.

THE AMBIGUITIES OF ENLIGHTENMENT: GUNNAR MYRDAL AND AFRICAN AMERICAN CULTURE

Richard H. King

"White people today simply do not have a bad conscience over the fact that Negroes were brought here into slavery a long time ago," observed Gunnar Myrdal in a round-table discussion printed in *Commentary* as "Liberalism and the Negro" in 1964.[1] Though delivered in passing, as it were, Myrdal's observation was a startling one, since it seemed to repudiate the central thesis of his massive *An American Dilemma* published two decades earlier—that Americans were committed to what he called "the American Creed" and the "American Dilemma" arose precisely from the bad conscience induced by the conflict between the commitment to equality and freedom and particularist beliefs in racial inequality.

Between the 1930s and the 1960s, large-scale, ambitious investigations of American life, a kind of epic sociology, reached its peak. One thinks of Helen and Robert Lynd's *Middletown* and *Middletown Revisited*, but, more to the point here, of the numerous studies which took the South, whether that of impoverished white farmers and mill hands or of black sharecroppers and African American city dwellers, as their focus. Such studies, emanating from Yale and Chicago, Fisk and the University of North Carolina and written by men and women of both races, were the building blocks of the President's 1938 *Report on the Economic Conditions of the South*, which recognized the South as the "Nation's No. 1 economic problem."

Indeed, Myrdal's two-volume work was perhaps the crowning achievement of progressive epic sociology and of the social policy derived from it. It was cited in Chief Justice Earl Warren's famous *Brown v. Board of Education* (1954) decision outlawing school segregation and had earlier exerted considerable influence on *To Secure These Rights* (1947), the path-breaking report of President Truman's civil rights commission. Books on race relations, studies of the psychological roots of prejudice, proposals for expunging the ugly legacy of racism that marred America's cold war moral leadership: all referred and deferred to the Swedish economist's work. With its publication, then, Myrdal joined such earlier foreign observers as Alexis de Tocqueville, James Bryce and Max Weber to offer a definitive interpretation of the American experience. More than that, Myrdal's *An American Dilemma* established the basic liberal orthodoxy in American race relations the mid-1960s when the huge controversy Daniel Patrick Moynihan's "Report on the Negro Family" appeared. From this perspective, the collapse

---

[1] Gunnar Myrdal, "Liberalism and the Negro," *Commentary*, 37 (1964), 30. The participants in the round table discussion were Sidney Hook, Nathan Glazer, James Baldwin and Myrdal.

of that framework of assumptions was foreshadowed by Myrdal's own statement in the *Commentary* symposium of 1964.

But that far from exhausts the significance of Myrdal's massive work. It belongs in an international context as well. Along with Theodor Adorno and Max Horkheimer's *The Dialectic of Enlightenment* (1944; 1947), Jean-Paul Sartre's *Anti-Semite and Jew* (1946) and Hannah Arendt's *The Origins of Totalitarianism* (1951), *An American Dilemma* attempted to come to terms with the disfiguring presence of racism and anti-Semitism in Western life and thought. But where the continued viability of the Western tradition of humanism was problematic in the works both of Adorno and Horkheimer and of Arendt, Myrdal's work largely shied away from any such historical or philosophical self-consciousness. Of course, Adorno and Horkheimer's now well-known claim that progress in Enlightenment entailed progress in domination and that the control of nature meant the control of human beings was not available to Myrdal. But though Myrdal, as we shall see, was aware of certain blind spots in the Enlightenment perspective, he would have thought it bizarre to indict the tradition of humanism and secular Enlightenment as part of the problem rather than of the solution. *An American Dilemma*, along with the rest of Myrdal's life work, was clearly a defense of the Enlightenment tradition of social analysis and prescription, rationality in the service of reform, enlightenment in the service of a progress toward freedom and equality. The question Myrdal's intellectual biographer, Walter Jackson, has identified as crucial for Myrdal's formative intellectual years in Sweden best captures the nature of his life-long commitments: "How could one recover the heritage of the Enlightenment and subject the irrational in human behavior to scientific analysis so as to plan for a more rational future?"[2] Whether in Sweden or in America (or later in studying Asian economic development), Myrdal maintained a generally optimistic vision of the possibilities of rational reform, based on the assumption, as Timothy Tilton has pointed out, that all "social goods are largely compatible."[3]

Still, no work addressing a topic as explosive as American race relations could have escaped criticism. Southern racial conservatives (rightly) charged Myrdal with challenging the idea that black people were inferior to whites, while Mississippi Senator James Eastland (wrongly) charged Myrdal in 1958 with being a "Socialist who had served the Communist cause."[4] More moderate white Southern academics and intellectual, the dean of regional sociologists Howard W. Odum among them, were afraid

---

[2] Walter Jackson, *Gunnar Myrdal and America's Conscience* (Chapel Hill, N.C., UNC Press, 1990), 55. See also David Southern, *Gunnar Myrdal and Black-White Relations* (Baton Rouge, LA.: LSU Press, 1987). Both works are invaluable sources of information and analysis, Jackson's in particular. In a sense this paper is but a footnote to it.

[3] Timothy Tilton, "Gunnar Myrdal and the Swedish Model, " in *Gunnar Myrdal and His Works* ed. by Gilles Dostales et al. (Montreal: Harvest House, 1992), 21. Tilton and other contributors to the volume underline Myrdal's strong commitment to the Enlightenment heritage and contrast Myrdal's "compatibilist" liberalism with Isaiah Berlin's tragic liberalism in which, for example, equality and freedom are not necessarily compatible in all (or any) situations.

[4] James O. Eastland, "An Alien Ideology is NOT the Law of Our Republic", *The American Mercury*, 86 (1958), 28.

that Myrdal's too liberal "take" on the racial situation would endanger the progress they thought had already been made in the South. Not surprisingly, Myrdal's Marxist critics accused him of not being radical enough, which is to say, of not being a Marxist but rather a bourgeois reformer. (Both charges were true.) According to critics such as Herbert Aptheker, Doxey Wilkinson and Oliver O. Cox, Myrdal's work only re-enforced the status quo rather than aiding in its destruction, since it took, not class, but race and caste as the central categories of analysis and explanation. On the other hand, Myrdal got his most consistent support from black intellectuals and academics, though even there responses were somewhat varied. More recently, historian Numan Bartley has charged that *An American Dilemma* played a crucial role in shifting the center of gravity of post-war liberalism from an emphasis upon social and economic issues to a morally charged obsession with dismantling segregation to the detriment of the economic progress of the less well-off of both races and in the North as well as in the South. From this perspective, the decline of the Democratic Party and the rise of a Wallace-ite politics of (white) resentment in the South seem all but inevitable.[5]

Though these are important issues, my interest here lies elsewhere. One of the striking things about an *American Dilemma*, at least in retrospect, was the way that Myrdal so underestimated the strength of African American culture and its central institutions in the struggle for black social, economic and political equality. In fact, behind this strange neglect of black culture were the very assumptions of a progressive, Enlightenment-derived sociology. I want to avoid any easy or cheap shots at the Enlightenment—such have become a dime a dozen; nor is it possible to imagine the genuine analytical or moral achievements of *An American Dilemma* aside from the Enlightenment tradition. But it seems undeniable that it did at least contributed to Myrdal's and his associates' understanding of the strengths—as well as weaknesses—of African American culture. Thus in *An American Dilemma*, the "other of reason" blocking black progress and racial justice, was not only the ideology of white racial superiority which provided the justification for the caste system in the South; more surprisingly, it was also the distorted nature of the dominant institutions and culture of black America, North and South.

The Context

The intellectual and political context in which Myrdal was chosen director of the Carnegie Corporation-funded project in 1938 is crucial to an understanding of *An American Dilemma*. Between the end of World War I and the conclusion of World War II, the Anglophone academic world witnessed a far-reaching paradigm shift in the study

---

[5] Numan B. Bartley, *The New South* (Baton Rouge, LA.: LSU Press, 1996). It is significant that C. Vann Woodward's *Origins of the New South* (1951) scarcely mentions the progressive racial implications of southern progressivism, the "party of enlightenment" if such existed in the turn of the century South. Indeed, Woodward described it as a progressivism "for whites only."

of race. In anthropology, biology, psychology, and sociology, the assumption of fixed racial differences came under withering intellectual scrutiny, even before the full horrors of Hitler's racial state came to light. Once they did begin to register, a consensus firmly opposed to racial differences grounded in biology emerged among intellectual and academic elites. Overall, in these years, the preoccupation with the allegedly objective traits of separate races gave way to an investigation of the subjective attitudes one group projected onto, or found in, another. "Prejudice" not "race" came much more to the fore in the study of race relations.[6]

Yet liberal politics and political thought in America underwent a subtle but important re-orientation in the interwar years. As Gary Gerstle put it, "a new liberalism that emphasized the 'economic' and neglected the 'cultural' was the choice of influential liberal thinkers to put their embattled creed on a more secure foundation."[7] While race and particularly ethnicity had played a prominent role in the political debates of the Progressive era and while post-World War II liberalism elevated civil rights and the pursuit of racial equality to near pre-eminence, New Deal liberalism stressed social and economic concerns to the distinct neglect of race and culture. Paradoxically, this shift in emphasis may have allowed a multi-ethnic and multi-racial New Deal liberal coalition to emerge. By 1936, most black Americans had joined the ranks of the Democratic Party, but on the terms set by the white political class and the white electorate generally. In *An American Dilemma*, Myrdal referred explicitly to the serious disparity between the academic elite hostility to white supremacy and the majority white public's resistance to abandoning white supremacy. It is precisely this gap that explained the reluctance of liberal intellectuals and politicians (of both races) to focus too much attention on race and ethnicity between the two World Wars. In times of economic depression, questions relating to racial equality or ethnic difference seemed of less than compelling importance at best and an irrelevance at worst. One has only to inspect the FSA-sponsored photography of the 1930s, a marvellous visual record in itself, to note the way that poverty was seen largely as a white phenomenon.

Yet on this and certain other issues, Myrdal, who had been selected because Sweden allegedly lacked a history of imperial domination and who was not in fact well-versed in the literature of American race relations, represented a partial exception to the dominant tendencies of American political and social science of the time. For instance, Myrdal's ideological commitment to Swedish social democracy distanced him radically from the Sumnerian idea that "Folkways" trumped "Stateways"; led him to challenge sociologist Robert Park's rejection of state intervention in the four stage process of racial and ethnic assimilation (competition/ conflict/ accommodation/ assimilation); and also

---

[6] For this shift from focusing on race to a concentration upon prejudice, see Franz Samuelson, "From Race Psychology to Studies in Prejudice," *Journal of the History of the Behavioral Sciences*, 14 (1978), 265-78.

[7] Gary Gerstle, "The Protean Character of American Liberalism", *American Historical Review*, 39 (1949), 1045. See also Tony Kushner, *The Holocaust and the Liberal Imagination* (Oxford, U.K.: Basil Blackwell, 1994) for an analysis of the shift in racial and ethnic consciousness during an after World War II in both the United States and Great Britain.

meant that he dismissed the Chapel Hill Regionalists' gradualism by supporting a direct intellectual and moral intervention in the Jim Crow South. Myrdal's outsider perspective, at once both rational and morally engaged, helped him avoid many of the conventional wisdoms of American race relations.

Yet in other respects. Myrdal felt right at home in America. The theory of the State assumed in Myrdal's Swedish-derived "Third Way" approach posited an activist, interventionist state which would see its task as one of adopting economic, social and educational policies to help remedy racial problems. If white American academics and politicians failed to see the way to translate Roosevelt's New Deal interventionist impulses into racial policy, the Swede could and would. Nothing in Myrdal's background or in the text itself suggested that education and moral suasion alone were enough. Intellectually, Myrdal was on familiar ground. Having spend 1929-30 in America, Myrdal and his wife Alva had been powerfully influenced by John Dewey's work. Thus the Carnegie-funded project Myrdal ruled over as an enlightened despot (one of Myrdal's most trusted associates, Ralph Bunche, once half-jokingly referred to Myrdal as a "Swedish Simon Legree") placed a Swedish, social-democratic spin on American liberal-progressive social science. Significantly, however, what Myrdal failed to adopt from the Deweyan perspective was the American philosopher's commitment to democratic participation in the social engineering schemes of the liberal social science elites. In short, Myrdal was no populist, either at home or abroad, a not insignificant fact in trying to figure out why Myrdal was tone-deaf to the nature of African American culture.[8] Overall, then, Myrdal rejected the notion that intervention in a racially biased and economically unequal society would be unwise or ineffectual, but his concern with the cultural sphere, particularly at the grass-roots level, remained largely undeveloped.

Of great importance, moreover, was that Myrdal bought into the new consensus on race and culture. But this in itself was a tricky issue. Though the biological bases for white superiority had been discredited, a new consensus on the issue of cultural difference had emerged: at least for the present, black American culture was distinctly inferior to the dominant white American culture. As James McKee has summed it up: "they[sociologists] discarded the idea that black people were biologically inferior, but, despite the arguments of anthropologists, they retained an image of them as culturally inferior."[9] Secondly, and symmetrically, the dominant white population was marked by deeply held prejudices. But these were not the expression of natural impulses; rather they were learned and could be changed over time. Overall, then, inherited racial inferiority by blacks and natural prejudices on the part of whites had been rejected only to replace them with the idea that blacks were culturally inferior and that whites were deeply prejudiced. On these issues Myrdal largely agreed with the dominant thinking,

---

[8] Jackson makes this point particularly clearly, while Robert Westbrook's *John Dewey and American Democracy* (Ithaca, N.Y.: Cornell University Press, 1991) presents a convincing case for Dewey's democratic (as opposed to technocratic) credentials.

[9] James B. McKee, *Sociology and the Race Problem: The Future of a Perspective* (Urbana and Chicago, IL.: University of Illinois Press, 1993), 6. McKee presents an invaluable intellectual history of the way American sociologists have dealt with race in this century.

though on the matter of white prejudice, as I have stated, Myrdal was to speak with much more urgency for active intervention to combat white prejudice. Though not a revolutionary, Myrdal was no gradualist either, content merely to let time heal all ills.

The American Creed

Though Myrdal explained the origins and definition of his best known concept "The American Creed" in various ways, it is best considered the moral foundation of American political culture and institutions, organized as it is around "a belief in equality and in the rights to liberty."[10] Myrdal duly acknowledged the influences of the Judaeo-Christian tradition and of English legal and political traditions; however, the chief sources of the American Creed were found in "the great tradition of the Enlightenment and the American Revolution." Indeed, as numerous commentators have noted, the last word of the study was "Enlightenment."[11] Interestingly, when Myrdal returned to Sweden once World War II had broken out, he became even more convinced of the importance of something like the "American Creed." From that distance, Americans seemed quite clear about what they were fighting to preserve. Thus, it was his experience, as Walter Jackson has noted, not any deep philosophical commitment to the priority of consciously held ideas and values over social and economic forces that pushed him to emphasize the importance of the Creed for resolving the American dilemma.

It is important to understand the complex and protean-like quality of the American Creed as posited by Myrdal. First, Myrdal treated the Creed as an empirical social fact which summed up the actual basis for the shared consensus among "most Americans"[12] of both races. Second, not only was the Creed a social fact, it also offered a normative standard to Americans (and to readers of *An American Dilemma*). In this sense, it anticipated what Robert Bellah later referred to as "the American civil religion" and what Jefferson had referred to in 1800 as the "text of civil instruction." In addition, Myrdal deployed the Creed as a methodological or heuristic tool, from which he could derive the standards by which American performance in areas of race relations could be judged and even predicted. Thus, for instance, discrimination was wrong in the American context, not because tolerance or equality was an eternal value inscribed in the nature of things, but because "equality of opportunity" was a value to which the American people had notionally set themselves to live up to. Finally, Myrdal used the American Creed in what might be termed a "performative" or pragmatic sense. In (William) Jamesian terms, truth "happens" to an idea. By positing and evoking the Creed, Myrdal succeeded to a degree in raising it to self-consciousness and thus strengthening it.

---

[10] Gunnar Myrdal, *An American Dilemma*, vol. 1 (New York: McGraw-Hill, 1964), 8.
[11] Myrdal, vol. II, 1024.
[12] Myrdal, vol. 1, lxxi.

Over and against the American Creed, Myrdal detected the great influence of specific, particularistic values and ideologies by which Americans lived but which were at odds with the American Creed. Specifically he had in mind notions of racial and caste superiority, found most explicitly among southern whites. What he called the "American Dilemma" arose from the "conflict between his moral valuations" on "the general plane which we shall call the 'American Creed' " and the "valuations on specific planes of individual and group living."[13] And though white and black Americans shared the Creed, the moral and psychological dilemma which arose from the conflict between the particular, racist creeds and the general American Creed of equality was obviously "the white man's problem."[14]

Presenting no theory of unconscious motivation nor thick description of intra-psychic conflict—Myrdal was an economist and social scientists not a psychoanalyst—he in fact often depicted the dilemma as a conflict between the white South and the rest of the country; that is, as one between groups as much as within individuals. At the time of writing roughly 75% of African Americans lived in the South, so focussing his attention on the South was not without justification. By the 1960s, when only around 50% of the nation's black population lived in the South, the southern focus of Myrdal's work would seem increasingly misplaced, this perhaps contributing to the growing sense the *An American Dilemma* had lost its cogency.

As mentioned, Myrdal resisted the notion that white prejudice was inevitable and stressed that there was a dilemma just because "people also want to be rational."[15] In fact, rationality and morality are all but synonymous in *An American Dilemma*. Formally, they refer to the desire to bring specific and general beliefs into harmony; substantively, the assume the equality of all people. Just as clearly, one motivation driving his analysis was the desire to undermine the power of the specific creeds: "The gradual destruction of the popular theory behind race prejudice is the most important of all social trends in the field of interracial relations." In keeping with the hot-house atmosphere of war-time optimism, Myrdal proposed "an educational offensive against racial intolerance," something which had "never seriously been attempted in America."[16] This was clearly the militant Enlightenment on the march against intolerance as a cast of mind and discrimination as a form of action.

Yet, Myrdal did more than offer a simple proposal for popular education against racial intolerance. He also proposed a more comprehensive, explanatory "vicious circle" model based on the principle of "cumulation." According to this analytical model, which put clear water between him and the Marxists, there was no one privileged cause of, or solution to, America's racial agonies. Myrdal admitted that the American Creed was "less specified and articulated in the economic field than, for instance, in regard to civil

---

[13] Ibid., lxxi.
[14] Ibid.
[15] Ibid., lxiii.
[16] Myrdal, vol. 2, 1003; vol. 1, 48-49. A good account of the war-time atmosphere of social hope, see Ellen Hermann, *The Romance of American Psychology: Political Culture in the Age of the Experts* (Berkeley, CA.: University of California Press, 1995).

rights" and that "'equality of opportunity' had always been challenged by the belief in the "'liberty' to run one's business as one pleases." But it was a measure of Myrdal's optimism that he predicted that equality of opportunity would become enshrined in the form of a social and economic right.[17]

Specifically, Myrdal identified:

> three bundles of interdependent, causal factors—1) the economic level; 2) [black] standards of intelligence, ambition, health, education, decency, manners and morals; and 3) discrimination by whites ...[18]

The key to halting, even reversing, the downward spiral of cumulative causation lay in introducing a positive change in one of these factors. Thus, when "a primary change, induced or unplanned, affecting anyone of the three bundles" occured, there would be accompanying "changes in the other two and, through mutual interaction, [they] move the whole system along in one direction or another."[19] Though presenting a complex, multi-factoral model, Myrdal's basic assumption was that things could and should be meliorated through outside intervention.

All that said, Myrdal's optimism was not as simplistic as it may now sound. It makes no sense to criticize *An American Dilemma* for its optimism as such, since it was just the point of the study to provide foundations for rational public policy decisions. Nor does the tension between the American Creed and particularist, racist beliefs have to be couched in regional rather than intra-psychic terms. Had Myrdal done the latter, his work might have had some of the dense complexity of the idea of "double consciousness" which DuBois had posited at the center of African American consciousness. That is, Myrdal could have developed a notion of white double-consciousness. Nor, strictly speaking, is it correct to see the moral dilemma of white Americans in terms of the conflict between "theory" and "practice," as it is often expressed. Rather, it was primarily a conflict between two sets—and types—of beliefs: the general and the specific. For Myrdal, racist views were irrational because they conflicted with the standards of the Creed which were themselves the measure of rationality.[20]

Nor was Myrdal's claim that white Americans wanted to be "rational" as naive or as easily achieved as it sounded. "Rational" for Myrdal meant that which involved a preference for the general over the particular, for equality over white supremacy, in keeping with the universalizing spirit of the American Creed. To Myrdal's way of thinking, rationality was an achievement, the overcoming of the "specific" beliefs in the light of the "general" belief in equality. In this sense the American Creed was not just a static, normative standard but, as mentioned, a performative utterance, a way of

---

[17] Ibid., 209. In this context, the Civil Rights Act of 1964 might be seen as an expression of such a guarantee, along with the expanded interpretation and application of the Fourteenth Amendment.
[18] Ibid., 208.
[19] Ibid., 208.
[20] See Rogers M. Smith, "Beyond Tocqueville, Myrdal, and Hartz: The Multiple Traditions in America," *American Political Science Review*, 87 (1993), 533.

bringing itself into being. Nor was the educational effort Myrdal recommended to fight prejudice to be one-dimensional or heedless of the type or depth of prejudice.

Still, it is not surprising that some white and especially black readers of *An American Dilemma* were sceptical of Myrdal's emphasis upon the white American dilemma. Sociologist, E. Franklin Frazier praised Myrdal's emphasis upon the American dilemma as "essentially a moral problem" but wondered whether it was "on the conscience of white people to the extent implied in his statement." Though Frazier failed to elaborate on the types of whites who might be more or less sensitive to the dilemma, he did suggest a kind of moral-metaphysical threshold beyond which the Creed might come into effect: "It is when the Negro emerges as a human being and a part of the moral order that discrimination against him is on the conscience of the white man."[21] Frazier's subtle criticism suggests that Myrdal might have paid more attention to the historical emergence among whites of the idea that blacks were fully human, but Myrdal was not primarily interested in taking the historical perspective.

Similarly, it may be appropriate to call Myrdal's position a "consensus" view of the American experience; but that consensus, like rationality, was something to be achieved or realized, not a comfortably shared set of values. Still, racist beliefs were aberrations from the American Creed; and in this claim, Myrdal of course, comes into conflict with later students of American race, such as historian Edmund Morgan and novelist Toni Morrison, who see white American identity as entailing the inferiority—and marginalization—of African-Americans. But Myrdal never claimed that racist beliefs were foreign to many white Americans or at least to white Southerners. Nor was the dominant position of the Creed quite so firmly at the center of Myrdal's analysis as it seemed, since it was somewhat at odds with the "principle of cumulation." While, according to the American Creed, the problem was one of rectification of conscience, of making rational what was irrational in the white psyche, the principle of cumulation, as already mentioned, depicted three equally crucial factors at work: economics, white racial consciousness and black life and culture. Any one, or a combination of all of them, had to be addressed to resolve the dilemma.

In other areas, the Creed was complex, even self-contradictory, as Myrdal himself recognized. For instance, the strong belief in laissez-faire (running one's business as one pleased) had nothing to do with racist beliefs or a defense of the caste system. Yet it could, and did, re-enforce the existing racial status quo. In addition, resolving the tension between equality and liberty by uniting them in the concept of "equality of opportunity" was a sleight-of-hand not a genuine resolution on Myrdal's part. The weight of past oppression and exclusion could scarcely be nullified just by opening up opportunities in the present. Yet, in 1964, Myrdal was opposed to early calls for preferential treatment and reverse discrimination: "I am convinced that this demand for discrimination in reverse, i.e. to the advantage of Negroes, is misdirected."[22]

---

[21] E. Franklin Frazier, Review of *An American Dilemma*, *American Journal of Sociology*, L, 556.

[22] Gunnar Myrdal, *The New Republic* (February 8 1964), 15. In the *Commentary* symposium of March 1964 (see footnote 1), Myrdal repeated this objection to what became affirmative action.

In addition, maverick Marxist sociologist, Oliver Cox, charged that Myrdal was much too sanguine about the workings of the principle of cumulation and thereby slighted the psychological complexities of white-black relations. Suppose, Cox suggested, that there was a rise in Negro standards (factor 2) and that this meant "Negroes increase their interest in white women."[23] The hostile reaction from white Southerners was not hard to imagine, thus suggesting that improvement in one of the three factors would not automatically lead to improvement in the other two. There did seem little room in Myrdal's model for white resentment of black efforts at self-improvement, even according to white standards. Finally, Cox contended that resistance to changing the racial order in the South was led by the white Southern planter oligarchy and failed to foresee—as many others also failed—that the planter oligarchy's days were numbered after 1945.

The Cultural Question

In retrospect, Myrdal's firm belief in black cultural inadequacy was the most striking thing about his two-volume study.[24] Ironically, the more conservative Robert Park paid greater attention to black cultural consciousness than did progressive sociologists such as Myrdal. For example at the beginning of chapter 43 ("Institutions"), Myrdal asserted that the black "family, crime, insanity and cultural achievements" were "not focal to our inquiry," despite the fact that one of the three crucial causal forces Myrdal identified as crucial in the deterioration of Negro life were "standards of intelligence, ambition, health, education, decency, manners and morals...."[25] In fact, Myrdal was so little concerned with black life that the initial draft of the two chapters dealing with them (chapters 43 and 44, consisting of 67 pages) were written by one of Myrdal's assistants, Arnold Rose. Not surprisingly, Myrdal asserted that Negro institutions "show little similarity to African institutions," thus rejecting Melville Herskovits's work on African cultural survivals in the New World as constituting the core of the beliefs and practices of a separate black American culture. Myrdal drove the point home when he announced his assumption—and by extension his conclusion—that:

> In practically all its divergences, American Negro culture is not something independent of general American culture. It is a distorted development, or a pathological condition, of the general American culture.

Following on from this, Myrdal concluded that

---

[23] Oliver O. Cox, *Caste, Class and Race* (New York: Monthly Review Press, 1948), 530.

[24] In *Gunnar Myrdal and America's Conscience*, Walter Jackson covers some of the major points in Myrdal's analysis of black culture, e.g. see 130-31; 119-27. See also Daryl M. Scott's very useful *Contempt and Pity* (Chapel Hill, N.C.: UNC Press, 1997) for a thorough exploration of the "damage" thesis regarding African American culture in this century.

[25] Myrdal, vol. II, 907; vol. I, 208.

it is to the advantage of American Negroes as individuals and as a group to become assimilated into American culture ... This will be the value premise here...here in America, American culture is 'highest' in the pragmatic sense.[26]

One thing in particular deserves comment: the way Myrdal moves almost imperceptibly from Negro culture as "not something independent" to it as a "distorted development" and finally to black culture as a "pathological condition". The escalation of rhetoric and hence (future) implication here was considerable.

Then just after these crucial passages, Myrdal both acknowledged and sidestepped the issue of culture equality. He first grants the salutary effect of "the notion popularized by anthropologists that all cultures may be good under the different conditions to which they are adaptations."[27] But then he honestly, if evasively, gives his judgement a pragmatic spin by suggesting that,in the American context, the abstract issue of cultural equality should be forgotten and that black Americans should adapt to, and adopt, the dominant "American" (that is, white) culture. As already mentioned, Myrdal deployed the binary opposition "general/local" to structure his normative judgements. As always, the more general, the better; the more particularized, the worse.

The specific criterion by which Myrdal judged black institutions, ranging from the family through to the churches, was their failure to nurture political change. In light of its later importance in the civil rights movement, Myrdal's dismissal of the black church as apolitical and as "an ordinary American church with certain traits exaggerated because of caste"), along with his failure to identify its potential for mass political mobilization was striking. The irony, according to Myrdal, was that modernization made the black church "a more efficient instrument" for advancement, while "reducing[its] relative importance." Only "the fighting press" received good marks for its political militancy.[28] This is not to say that Myrdal totally neglected recent political ferment. But his emphasis fell upon the need to improve black leadership and their need to forge political alliances with white groups. No political movement originating exclusively among African Americans and under their leadership seemed possible or desirable. Myrdal did treat Marcus Garvey with a certain wary respect but also with hardly any enthusiasm. The main lesson he drew from the rise and fall of Garvey was that support for the UNIA "testifies to the unrest in the Negro community" and that "a Negro movement in America is doomed to ultimate dissolution and collapse if it cannot gain white support. This is the real dilemma."[29] Indeed, it might be added: that was, and still is, the African American political dilemma. The parallel with the cultural question is clear—the more general, the better.

To ears attuned to post-1965 assertions of black pride, the rediscovery of black history and the reconstruction of the black family and culture within and after slavery, Myrdal's position seems to anticipate the position Stanley Elkins was later to adopt in

---

[26] Myrdal, vol. II, 927-28.
[27] Ibid, 929.
[28] Ibid., 873; 878; 908.
[29] Ibid., 749.

his *Slavery* (1959) and which Elkins would describe still later as representing the "literature of damage" on slavery.[30] But lest we attribute that judgement to racial hostility or even to cultural tone-deafness, it should be noted that very few black academics or intellectuals challenged Myrdal on this point. E. Franklin Frazier and Ralph Bunche, his two most trusted black advisers—and here it should be noted that Myrdal involved black social scientists in his project to an unprecedented degree and in a way not matched before or since—had no problem with Myrdal's judgement. In general they were no yes-men. Frazier's review of *An American Dilemma* did question the depth of white commitment to the "American Creed" and Bunche favored the pursuit of an alliance between black Americans and working class whites, neither of which positions Myrdal preferred. But on the question of the strengths and weaknesses of black institutions and culture, there was general agreement.

Other black intellectuals at the fringes of the project failed to challenge Myrdal's cultural judgements. Even though W.E.B. DuBois advocated the development of autonomous black institutions in *Dusk of Dawn* (1940) and earlier in *The Souls of Black Folk* (1903) created the terms for discussing black cultural psychology, he never challenged the Swede on the centrality of the cultural issue which he (DuBois) had so trenchantly raised in *The Souls of Black Folk* (1903), perhaps due to DuBois's own ambivalence about the strength of black institutions. (Though Myrdal cited DuBois extensively in *An American Dilemma*, he did challenge DuBois's advocacy of separation in *Dusk of Dawn* as providing "the caste system with a certain moral sanction."[31]) The "founder" of Negro History, Carter Woodson, was severely critical of *An American Dilemma*, but his animus could be dismissed as sour grapes, since in *An American Dilemma* Myrdal accused Woodson of turning out racial propaganda marked by a "distortion in emphasis and perspective" rather than encouraging a historiography that could be respected.[32] Richard Wright failed to voice any strong objections, which was scarcely surprising in light of his bitter indictment of black southern culture—or the lack of it—in *Black Boy* and his general ambivalence on the topic. Zora Neale Hurston, a student of Franz Boas and one-time assistant to Herskovits, certainly celebrated the African American folk culture of her time, but her response to *An American Dilemma* on such matters is unknown. Thus there seemed to be a general consensus, or at least a lack of strong conviction, that African American culture was not worth defending in explicit terms.

Nor did Marxists in general do any better. Oliver Cox, Myrdal's most formidable black adversary, scored Myrdal's neglect of a class analysis and questioned his preference for a "caste" approach adopted from the "caste and class" school of sociologists of the 1930s. But Cox assumed in Myrdalian terms that black Americans were "a people without a culture to itself, but having only a truncated pattern of the

---

[30] Stanley Elkins, "The Two Arguments on Slavery" (1975), in *Slavery*, 3rd. ed. (Chicago, IL.: University of Chicago Press, 1976).
[31] Myrdal, vol. II, 798.
[32] Ibid., 752.

general culture within which it lives." For that reason, they were bent on assimilation.[33] Except for Herbert Aptheker, who questioned just about everything in *An American Dilemma*, including Myrdal's anti-Nazi credentials in the war, hardly anyone raised the cultural issue or insisted on the usability of the black American past. Only Ralph Ellison's unpublished review of *An American Dilemma* noted the bias in Myrdal's approach and thereby kept the DuBoisian tradition of cultural consciousness alive:

> can a people ... live and develop over three hundred years simply by reacting? Are American Negroes simply the creations of white men, or have they at least helped to create themselves out of what they found around them?

Ellison's views first saw the light of day in *Shadow and Act* (1964) and were then increasingly expanded upon by the newly articulate advocates of black consciousness and the champions of black culture. Particularly biting were Albert Murray's attacks on social scientists. Murray scored the "folklore of white supremacy and the fakelore of black pathology" in his *The Omni-Americans* (1971). Murray savaged social scientists ranging from Daniel Patrick Moynihan to Kenneth Clark and included Myrdal in his strictures, though conceding that Myrdal had been "relatively fair-minded."[34] Harold Cruse's *The Crisis of the Negro Intellectuals* (1967) urged black Americans to seize control of the means of cultural production and reproduction, while Leroi Jones (Amiri Baraka), Larry Neal and Addison Gayle, among others, advocated the development of a black aesthetic and black arts movement, explicitly grounded in black American and African experiences and rejecting white European forms of expression and ideas. In the course of a quarter-century, the tide had significantly turned, even reversed itself. African American culture, far from pathological and damaged, had become the source not only of artistic but also political health.

But how can we explain this overwhelming uniformity of attitude among early readers of *An American Dilemma* and among members of Myrdal's team, black and white? First, as mentioned, most progressive social scientists of both races assumed the priority of the social and economic to the racial and ethnic; certainly both Bunche and Frazier did. From their perspective, a focus on black culture was a diversion from the main business at hand and perhaps also harkened back too strongly to Garveyite black nationalism of the 1920s which had become the bugbear of many liberal and left-wing black academics and intellectuals. Frazier's chief objection to emphasizing a separate black culture or racial pride arose from his suspicion that white conservatives thought that races "should maintain their purity just as flowers do" and "believe that the Negro

---

[33] Cox, *Caste, Class and Race*, 569.
[34] Ralph Ellison, "*An American Dilemma*: A Review", *Shadow and Act* (New York: Signet Books, 1964), 301; Albert Murray, *The Omni-Americans* (New York: Avon Books, 1970), 20; 57. See also Joyce Ladner (ed), *The Death of White Sociology* (New York: Vintage Books, 1973).

should develop race pride." They hoped that the development of racial pride would, and should prevent blacks from attacking segregation.[35]

Indeed, if anyone was responsible for excluding Herskovits's claims for the importance of African survivals from *An American Dilemma*, it was Frazier. His letter to Arnold Rose, who had drafted the two chapters on black life and institutions after Myrdal's departure for Sweden in September 1942, insisted that Rose had given too much weight to the Herskovits thesis. Observed Frazier: "I would say there is some truth in the assumption about African origins rather than a 'great deal of truth'." Frazier added in another letter to Rose in December 1942 that "isolation" was "responsible for the incomplete assimilation of white man's culture." And in the same letter, Frazier further developed his reasons for rejecting the African origins thesis: "if whites came to believe that Negro social behavior was rooted [in] African cultures, they would lose whatever sense of guilt they had for keeping Negroes down."[36] Nor should it be forgotten that in the context of the early 1940s, one logical destination of emphasizing cultural and racial autarky was Hitlerian nationalism and racism. In a world where the global perspective and internationalism seemed the wave of the future, particularistic ideologies of blackness seemed little more appealing or justifiable than the white racial particularism that so pervaded the white South.

Second, though Warren Susman once suggested that the rediscovery of local and regional cultures was a central theme in America intellectual and cultural life during the Depression, those "folk" cultures which were rediscovered and celebrated were overwhelmingly, as Gary Gerstle has noted, white Southern or Yankee New England or rural people of long-standing residence. This is not the entire story, since during the 1930s significant collections of interviews with former slaves were carried out and much of the black music of the rural South was recorded or transcribed. Still, it was true enough to make the point about the selective rediscovery— and selective definition—of the American folk.[37] Apparently the "New Negro" created by the Harlem Renaissance moved in such rarefied, even decadent, cultural circles as to be of little use.

Still in fairness to Myrdal and his associates, and contrary to Myrdal's later reputation as a kind of naive, overly rational (and flattering) foreign visitor, neither segment of America culture—black or white—emerged from his study looking very impressive. If black culture was dysfunctional, white culture and institutions were disfigured by racist assumptions and compromised by divided moral loyalties. Moreover, there was *something* to be said for Myrdal's position. Black life had been

---

[35] Letter from Frazier to Myrdal, June 27, 1942, in E. Franklin Frazier papers, Moreland-Spingarn Center, Howard University Library, Washington, D.C., Box 131, Folder 16 (1942). The specific person Frazier had in mind was a southern racial moderate, Willis Weatherford.

[36] Frazier to Arnold Rose, n.d. (late 1942); Frazier to Rose, December 14, 1942. The last comment about African culture was incorporated into chapter 35, note 32 of *An American Dilemma*, vol. II, 1394.

[37] See Warren Susman, "The Thirties," in *The Development of American Culture* ed. by S. Coben and L. Ratner (New York: St. Martin's Press, 1983), 215-60; Gerstle, 1068-69. For additional background on this issue, see Robert Dorman, *The Revolt of the Provinces: The Regional Movement in America, 1920-1945* (Chapel Hill, N.C.: UNC Press, 1993). There was a revival of interest in American Indian life and culture in the 1930s which didn't seem to arouse much apprehension.

profoundly affected by the history of slavery and oppression under segregation, including of course poverty and deprivation. In certain areas, African American culture was as much a "culture of damage" as much as it was one of "creativity." Black institutions did suffer from the negative effects of limited resources; nor, as of the mid-1940s, was there a lengthy, successful history of black political autonomy or mobilization. Finally, Myrdal's motives for being so critical were honorable, since he emphasized that if there was a choice between praising or criticizing black institutions, he would choose the latter stance in order hopefully to goad those institutions into great political awareness.

Other factors were also at work. Myrdal himself had little interest in the culture sphere, whether high or folk or popular; nor was there a profound philosophical or moral intelligence at work in *An American Dilemma*. Both Stanley Elkins and more recently Ivan Hannaford have emphasized the "moralizing" nature of Myrdal's approach, along with his preference for a "rational mechanical, social-engineering remedy," a combination not noted for its sensitivity to political complexity or to expressive culture.[38] While it is hard to imagine Hannah Arendt's *Origins of Totalitarianism* (1951) without the Kafkaesque and Heideggerian motifs informing it or to understand Theodor Adorno and Max Horkheimer's *The Dialectic of Enlightenment* (1944) apart from the sensibility of the European avant-garde which dominates it, no such literary or philosophical reference points come to mind when reading Myrdal's *An American Dilemma*. At best, its philosophical underpinnings remind the reader of John Dewey's combination of science and morality or Jefferson's Enlightenment faith in reason.

Perhaps this what Richard Wright, one of Myrdal's champions and later a close friend, was driving at when, in the introduction to *Black Metropolis*, he wondered how it was possible to do justice to the complexities of black urban life:

> We have the testimony of Gunnar Myrdal, but we know that is not all. What would life on Chicago's South Side look like when seen through the eyes of a Freud, a Joyce, a Proust, a Pavlov, a Kierkegaard?[39]

Even more importantly, none of Myrdal's close advisers worked against the grain of these temperamental and intellectual inclinations. Those like Melville Herskovits and Alain Locke who might have helped Myrdal understand such matters were only marginal to the whole *An American Dilemma* enterprise, even though Herskovits's book on the African origins of black American culture was financed by the Carnegie-funded project.

Furthermore, it is important to note the limitations of a public policy approach to a cultural problem as complex as the one Myrdal addressed in *An American Dilemma*.

---

[38] Besides Elkins' *Slavery* (1959) for the source of the comment about Myrdal's "moralizing," see also Ivan Hannaford, *Race: The History of an Idea in the West* (Baltimore, MD.: Johns Hopkins Press, 1996), 395-96.

[39] Richard Wright, "Introduction" (1945), in *Black Metropolis: A Study of Negro Life in a Northern City* by St. Clair Drake and Horace Cayton (New York: Harcourt, Brace and World, Inc., 1970), xxx.

While the weaknesses of social institutions and conditions can be addressed by the social (and policy) sciences, the quality of everyday experience and the cultural articulations arising of that experience resist treatment in terms of public policy recommendations. Analytically, for instance, Myrdal and his associates failed to distinguish the problems of the black family, which may have been in need of bolstering, or of the black church, which may have been too acquiescent politically, from the real achievements of an expressive culture of music, dance, painting, literature and even scholarly achievement. Thus the picture presented by Myrdal seemed to grant black Americans hardly any intellectual or moral reserves, scarcely any cultural resources. More simply, Myrdal or his associates failed to envisage the political relevance of cultural "productions" altogether. In his review, Ellison didn't deny that African American institutions had problems; only that was the whole story. Overall, though it is not right to suggest that it makes no difference whether black inferiority a matter of race or a matter of culture, a biological fact or the force of circumstances, in this instance, the badge of inferiority —and picture of institutional pathology—seemed ineradicable.

Finally, the cultural tone-deafness of Myrdal and the social science biases embedded in his project were closely related to his emphasis upon rationality as the crucial value in explaining why the American Creed would triumph and upon the Enlightenment as the primary source of America's moral salvation. Myrdal was no crude positivist, since he explicitly rejected value-neutrality or so-called objectivity in his approach to his highly charged subject. Indeed, Myrdal himself noted that the Enlightenment tended to emphasize "equality in the 'natural rights of man' rather than equality in natural endowments" but added that "natural equality" and "moral equality" nevertheless tended to be linked. Even more perceptively, Myrdal observed that scientific racism was one of the outgrowths of the Enlightenment in part because the moral triumph of egalitarianism (Tocqueville's "democratic revolution") meant that the only way to justify the exploitation and exclusion of blacks was to claim scientific status for racial rankings: "the dogma of racial inequality may, in a sense, be regarded as a strange fruit of the Enlightenment." Furthermore, the claims of scientific prestige and the increasing desire over the course of the nineteenth century to offer materialistic, naturalistic support for claims about racial and cultural difference—here one thinks of racial taxonomies, the use of phrenology and the argument for polygenesis—led many to prefer racial explanations for group behavior to religious teachings about the unity of the human species or a single creation.[40]

This is by no means to imply that Myrdal bought into scientific racism. The first volume of *An American Dilemma* explicitly and carefully rejected the scientific basis of alleged racial inferiority and caste inequality. But it is to say that rationality generated considerable ambiguities of its own. Myrdal's study itself demonstrated one such ambiguity between substantive rationality as a common human capacity and hence the basis for human equality and technical or instrumental rationality, embodied in the systematic procedures of empirical investigation, which revealed significant differences

---

[40] Myrdal, vol. 2, 84, 89. See also Hannaford, *Race*.

between whites and blacks. This ambiguity had itself been perpetuated in the tension, already mentioned, between the fact of racial equality and the fact of black cultural inequality.[41]

Just as his predecessors in the Enlightenment were often unable to see Africa and peoples of African descent as anything but lacking history and a culture of rationality,[42] Myrdal's own *Bildung*, grounded as it was in the Enlightenment tradition, led him to consider African American life and culture too emotional, too disorganized, too backward and too religious to be of much political use. By so emphasizing the normative status and power of the American Creed, the cultural and political potential of the black southern church, for instance, was bound to appear meager. For 1930s liberals and social democrats, not to mention Marxists, there was a sneaking suspicion, even a firm contention, that Marx had been right: religion was "the opiate of the masses," part of the problem not of the solution. For Myrdal, the possibility of rational social change was bound up with the power of social science and of political elites rather than invested in southern black "folk" or northern urban masses as subjects for political mobilization.

And yet, it is important to remember that when Martin Luther King was an undergraduate in the late 1940s, he resisted the call to the ministry in the South, so repelled was he by the hyper-emotionality of the southern black church. If King had this difficulty, think how much more difficult it would have been for Gunnar Myrdal and his associates, black and white, less than a decade earlier. The "genius" of King and the civil rights movement was to forge a new sort of black political culture oriented toward the general, what we would call "liberal," Enlightenment goals expressed in the "American Creed"—especially equality and liberty—but driven by, and often articulated in terms of, beliefs, values, and practices grounded in the "communitarian" nexus of black culture that Myrdal felt was so lacking in cultural richness, moral standards or political possibility. Rather than being a burden or hindrance, a drag or a drug, black southern culture was a vital resource in the assertion of black self-determination in the two decades after *An American Dilemma* first appeared.

---

[41] Though he expresses it in a somewhat different way, John Diggins made this essential point about the Enlightenment in his "Slavery, Race and Equality: Jefferson and the Pathos of Enlightenment," *American Quarterly*, 28, (1976), 206-28. But see also of course Adorno and Horkheimer, *The Dialectic of Enlightenment*.

[42] See E.C. Eze (ed.), *Race and the Enlightenment: A Reader* (Oxford, U.K.: Blackwell Publishers Ltd.) for the thoughts of several key Enlightenment figures on racial and cultural equality.

THE MULTICULTURAL ROUTES OF HISTORICAL MEMORY: A CRITIQUE OF PIERRE NORA'S CONCEPT OF *LIEUX DE MEMOIRE*[1]

Peter Ling

Multiculturalism has been the contested ideal within the culture wars that have raged across American campuses in the last decade. But a much more visible, and in some cases, bloody reality in both Europe and the United States has been cultural nationalism.[2] Part of this nationalism for African Americans has been an insistence that their common identity has endured not simply because of the persistence of white racism but because of their inheritance of a rich distinctive cultural heritage. African-American scholars, such as Sterling Stuckey, have spent their careers arguing that, despite white efforts to eradicate African traditions, such folkways not only persisted within American slavery but that this Africentric ethos was transmitted down the generations to contemporary African-Americans. Writing in the late 1960s, Stuckey concluded a famous essay, "Through the Prism of Folklore" by declaring:

> What [the slaves] learned about handling misfortune was not only a major factor in their survival as a people, but many of the lessons learned and the aesthetic standards established would be used by future generations of African Americans in coping with a hostile world. What a splendid affirmation of the hopes and dreams of their slave ancestors that some of the songs being sung in antebellum days are the ones African Americans sang in the freedom movement: 'Michael, row the boat ashore'; 'Just like a tree planted by the water, I shall not be moved.'[3]

More recently, the black British scholar Paul Gilroy has also pointed to the importance of music as a medium of cultural transmission within the various cultures of the African diaspora. At the same time, however, he has tried to distance himself from what he terms the ontological and strategic varieties of racial essentialism in the multiculturalism debate. For Gilroy, the ontological variant is "characterised by brute pan-Africanism" and is "a symptom of the growing cleavages *within* the black communities." It is especially a sign of the remoteness of a black cultural elite whose "most consistent trademark," he declares, "is the persistent mystification of that group's increasingly problematic relationships with the black poor." Gilroy regards the strategic variant of

---

[1] A version of this essay was published as "Spirituals and Freedom Songs: African American Music as Sites of Memory," in *Prospects: An Annual of American Cultural Studies* 24 (1999).

[2] James Davidson Hunter, *Culture Wars: The Struggle to Define America*, (New York: Basic Books, 1991). Richard Bolton, *Culture Wars: Documents from Recent Controversies in the Arts*, (New York: New Press, 1992).

[3] Sterling Stuckey, "Through the Prism of Folklore: The Black Ethos in Slavery,"[first published in *Massachusetts Review*, IX, (1968)] in *Going Though the Storm: The Influence of African American Art in History*, (New York: Oxford University Press, 1994), 18.

black essentialism more sympathetically. Its advocates celebrate "the polyphonic qualities of black cultural expression." They nominally see race as a social and cultural construction, but remain strategically reluctant either to denounce their Africentric contemporaries or to uncover the lingering racialised forms of subordination within the totalising tendency of post-modern thought.[4] Gilroy himself favours a fractal view of black cultures with an emphasis on *routes* rather than *roots* as a keyword to explain the historical development of a diasporic, hybrid, cultural network. He suggests that the vitality and complexity of black music in particular "offer(s) a means to get beyond the related oppositions between essentialists and pseudo-pluralists on the one hand and between totalising conceptions of tradition, modernity, and post-modernity on the other. It can also provide a model of performance which can supplement and partially displace concern with textuality."[5]

A few years before Gilroy's attempt to establish a new position for blacks within the global history of modernity, the French scholar Pierre Nora edited a highly influential collection of essays on French history that took as its theme, the emergence of what Nora termed *lieux de mémoire*. In the pre-modern era, such sites of memory had not existed because their purpose as a source of group identity had been met by what Nora neatly calls *milieux de mémoire*. Since modernization has proceeded at different rates in different parts of the world, Nora sees the transition he describes as occurring more recently in non-European nations and among minority cultures. Thus, he writes that:

> Among the new nations, independence has swept into history societies recently roused from their ethnological slumbers by the rape of colonisation. At the same time a sort of internal decolonisation has had a similar effect on ethnic minorities, families, and subcultures that until recently had amassed reserves of memory but little in the way of history. Societies based on memory are no more: the institutions that once transmitted values from generation to generation—churches, schools, families, governments—have ceased to function as they once did.[6]

As the above quotation makes clear, Nora's original terminology would place traditional African-American culture in the South clearly under the rubric of the *milieux de mémoire*. His description of the lost *milieux de mémoire*, or "settings in which memory is a real part of everyday experience," would seem to fit the experience of isolated, rural African-American communities well into the twentieth century. It might truly be said of them that they "had amassed abundant reserves of memory."[7] To many observers over the course of this century, it has appeared that in such communities memory continued to function un-self-consciously, pervasively, and via spontaneous expression.

---

[4] Paul Gilroy, *The Black Atlantic: Modernity and Double Consciousness*, (Cambridge, Mass.: Harvard University Press, 1993), 31-33.

[5] *Black Atlantic*, 36.

[6] Pierre Nora, "General Introduction: Between Memory and History," in Lawrence Kritzman, *Realms of Memory: Rethinking the French Past*, vol. 1, *Conflicts and Divisions*, (New York: Columbia University Press, 1996), 1-2.

[7] *Realms of Memory*, 1-2.

In the absence of widespread literacy, oral traditions have preserved a folk memory that might be seen as being, in Nora's words "in permanent evolution, subject to the dialectic of remembering and forgetting, unconscious of the distortions to which it is subject." Fulfilling Nora's image of pre-modern communities, memory had thus continued to be magical and affective, nourishing and situating "remembrance in a sacred context" yet having its roots "in the concrete, in space, gestures, image, and object."[8]

The opposition that Nora set up between *milieux de mémoire* and *lieux de mémoire* sharpens his thesis. For, in contrast, he declares that *lieux de mémoire* "originate with the sense that there is no spontaneous memory, hence that we must create archives, mark anniversaries, organise celebrations, pronounce eulogies, and authenticate documents because such things no longer happen as a matter of course."[9] The emergence of *lieux de mémoire*, according to Pierre Nora, is a major rift or rupture in historical consciousness, marking the permanent loss of "the kind of inviolate social memory that primitive and archaic societies embodied, and whose secret died with them."[10] Nora's thesis in this respect becomes empirically untestable since we cannot retrieve even a trace of the kind of social memory that comprised the *milieux de mémoire*. Although the study of *lieux de mémoire* that Nora sponsors is far from confined to the textual, universal literacy seems fundamental to its central phenomenon of the "disappearance of peasant culture" that he sees as launching a disorientating *acceleration of history*.[11] However, as Gilroy's insistence on performance rather than simply text suggests, it is a distortion to see modernity as a straightforward shift from the spoken to the written word. Orality has co-existed, survived, and arguably flourished in new ways within literate cultures and what follows hopefully illustrates the problematic relationship between memory, history and orality that Nora's work fails to incorporate.

Heeding Paul Gilroy's admonition to look for *routes,* I will take Charleston, South Carolina as my port of departure for an examination of an episode in African-American musical history. Charleston was the major southern port for slave imports from Africa before the Civil War, and the state of South Carolina had a black majority population for over a hundred and fifty years after 1740. When the Civil War brought freedom to the mainland and Sea Island plantations around Charleston, the liberated slave-holdings were among the largest in America. This numerical concentration of African-Americans helped the development and persistence of a distinctive black community with its own folkways. Among the islanders, African cultural retentions were most evident in their religion. However, the continuation of the African-style "ring-shout" at the islands' praise houses was jeopardised by Emancipation. As Lawrence Levine pointed out twenty years ago, traditional modes of African-American worship were criticised after the Civil

---

[8] *Realms,* 3. Walter Benjamin's comment that the story teller makes his recollection of experience into "the experience of those who listen to his tale" captures the collective, contingent, interactive nature of this process; in his essay, "The Story Teller: Reflections on the Works of Nikolai Leskov," *Illuminations,* translated by Harry Kohn, (New York: Schocken, 1968), 77.

[9] *Realms,* 7.

[10] *Realms,* 2.

[11] *Realms of History,* 3, 1.

War by both whites and blacks. Perhaps predictably, Northern white teachers like Laura Towne on St Helena Island condemned the shout's savage character but so, too, did the black African Methodist Episcopal (AME) bishop, Daniel Payne. With his usual acuity, Levine linked this condemnation, and the cultural defensiveness it induced in the islanders, to the transition from an oral to a written cultural worldview. Levine concluded that "the introduction of literacy inevitably dilutes the predominance of the oral tradition and just as inevitably produces important shifts in the *Weltanschauung* of the group."[12]

However, this dilution, which corresponds in many respects to Nora's irrevocable breach with peasant culture, was neither immediate, nor complete, nor irreversible. There is a sizeable scholarly literature on the so-called "Gullah" culture of the Sea Islands, and one of its shared characteristics over several generations is a lamentation that the culture would soon be lost.[13] Historians have come to share this sentiment and have attributed to such folklore a special authenticity.[14] Sterling Stuckey, for instance, contends that "folklore, in its natural setting, is of, by, and for those who create and respond to it, depending for its survival upon the accuracy with which it speaks to needs and reflects sentiments." Stuckey cites pioneer ethnomusicologist, Alan Lomax's observation that folk songs "can be taken as signposts of persistent patterns of community feeling and can throw light into many dark corners of our past and present."[15] But if there are fading drumbeats of a *milieu de mémoire* to be detected in Gullah folk songs, the feelings they evoke in us must surely, by Nora's standards, be symptomatic of our depleted historicized condition.

This outside reverence for folk culture was evident in the late 1950s when a civil rights movement developed in the area. In late 1959 folk singer Guy Carawan, a young white staff member of the Highlander Folk School, came to Charleston to help a local black activist Septima Clark supervise some widely scattered adult literacy classes.[16]

---

[12] Lawrence Levine, *Black Culture and Black Consciousness: Afro-American Folk Thought From Slavery to Freedom* (New York: Oxford University Press, 1977), 158.

[13] Major older works include: Guion G. Johnson, *A Social History of the Sea Islands*, (Chapel Hill, N.C.: University of North Carolina Press, 1930); Guy B. Johnson, *Folk Culture on St Helena Island, South Carolina*, Chapel Hill: University of North Carolina Press, 1930); Elsie Clews Parsons, *Folklore of the Sea Islands*, (New York: American Folklore Society, 1923); and Lorenzo Turner, *Africanisms in the Gullah Dialect*, [1949], New York: Arno Press, 1969); more recent scholarship includes Patricia Jones-Jackson, *When Roots Die: Endangered Traditions on the Sea Islands*, (Athens, Ga.: University of Georgia Press, 1987), and Mary Twining & Keith Baird, eds., *Sea Island Roots: Studies in African Cultural Continuities in Georgia and South Carolina*, Trenton, N.J.: African World Press, 1988).

[14] Major historical works on African-American culture in this area include Margaret Creel, *A Peculiar People: Slave Religion and Community Culture among the Gullah*, New York: New York University Press, 1988); and Charles Joyner, *Down By the Riverside: A South Carolina Slave Community*, Urbana: University of Illinois Press, 1984). On singing in particular, see Thomas E. Hawley, "The Slave Tradition of Singing Among the Gullah of Johns' Island, South Carolina," unpublished Ph.D, University of Maryland-Baltimore, (1993), [DAI ref. 9324164].

[15] "Prism of Folklore," 4, note 6.

[16] For accounts of Highlander and of its projects, see John Glen, *Highlander: No Ordinary School, 1932-1962*, (Lexington, Ky.: University Press of Kentucky, 1988); Aimee Horton, *The Highlander Folk School: A History of the Development of Its Major Programs Related to Social Movements in the South*,

Carawan had a master's degree in sociology and a deep interest in folklore. As well as acting as Clark's chauffeur, he was keen to encourage the incorporation of folk music into the classes. Like Zilphia Horton of Highlander before him, Carawan believed that folk music was an important resource for democratic movements. Especially in its collective modes, it seemed to convey a vernacular interpretation of a people's history in a way that conflicted with the official version. During its Popular Front period of the 1930s in particular, the American Left was especially drawn to folk song as a vehicle for political mobilisation and both Carawan's contacts with Pete Seeger and his work for Highlander should be viewed in this context. Carawan's recently issued second album had carried liner notes by Alan Lomax urging "folkniks" like Carawan, to go out into the field, to learn authentic styles.[17]

Taking Lomax's advice, Carawan found that the more established and educated black congregations in Charleston itself, "tended to be complete imitations of the white elite churches." Even on the neighbouring islands, he reported that wherever "the more educated ministers and music masters are in control of the situation the respectable protocol of the white city churches is followed." As a result, the old style spirituals existed only as an oral tradition among some older people who gathered on weekday evenings, especially in the summer, to hold "praise meetings." Carawan learnt of this practice from the Sea Islanders who attended the five Citizenship Schools around Charleston. Between forty and sixty years old, most of these students, according to local reports, were direct descendants of plantation slaves. Younger islanders did not attend the praise meetings and Carawan lamented that the combination "of the schools, the organized churches, and the mass commercial culture ... have been too much for the young people to resist." Thus, African-American blood lines would not in themselves ensure the preservation of traditions.

Carawan set up singing sessions after the regular adult literacy classes. He began the sessions by singing songs from Highlander's extensive protest song repertoire and then encouraged students to sing their own songs. He reported that they often also gave "beautiful testimony" about how these songs had enabled them to "overcome their many

---

(Brooklyn, N.Y.: Carlsen Publishing, 1990); and Carl Tjerandsen, *Education for Citizenship: A Foundation's Experience*, (Santa Cruz, Cal.: Emil Schwartzhaupt Foundation, 1980). For Septima Clark, see her *Echo in My Soul*, New York 1962 and with Cynthia S. Brown, *Ready Within: A First Person Narrative: Septima Clark and the Civil Rights Movement*, (Trenton N.J.: Africa World Press, 1990). I describe the slow development of these classes in Ling, "Local Leadership in the Early Civil Rights Movement: The South Carolina Citizenship Education Program of the Highlander Folk School," *Journal of American Studies*, 29 (Dec 1995) 399-422.

[17] I use the concepts of vernacular and official cultures expounded by John Bodnar in *Remaking America: Public Memory, Commemoration, and Patriotism in the Twentieth Century*, (Princeton: Princeton University Press, 1992). The political use of folk music is discussed in the following: Serge Denisoff, *Great Day Coming: Folk Music and the American Left*, (Urbana, University of Illinois Press, 1971); Robbie Lieberman, *"My Song is My Weapon": People's Songs, American Communism, and the Politics of Culture, 1930-1950*, (Urbana, University of Illinois Press, 1989); and Robert Cantwell, *When We Were Good: The Folk Revival*, Cambridge, Mass.: Harvard University Press, 1996). Lomax's liner notes to *Guy Carawan Sings, Volume 2*, Folkways FG 3548 (New York, 1959) are reprinted as Alan Lomax, "The 'Folkniks'—and the Songs They Sing," *Sing Out!* 9 (1959), 30-31.

hardships and come through them still full of love for their fellow men." Songs such as "Lay Down Body" and "Been in the Storm So Long" belonged to the rich Sustainer tradition of the slave preacher within African-American Christianity. Like the sermons within that tradition, the songs articulated a faith in the fundamentality of divine justice: a belief that the tired would be rested; that the storm-tossed would find shelter, and that the wicked would be punished. Far from being an opiate that stifled resistance, the religion simultaneously underpinning, and being itself reinforced by this sustaining repertoire of songs, was a powerful and therapeutic cultural artifact.[18] It supported the collective identity and consciousness of local African-Americans in a manner comparable to that which Pierre Nora sees as the function of "history-memory" for the French nation after its defeat by Prussia.

With a certain wistfulness, Nora recounts how between the publication of Augustin Thierry's *Lettres sur l'histoire de France* (1827) and of Charles Seignobos's *Histoire sincère de la nation française* (1933), "History, memory, and the nation enjoyed an unusually intimate communion, a symbiotic complementarity at every level—scientific and pedagogical, theoretical and practical." Thereafter, he writes, the sacred union between state and nation "was supplanted by a new one: state and society." However, the new alliance could not preserve the communion between history and memory. "Once society had supplanted nation," writes Nora, "legitimation by the past, hence by history, gave way to legitimation by the future." He goes on to argue that "a society fundamentally absorbed by its own transformation and renewal ... values the new over the old, youth over old age, the future over the past."[19]

There are strong parallels here with the American experience. According to Michael Kammen, prior to around 1870, "Americans were much more likely to allude to the *burden* of the past than to the possible *uses* of the past" and at times displayed a "simplistic present-mindedness and future-orientation."[20] The Jeffersonian rhetoric of escaping the dead hand of bygone generations was compounded by an increasing emphasis in the Jacksonian era on "natural" over "cultivated" traits. Concurrently, the celebration of the free market within liberalism insisted on the importance of the independence of men, not only from each other, but from cultural and communal attachments. In this respect, transcendentalism (which Emerson characterized as "a poetry and philosophy of insight and not of tradition") and the personal experience of God at the heart of the Second Great Awakening were symptomatic of the culture of a nation of newcomers. America was legitimized by her future; her destiny was more

---

[18] See Richard Lischer, *The Preacher King: Martin Luther King and the Word that Moved America*, New York: Oxford University Press, 1995, 28-32. Lischer compares his Sustainer preacher typology to that of Peter Paris, "The Bible and the Black Churches" in Ernest Sandeen, ed., *The Bible and Social Reform*, (Philadelphia: Fortress Press, 1982), 136-44, and that of Benjamin Mays, *The Negro's God*, (Boston: Chapman & Grimes, 1938), 14-15.

[19] *Realms of Memory*, 5-6.

[20] Kammen, *Mystic Chords of Memory: The Transformation of Tradition in American Culture* (New York: Alfred Knopf 1991) 35, 59.

manifest than her history.[21] Thus, the social change that Nora depicts resembles not only the impact of modernization but the onset of Americanization.

Between the Civil War and the First World War, what Kammen calls the party of Memory but what Nora would dub the party of History triumphed in America. It was also the period in which the professionalization of history occurred. The same period is commonly regarded by American historians as an era of modernization and by historians of the African-American experience as the time when the development of segregation and the codification of racism melded memories of slavery and aspirations for freedom into new forms of black cultural expression. For many Americans, black and white, it was an epoch in which the world was turned upside down. The reaction to this turmoil included a quest for identity among African-Americans faced with the psychic tensions of an ingrained double-consciousness.[22] This search led some African-Americans towards Africa so that by the time of the First World War, they were primed to embrace Marcus Garvey's doctrines of racial pride. However, as Garvey's turbulent career illustrated, others, particularly middle-class blacks, chose to affirm their Americanness.[23] Nora's work does not easily accommodate such ambiguous forms of consciousness.

On the contrary, Nora prefers to embrace an old-fashioned notion of American exceptionalism. He writes:

> In countries where the history has not assumed the same didactic role in forming the national consciousness, the history of history need not burden itself with such polemical content. For example, in the United States, a country of plural memories and diverse traditions, historiographical reflection has long been part of the discipline. Different interpretations of the American Revolution or the Civil War may involve high stakes but do not threaten to undermine the American tradition because, in a sense, there is no such thing, or if there is, it is not primarily a historical construct. In France, by contrast, historiography is iconoclastic and irreverent.[24]

This is Nora's most explicit discussion of the United States and it suggests that his concept of a transition from the peasant *milieux de mémoire* to the modern state's *lieux de mémoire* may be far less applicable to America than to France. As a historian of the United States, and of African-American history in particular, I would disagree. Historians, such as Michael Kammen, have also considered at length the didactic role that history has assumed in the evolution of American national consciousness.[25] There

---

[21] For a fuller review of Kammen's work, see Peter Ling, "Michael Kammen's Commemoration of the Americanist Tradition," *Journal of American Studies*, 27 (1993) 2, 249-254.

[22] W.E.B. DuBois, *The Souls of Black Folk* (1903) in *Three Negro Classics*, (New York: Avon Books, 1965), 214-15.

[23] E. David Cronon, *Black Moses*, (Madison: University of Wisconsin Press 1968); and Judith Stein, *The World of Marcus Garvey*, (Baton Rouge: Louisiana State University Press, 1986).

[24] *Realms of Memory*, 4.

[25] See Kammen, *Mystic Chords of Memory*. This book was the third in a series which began with Kammen's *Season of Youth: The American Revolution and the Historical Imagination*, (New York: Alfred Knopf, 1978) and *A Machine That Would Go of Itself*, (New York: Alfred Knopf: 1986) as well as a collection of essays, *Selvages and Biases: The Fabric of History in American Culture*, (Ithaca, N.Y: Cornell

is also the role it has played in American racism, a function that has definitely loaded American history with polemical content, and high stakes. Few traditions are as venerable among Americans as the assumption that theirs is properly a white man's country.[26] The intellectual challenge to this tradition by African-Americans, native Americans, other minority groups and their allies has been partly based on the use of historical scholarship to critique a highly selective national memory. The images of damage and desecration that Nora offers for such critical historiographical practice should not lead us to underestimate its benefits.[27]

Placed in Nora's theoretical framework, Carawan's work involved the construction or reconstruction of what Nora would term a *lieu de mémoire*. Carawan offered the Sea Islanders a new perspective on their own music. "Each week," he wrote, "I've read something to them about the spirituals by various writers who hold them in high esteem and have attempted to describe the conditions of life, which created them." He reported that the students responded positively to this external affirmation of the spirituals' worth. "They were genuinely moved," he wrote, "when I read them some parts of Alan Lomax's new book *The Rainbow Sign*." To promote an appreciation of the old spirituals and to publicise the goals of the adult schools in the African-American community, Carawan organized a concert of singers from the classes for the closing ceremony of the Citizenship Schools' three-month term.[28] Between 1963 and 1966, he expanded these concerts to include Georgia Sea Island Singers and the Freedom singers from the broader Movement. Moreover, a group of Johns Island singers, taking their name from the community lodge where they had originally gathered—Moving Star Hall—not only performed on the island but on the established folk music revival circuit, including the Newport Folk Festival of 1964. They thus became part of the folk music revival that swept the United States in the late Fifties and early Sixties and their involvement in this commodified pop culture underlines how far removed they were from any *milieu de mémoire*.

University Press, 1987).

[26] There is a vast literature on the subject, most recently on the social construction of whiteness v. Ronald Takaki, *Iron Cages: Race and Culture in Nineteenth Century America*, (New York : Oxford University Press,1979); Reginald Horsman, *Race and Manifest Destiny: The Origins of American Racial Anglo-Saxonism*, (Cambridge, Mass: Harvard University Press, 1981); Alexander Saxton, *The Rise and Fall of the White Republic: Class Politics and Mass Culture in Nineteenth Century America* (London: Verso, 1990); David Roediger, *The Wages of Whiteness: Race and the Making of the American Working Class*, (London: Verso 1991), Ruth Frankenberg, *White Women, Race Matters: The Social Construction of Whiteness*, (Minneapolis: University of Minnesota Press, 1993); Audrey Smedley, *Race in North America: Origin and Evolution of a Worldview* (Boulder, Co.: Westview, 1993) and Tomas Almaguer, *Racial Fault Lines: The Historical Origins of White Supremacy in California*, (Berkeley, University of California Press, 1994).

[27] For example Nora writes: "historiography sows doubt; it runs the blade of a knife between the heartwood of memory and the bark of history." Or again, "The memory we see tears at us, yet it is no longer entirely ours; what was once sacred rapidly ceased to be so, and for the time being we have no further use for the sacred." *Realms of Memory*, 4, 7.

[28] HP-SHSW reel 34: sheet 1.

However, this may also serve to expose the mythic status of this concept. Certainly, the way Nora describes the *milieu de mémoire* is similar to the romantic way scholars used to refer to the *folk*. Contemporary ethnographers would be uncomfortable with Nora's reference to "ethnological slumbers." They are, as Robert Cantwell points out, "at great pains to avoid what, a generation ago, was freely avowed to be the salient characteristic of folk performance: its immediacy, spontaneity, and ingenuousness, its 'unself-consciousness'." These characteristics are now regarded as products of the spectator's non-folk status and of the media through which folk culture is encountered. To quote Cantwell again:

> folklore is reborn in each incarnation through a series of syntheses that mark its intersection with literary and political forces, which seem diverted or disturbed in haunting and mysterious ways by its influence. The oral traditions themselves, however ancient or contemporary, remain out of reach. ...[29]

Nora accepts that the "inviolate social memory" that is the essence of the *milieu de mémoire* is out of reach. Yet it still constitutes the criterion by which he evaluates the realms of History that have displaced it.

Contemporary folklorists suggest that Nora's judgement on History may be too harsh. In one of the most important introductory texts to folklore, Barre Toelken defines a folk group as "people who share some basis for informal communal contacts, some factor in common that makes it possible, or rewarding or meaningful, for them to exchange materials in a culturally significant way." He adds that "we would expect to find that the group will have maintained itself through its dynamics for a considerable time and that the expressive communications have thus become the educative matrix in which children of the group—or newcomers to it—are brought up."[30] While it is clear, as it was to Carawan in 1959, that the Sea Islanders are a folk group under these terms, they are not timeless relics. A feature of contemporary ethnology is a new emphasis on the ongoing collective process of constructing and representing meaning that means that such groups can continue to evolve today.

This is captured in an essay by I. Sheldon Posen, a Canadian folklorist and public historian, which deals with misgivings he had about the folk festival phenomenon. Posen was struck by the gulf between the nature of singing as an activity shared by resident Newfoundlanders around an old stove in a family kitchen, on the one hand, and his own performance of the same songs at the Mariposa Folk Festival in Toronto, on the other. The latter was so alien a context that it struck him as ridiculous to use terms like "traditional," "authentic," or even "folk" to describe what he did on stage, and so Posen gave up performing at festivals. However, he then pursued a close study of singing at children's summer camps. He subsequently argued that "items are not intrinsically 'folk'; rather their 'folkness' lies in the functions and processes and ultimately the

---

[29] Robert Cantwell, *Ethnomimesis: Folklife and the Representation of Culture*, (Chapel Hill, University of North Carolina Press, 1993) 7, 16.

[30] Toelken, *The Dynamics of Folklore*, (Bosto: Houghton Mifflin, 1979), 33, 51.

contexts of which they are a part." Moreover, "since 'folklore' was the result of a process taking place within a certain order of context, then middle-class urban people like [Posen himself] 'had' folklore too, which we performed in appropriate surrounds involving interaction with peers and reflecting the values of our group. I had met the folk," Posen concluded, "and they were us."[31]

In this sense, the Civil Rights Movement became Carawan's folk grouping. When the Moving Star Hall Singers performed at the closing concert for the Southern Voter Education Internship Program on Johns Island in March 1963, they illustrated how traditional cultural forms had a role to play in political mobilization, aspects of which activists from across the South had come to study in the context of the new Charleston County Coordinating Committee.[32] In late 1965, Carawan wrote to Highlander at length about what he had done "so that people will neither ignore nor overrate my work."[33] By this stage, the Civil Rights Movement had established itself as a singing protest movement with "We Shall Overcome" as its anthem. It had created this *lieu de mémoire* just as surely as the French Revolution created *La Marseillaise*. Just as the latter was adopted by other revolutionary movements in the nineteenth century, so "We Shall Overcome" was sung by crowds during the revolutions of 1989 in eastern Europe.

Carawan believed that people might assume that "freedom singing" had developed spontaneously. On the contrary, there had been various obstacles to its development. He reiterated in 1965 his belief that most "college educated Negroes and students have been educated out of their folk heritage." Indeed, they had become "ashamed of the ways their parents or grandparents from rural and working class backgrounds express themselves in song, speech and worship." This was not just true of Charleston's well-established black churches but across the South. Until after the sit-ins of 1960, Carawan reported, "most mass meetings were conducted in an overly formal manner by professional and educated Negroes who led stiff hymns like 'Onward Christian Soldiers' or Rotarian type songs like 'The More We Get Together, The Happier We'll Be'."[34] Even many of the Nashville students at colleges like Fisk, who became the nucleus of the early Student Non-violent Coordinating Committee [SNCC], had "initially reacted with embarrassment to new freedom songs that were sung with hand clapping and in a rural free-swinging style." According to Carawan, the local sit-in campaign had

---

[31] Posen, "On Folk Festivals and Kitchens: Questions of Authenticity in the Folksong Revival," in Neil Rosenberg, *Transforming Tradition: Folk Music Revivals Examined*, (Urbana: University of Illinois Press, 1993), 130-36; quotation, 135.

[32] HP-SHSW, reel 34: 8; v. also Southern Regional Council Papers, Series VI, Voter Education Project, microfilm reel 181, sheets 728-833.

[33] Memo, Guy Carawan to Myles [Horton] & Connie [Conrad] on work in the South since 1959, HFS Papers, 7:347-353. Unless otherwise indicated, all quotations are from this report.

[34] The documentary series *Eyes on the Prize* unwittingly captures this in its episode on the Montgomery Bus Boycott when the Reverend Ralph Abernathy recalls how the congregation at the mass meeting sang "Leaning on theEverlasting Lord," a mainstream Protestant hymn familiar to most southerners, black and white. More importantly, the song is rendered in a formal "white" scanned way. See the first episode, "Awakenings," Blackside Productions, Boston, (1987).

overcome this reticence, making Nashville "the first city to develop a diversified repertoire of freedom songs."

However, the class barrier was not the only cultural impediment to the development of the Freedom Songs. Carawan also found that in the rural communities in which the old singing traditions were most vibrant, it went "against the reflexes of the older people at first to hear new words and new meanings put to their old church songs." Elaborating on this resistance, Carawan claimed for himself a clear but short-term role in developing the Freedom Songs at Highlander workshops and other movement gatherings. He had recognised that African-Americans:

> were not taking advantage of what their heritage had to offer. So many great old spirituals that express hatred of oppression and a longing for freedom were being left out of this growing freedom movement. It was an exceptional case when a Negro took a spiritual or gospel song (for example 'Amen') and substituted a word or two to make it applicable (like 'freedom') or followed the example of the labor movement and adapted a song like 'I Shall Not Be Moved.'

The sense of the sacred which Nora links expressly to the oral *milieu* had in this sense stifled the spontaneity that Nora sees as another vital characteristic. This reinforces the importance of recognizing that orality potently co-exists within literate cultures.

Carawan's importance in encouraging the improvisational use of African-American folk song in the Civil Rights Movement was for a very limited period, 1960-1961. In April 1960, first at a conference for sit-in students at Highlander, then at Fisk University, and finally at Student Nonviolent Coordinating Committee's founding conference in Ralegh, North Carolina, he led the singing and helped to introduce "We Shall Overcome" and other Freedom Songs to activists from different movement centres. In the summer of 1960, he visited major Southern Christian Leadership Conference (SCLC) affiliates in Birmingham, Alabama and Petersburg, Virginia, and ran a workshop for activists at Highlander entitled "Sing for Freedom." This produced the first mimeographed book of freedom songs. At the SCLC and SNCC conferences that autumn, Carawan passed out this songbook to movement leaders.

By Carawan's own estimate, his preeminence in the development of the Freedom Songs ended in the summer of 1961. This was a difficult period for Highlander itself as the school was forced to close when it lost its Supreme Court appeal against the state of Tennessee's revocation of its charter. Carawan's singing project, like other Highlander initiatives, had to find support from local movement organizations and this took Carawan to Mississippi to help the local Jackson movement and the incoming Freedom Riders. The latter subsequently "carried back to their home communities many, many songs." The Freedom Song repertoire was now large, well established, and widely known.

The mass meetings in Jackson in August 1961 convinced Carawan that there were others better equipped than he himself was to lead the Freedom songs. Not least, the new African-American singers—like SNCC's Cordell Reagon and Charles Sherrod who had just started fieldwork in Albany, Georgia—could draw more readily than Carawan on the broader percussive musical and dance traditions of their own rural church background. In 1962 the struggle moved deeper into the Black Belt where these musical practices were more prevalent. College students like Reagon and Sherrod found that singing was one tool they could use to get a movement going in these areas and to develop local people not just as song leaders but as protest leaders as well. This emphasis on cultural forms as mechanisms for African-American consciousness-raising was also evident in the innovative curricula of the Freedom Schools both in the Northern schools' boycott of 1963 and the Mississippi Freedom Summer of 1964.[35]

Carawan also publicised the Movement's activities to the larger folk music revival audience by his documentary records of songs, speeches, and interviews, beginning with *The Nashville Sit-In Story*—issued on the well-established Folkways label. His 1962 record *Freedom in the Air* documented the Albany movement and was a fund-raising device for SNCC for whom Carawan also produced the songbook *We Shall Overcome* and a documentary record, *The Story of Greenwood*, about a voter registration project in Mississippi in 1963. By this stage, more famous white folk singers than Carawan were being invited to movement events. Joan Baez attended mass meetings during the Birmingham campaign and later in 1963 Bob Dylan performed in Greenwood. It was at this point that Carawan and his wife Candie, moved to Johns Island to work more intensively on nurturing the Gullah folk heritage throughout the Sea Islands of the Carolinas and Georgia, and to help local leader Esau Jenkins with the Southwide Voter Education Internship Program. When the SNCC Freedom Singers attended a folk festival on the island in December 1963, Carawan reports that they "added several of the old sea island songs to their repertoire" and took "lessons in complicated clapping." Carawan thus continued to facilitate the transmission of cultural traditions across the generations and to ensure that the African singing style was a living heritage not just a museum piece. In this sense, he achieved a communion of history, memory and movement: a very distinctive type of *lieux de mémoire*.

Ironically, Carawan's efforts to alert young African-American activists to the hidden riches of their own tradition strengthened the black separatist tendencies already stirring within SNCC. He himself noted that:

> For most of these young freedom singers, hearing Dock Reese [from Texas] and the Georgia Sea Island Singers was a revelation. It was the first time they'd heard many of these prison songs and songs from the days of slavery that sang of freedom in their own way. They began to realize how much of their heritage had not been passed on to them.

Certainly by the end of 1964, with the traumas of Freedom Summer and the Mississippi Freedom Democratic Party's convention challenge behind them, SNCC activists became interested in the political potential of folk festivals in the areas where they were working—Mississippi, Alabama, Southwest Georgia and Arkansas. From their perspective, such activities added, in Carawan's words:

---

[35] Daniel Hinman-Smith, "'Does the Word Freedom have a Meaning?' The Mississippi Freedom Schools, the Berkeley Free Speech Movement, and the Search for Freedom through Education," Ph.D. thesis, University of North Carolina, Chapel Hill, 1993 (DAI 9415322), 45.

another dimension to COFO's [Council of Federated Organizations] primary objective [namely] —trying to convince Negroes in these areas that they do have validity as people, that they can make their own decisions, that they do have as much (or more) to offer both politically and culturally as those who have been doing all the decision-making in the past.

Examining Guy Carawan's work thus provides a valuable perspective not only on Pierre Nora's distinction between *milieux* and *lieux de mémoire*, but on multiculturalism and the complicated *routes* of cultural transmission and development.[36] Carawan was unwilling simply to resuscitate the singing of old Gullah spirituals whose communal role had weakened over time. Put more positively, he was sensitive to the need to create a fresh *milieu*—a participatory, popular, dynamic context in which local people developed their own tradition; in other words, 'a setting in which memory was a real part of everyday experience.' Ironically, it might be argued that those who have subsequently pressed for the formal, Africentric celebration of the culture of African-Americans, who have developed "folk festivals," and appealed to the larger apparatus of federal and local governments for support in the preservation of African-American folkways, have tilted the cultural balance towards a more rigidified *lieu de mémoire*.

---

[36] See Charles Joyner's recent comment that:
Every black southerner has a European heritage as well as an African one, and every white southerner has an African heritage as well as a European one. That shared heritage constitutes the cardinal test of southern identity and the central theme of southern culture.
Joyner, "African and European Roots of Southern Culture; The 'Central Theme' Revisited", in Richard H. King and Helen Taylor, eds., *Dixie Debates: Perspectives on Southern Cultures*, (London:Pluto Press,1996), 28. The new immigration into France from Francophonic Africa, the Caribbean, Pacific, and Asia, and the recognition by scholars such as Gérard Noiriel of the importance of immigration within twentieth-century French history suggest that Joyner's statement may eventually be transferable to the French experience. See Noiriel's essay "French and Foreigners" in *Realms of Memory*.

LIST OF CONTRIBUTORS

Reinhard Isensee
Assistant Professor of American Studies at Humboldt University, Berlin, Germany. Publications in the field of American literature on American naturalism and, particularly, on 20th century young adult literature, as well as in cultural studies on identity formation and digital media (Internet). Major research interests: American adolescent novel, especially its narrative paradigms and strategies of fictionalizing non-peer readers, and in digital media and their impact on the production and distribution of knowledge in American culture.

Richard H. King
Professor in the School of American and Canadian Studies at the University of Nottingham, Great Britain. Selected publications: *Southern Renaissance: The Cultural Awakening of the American South, 1930-1955* (1980). The essay in this volume will be part of a larger comparative intellectual history of ideas of race and culture between 1945 and 1970 in Europe and the United States.

Rob Kroes
Professor and Chair of American Studies at the University of Amsterdam, The Netherlands. Studies at the University of Amsterdam and Chicago. Ph.D. in sociology from the University of Leiden. He is immediate past president of the European Association for American Studies (EAAS). He is the author, co-author, or editor of 29 books. Among his recent publications are: *If You've Seen One, You've Seen The Mall* (1996); *Predecessors: Intellectual Lineages in American Studies* (1999) (ed.); *Citizenship in a Globalizing World* (forthcoming).

Günter H. Lenz
Professor and Chair of American Studies, Humboldt University, Berlin, Germany. Recipient of the Carl Bode-Norman Holmes Pearson Prize of the American Studies Association for Lifetime Achievement in American Studies, 1999. Numerous publication in the areas of the history and theory of American Studies in a comparative perspective, (multi)cultural theory, 20th century U.S. American literatures and criticism, U.S. American culture in Europe, African American Studies, documentary film. Working on a book about multicultural critique in the U.S. and the international, intercultural dimensions of American Culture Studies.

Peter J. Ling
Senior Lecturer in American History in the School of American and Canadian Studies at the University of Nottingham, Great Britain. He is currently writing a biography of Martin Luther King, Jr. for Routledge's Modern Biographies series and completing a study of forms of political education in the Civil Rights Movement. His most recent publication is *Gender in the Civil Rights Movement* (1999).

Klaus J. Milich
Assistant Professor of American Literary and Cultural Studies at Humboldt University, Berlin, Germany. He is the author of *Die frühe Postmoderne: Geschichte eines europäisch-amerikanischen Kulturkonflikts* (1998) and co-editor of *Multiculturalism in Transit: A German-American Exchange* (1998) and *American Studies in Germany: European Contexts and Intercultural Relations* (1996). He currently works on a book on race-gender relations in American realism.

Berndt Ostendorf
Professor of North American Cultural History and Director of the Amerika-Institut, University of München, Germany. He has widely published on African American culture, Louisiana creoles, working-class culture, photography and advertising, ethnicity and minority cultures, the politics of difference, and the crisis of civil society. Publications: *Die Vereinigten Staaten von Amerika*, Bd. 2, 2nd ed. (1992) (ed.); *Die multikulturelle Gesellschaft: Modell Amerika?* (1995) (ed.); *Creoles and Creolization: The Concepts and Their History* (1997). Current project: "Why is American (Popular) Culture so Popular: A View From Eureope."

Meike Zwingenberger
Lecturer at the Amerika-Institut of the University of München, Germany. She holds an M.A. degree in American Cultural Hisotry from the University of München and is currently working on her dissertation with the title "Social capital and community building." Her major research interests are urban and immigration history, ethnic identities, social networks and community structures. Publications: *Einwanderungsland USA—Einwanderungsland Bundesrepublik: Migration im internationalen Vergleich* (1999) (with Götz D. Opitz).